MEANINGS
OF THE MEDIUM

Media and Society Series

J. Fred MacDonald, General Editor

MEANINGS
OF THE MEDIUM

Perspectives on the Art
of Television

Edited by
Katherine Usher Henderson
and
Joseph Anthony Mazzeo

Media and Society Series

New York
Westport, Connecticut
London

Library of Congress Cataloging-in-Publication Data

Meanings of the medium : perspectives on the art of television /
   edited by Katherine Usher Henderson and Joseph Anthony Mazzeo.
         p.   cm. — (Media and society series)
   ISBN 0–275–93390–3 (alk. paper)
   1. Television broadcasting.   I. Henderson, Katherine U.
II. Mazzeo, Joseph Anthony, 1923–   .   III. Series.
PN1992.5.M36   1990
791.45—dc20   89–16171

Library of Congress Catalog Card Number: 89–16171
ISBN: 0–275–93390–3

First published in 1990

Praeger Publishers, One Madison Avenue, New York, NY 10010
A division of Greenwood Press, Inc.

Printed in the United States of America

The paper used in this book complies with the
Permanent Paper Standard issued by the National
Information Standards Organization (Z39.48–1984).

10 9 8 7 6 5 4 3 2 1

To Our Parents
May and Munroe Usher
and
the Memory of
Lia and Joseph Mazzeo

Contents

Acknowledgments

We wish to thank the CBS Broadcast group, especially John P. Blessington and Philip A. Harding, for supporting our vision of this book through both personal interest and generous funding. As the reader will readily discern, their financial support has not influenced or determined our findings in any shape or fashion whatsoever.

We also thank the following scholars who served as consultants to the project: Cynthia Griffin Wolff and David Thorburn, both Professors of Humanities at the Massachusetts Institute of Technology, Rolf Meyersohn of the City University of New York, Jane Shapiro Zacek of the State University of New York, and Ann Pope Stone of Santa Monica College. The General Editor of the Series, J. Fred MacDonald, has been unfailingly available and the most astute possible advisor; our editor at Praeger, Alison Bricken, has been patient and intelligent with our many questions. Above all, we thank the contributors, who have sustained us through their enthusiasm for the project and taught us through their radiant insights.

Introduction

Katherine Usher Henderson
and Joseph Anthony Mazzeo

Television has wrought perhaps the fastest transformation of American life in modern times. As James M. O'Brien points out in his essay in this collection, "In the seven years between 1948 and 1955 . . . television became what it remains today: the major consumer of leisure time for all segments of American society, the dominant medium for both news and entertainment, and the bestower of celebrity and notoriety with an unmatched swiftness and intimacy."

The transformation is not yet complete, for American television has in the past two decades entered a new stage of its history. The proliferation of cable channels has created an almost endless potential for viewer choice, while the introduction of the video cassette recorder has enabled programs to be preserved much as books are—to be opened, closed, and experienced at the viewer's convenience. It is a crucial time for us to examine the past, present, and future of the medium, and to ask precisely what television and its programs "are" and what they "mean."

Our book differs from many others engaged in this task in its premise that scholars from the traditional humanistic disciplines can contribute substantially to this intellectual venture. Our authors are for the most part not experts in communications theory or mass culture, but literary critics, philosophers, rhetoricians, and historians. We are television watchers who enjoy analyzing what we watch. In this book we have used the intellectual tools and scholarly methods of our own disciplines to examine a series of related themes: the origin and meaning of American attitudes toward television, the relationship between "high" art and the popular art of television, and the relationship between particular kinds of programs and the sensibilities of their audiences. Each essay in this collection treats at least one of these themes, and in most, two—or even all three—are interwoven.

Authors of the book's first section, "Television and Society," stress the dynamic relationship between a particular genre and the sensibility of its audience. (By "sensibility" we mean not morals or behavior, but the capacity to respond to and discriminate among a wide range of emotional and cognitive impressions.) In the first essay rhetorician Robert Cluett analyzes the talk show, a genre that has captivated American audiences for decades, revealing its unique conventions and querying the meaning of its appeal. In "Television Intimacy: Paradoxes of Trust and Romance" women's studies scholar Judith Kegan Gardiner argues that the structure and content of programs like *The Love Connection* and *Moonlighting* attract viewers through their reflection of the current crisis in heterosexual relationships. Michael Seidel, noted historian of the meaning of sports heroes in American society, demonstrates in his essay that television viewers of major league baseball experience a very different game from that seen by fans in the stadium. In the final essay in this section Harriet Blodgett discovers that, despite overt changes in women's televised roles, old myths and archetypes still inform their images. The four essays in this section focus on the complex relationship between the viewer and the program viewed, the audience and the medium.

In the second section of the book, "Television Programming as Art," humanities scholars trace subtle connections between the texts of "high" culture and particular contemporary television programs; their essays embrace both formal qualities of the programs and the quality of the audience's experience. In the first piece comparative literature scholar James V. Mirollo discovers a series of striking resemblances—even identities—between the narrative forms of a great poem of the Italian Renaissance and *Hill Street Blues* and *L. A. Law*. In the same section philosopher Mary Sirridge discovers that Leo Tolstoy's concept of popular art gives us something we need and lack—clear and viable criteria for distinguishing "real" from "counterfeit" art on the contemporary television screen. In "Richard Chamberlain's *Hamlet*," Theoharis C. Theoharis explores the consequences of casting an actor well-known as a romantic hero in the lead role of Shakespeare's great tragedy. At the same time he demonstrates how televised drama, "working with synchronized electronic sounds and images instead of living bodies moving in three dimensional space, . . . can articulate the action of a play, its pace and structural values, with much more precision than virtually any theatrical performance." Taken as a group, these essays challenge our conventional ideas of art and culture, particularly the notion that "high" and popular culture are completely insulated from each other, existing on parallel but never intersecting planes.

Authors in the final section, "Television and Its Critics," are television "experts," scholars and teachers and professionals in the field of television. These pieces provide a context for the first two sections by documenting the development of American attitudes toward television. They also provide a historical view, showing the need for the kind of serious treatment which television is accorded throughout our collection. Barbara Lee describes the curve of high expectations falling into gloomy judgments that has defined the appearance of each new medium in the twentieth century. She suggests that instead of global pronouncements, we need to look at some of the positive social roles played by television in American culture. While Lee studies the reception given new media by the popular press, in "Mass Culture, Class Culture, Democracy and Prime Time," David Marc explores the negative—almost paranoid—reception of television in midcentury America by the intelligentsia, as well as the few critics who represented exceptions to this rule. He concludes by looking toward the future, speculating upon the quality of programming in today's highly fluid period as viewer choices are multiplied by cable channels. James O'Brien provides an overview of the birth and growth of television criticism over the last fifty years which is especially valuable for its revelation of the precursors of current schools of criticism. O'Brien's piece serves as commentary on the whole field of television scholarship, enabling the reader to locate our book within this field.

It took more than seven years for television to enter the ivy walls of higher education, and for many years it was but a stepchild in the curriculum of the academy. Now, however, it is a full-fledged part of that curriculum, viewed by some as favorite son and by others as black sheep, tainting the purity of the liberal arts. In the course of its acceptance by the academy, the subject of television has generated a large body of scholarly literature. For the editors of this anthology—and those contributors whose former scholarship has been grounded in other disciplines—working with this literature for the past two years has been an exciting, at times intimidating task. There was always the chance that, as scholars of the traditional humanities, we would have everything to learn, but nothing to say.

We found that as valuable and illuminating as much of this literature is, it tends to slight the historical and aesthetic dimensions of television in favor of the economic, the psychological, and the ideological. To draw a parallel with Renaissance drama, it is as if we understood the economic basis of the Elizabethan theater without a way of describing and studying the structure of *Macbeth*, or could examine whether Shakespearian tragedies bred violence on the streets of London without understanding the conventions governing those tragedies. While there is some excellent criticism from a traditional humanistic perspective—the names of Gilbert Seldes and Horace Newcomb are only two that come readily to mind—most contemporary criticism, like all current criticism in the humanities, is more oriented toward theoretical speculation. The methods of semiotics and deconstruction certainly have value, but the products of these methods are seldom anchored in the immediate experience of television viewing and programming. This book, on the other hand, stressing an aesthetic and historical approach, addresses the questions of precisely why people watch particular programs and what these patterns tell us about ourselves.

It also differs from most writing on the medium because it is neither polemical nor defensive. It does not attempt to demonstrate whether or not the ''effects'' of television on the viewer are good or bad, or to prove that television either uplifts or degrades its audience. What it does do is exemplify the kinds of insights that historians, philosophers, and literary critics can bring to the subject of television. Because it eschews esoterically theoretical or technical vocabularies, we hope that it will reach students and scholars in many disciplines, encouraging a richer, more historically and aesthetically nuanced sense of television's place in our culture.

Part I
Television and Society

1

Telegenic Colloquies: Paradigms of Society in the TV Talk Show

Robert Cluett

THE GENRE

James Reston once made the observation that talking is the one thing that Americans cannot be prevented from doing. We are a "talk" culture in every sense. It is hard to conceive of any other culture producing the "fireside chat" as a device for mobilizing the political energies of its people. And in no other place in the world is talk so prized as a spectator sport: what we love to do we also love to watch. The TV talk show—the TV interview conducted for purposes other than generating news or propagating ideas and information—is more pervasive in America than anywhere else. In Great Britain, for example, one's TV set is overwhelmed by news, health-giving analysis, and information, but of talk there is not much. Similarly, in Zürich, where the helpful owner of a three-star hotel is likely to provide his guest with an eighteen-channel, trilingual color TV, one will find barely a handful of talk in a week's viewing: sport, news, analysis, and information will all abound, but precious little talk.

In heartland America, by contrast, the airwaves are saturated daily by Johnny, Arsenio, Sally Jessy, Dave, Pat, Geraldo, Oprah, Jay, Morton Jr., and other heirs to the great oral kingdom once ruled by Jack, Merv, Steve, David, and Dick. Even where I sit, at the fringes of heartland America, on the Canadian shore of Lake Ontario, it is possible to watch between nine and fourteen hours of talk show per day without benefit of a cable hookup. Why is it that we are so fascinated with talk—and not just with real talk but with the manufactured talk of the TV show? And what does the talk show imply about some of the distinctive currents moving in our society, in the politics of America? I believe that the answers to these questions can be provided by the talk shows themselves, and by the consistencies that have developed over the years in the talk show as genre. Within the genre I would include, at the conservative end of the generic spectrum, the single-guest shows of David Susskind's *Open End* in the late 1950s and early 1960s; at the less conservative end, I would take in some of the one-on-one work of our latter-day hosts and hostesses such as Oprah Winfrey. I believe all the generic properties present in the one-on-one format to be present also in the multi-guest format, though often in attenuated form. But the freak-show features that are likely to go along with concurrent multiple guests (as with Geraldo, the American Nazis, and Roy Innes) constitute a distraction. I shall therefore restrict myself largely to the one-on-one situation with only incidental reference to the other. First, we need a few ground rules: who is the host, who the guest?

The host must be a person of what psychologists call "bright normal" intelligence—or, at least, he must give that impression. Bertrand Russell or Stanley Fish would probably be over-qualified in this respect; no Ph.D.'s or previously published authors need apply. The intelligence level required is high enough to make a quip but not so high as to escape identification on the part of the audience. A show of solidarity with average people in matters of grammar and usage can be an important asset: Susskind's phrase, "so incredible I don't believe it," despite the often highbrow content of his show, no doubt endeared him to many people out there in viewer land. In the same category is the habit of a current host who is likely to say, with the great multitude, "Each of them are . . ." and "There's three reasons for this . . . ."

As for appearance, ordinary good looks—the cosmetic equivalent of "bright normal" intelligence—constitute the requirement. Richard Gere, Steve Reeves, Lena Horne, and Bo Derek are too richly endowed with physical beauty. The talk show host can be more presentable than eight out of ten members of the public but not more presentable than nine out of ten. The case is similar with visible personal skills and accomplishments: the host can possess nothing that is truly excellent or exceptional. Ted Williams, Van Cliburn, Philip Roth, Walter Payton, Florence Griffith-Joyner would all make terrific guests on a talk show, but their excellences are too visible and too well-known to qualify them as hosts.

In short, the host is an ordinary guy (or gal) out there doing what most of us do a lot of every day—chatting up other people. He must be bright enough to know how to put his guest on display in an interesting way but not so bright as to short-circuit the fantasy of the ordinary viewer, "Hey, I could be up there." This person of ordinary intelligence, looks, and accomplishments has his strongest literary affinities with the heroes of stage comedy,[1] low-definition people whose most consistent visible attributes are a certain flexibility and a face that appears to be turned towards the future. The ratings catastrophe of Joan Rivers stands as a warning to the entire industry about the hazards of letting a high-profile personality host a talk show in an important time slot.

The guest, on the other hand, is utterly opposite: exotic, celebrated, often brilliantly accomplished. Eminent politicians, actors, comedians, celebrities

(Jimmy the Greek, Olympic athletes, Donald and Ivana Trump) are all perfect. A certain element of showmanship, or a flair for exhibitionism, can be a substantial asset. Potentially ordinary people who have undergone extraordinary experiences—victims of incest, for example—are also good, especially in the group format. Phil Donohue has gotten himself into drag to do cross-dressing.[2] Where is the limit to the extraordinary, the deviant, and the exotic, in talk show theme?

"Necrophilia," says Sally Jessy Raphael, and continues with emphatic indignation, "I definitely would not do a show on necrophilia."[3] In any case, the rule for the guest or for the subject represented by the guest is: the higher the definition and the more exotic, the better. Some kind of appeal to the voyeur that lurks in every member of the audience is essential.

LIFE AND ART

So pervasive is the talk show and its rhetorical modes in our daily lives that it sometimes requires extensive reflection for us to discriminate Life (real conversation) from Art (the conversation of the talk show). Consider the following occurrence, to which I was recently witness and audience.

It was a dinner for sixteen, held in a restaurant after a university graduation, and we were seated, eight to a side, at a long table: two graduates with assorted parents, aunts, uncles, friends, and siblings. The graduate on my left, Willa, perhaps twenty-five years of age, was exchanging small talk across the table with her older brother John, perhaps thirty-five, whom she had not seen in some time. The information floated down the table that one couple present had just rented and moved to a small farm, a former sheep spread, on which extensive presence of coyote had been confirmed and possible presence of wolf had been suspected.

John spoke, and in speaking silenced everyone:[4] "There are definitely wolves there. Though Madoc is in the southern part of their range, it *is* in their range, and in that part of Ontario wherever there are sheep there are wolves."

As I silently wondered whether he had gleaned this information from Aesop or from Roger Tory Peterson, Willa provoked her brother to continue.

"That's fascinating," she said, "how did you know this?"

"When I worked for the Ministry of Natural Resources, I took a course on wolves up near Lake Superior, and there are definitely wolves on that place of the Johnsons."

There was no time to meditate Willa's easy capacity for fascination. She was upon him again, in full eye contact, with another question: "But the sheep operation was shut down two years ago. Would the wolves still be there?"

"They certainly *could* be there, especially if there are other sheep operations in the area. And *if* these are nearby, then there are certainly wolves still there."

"How would you check? How could you definitely verify their presence?"

"Well, there are several ways. Easiest is that of listening carefully for their call at night, downwind of them. It is an easy call to recognize—a tenor monotone, as opposed to the treble warble of the coyote.''

"Fascinating. How would you know it wasn't a dog?"

"You might not be able to tell, especially if you are a wolf neophyte. The larger, more deep-chested dogs like the Greenland Husky or the Alaska Malamute have a monotone call that is virtually indistinguishable from a wolf's.''

"But there are other ways. . . . ''

"Yes. There is the track, which is especially visible after recent rain or snow, and there is the stool, or scat as the naturalists call it. . . . ''

And on it went for a full seven and a half minutes, with Willa continually giving off both the words and the body language of fascination, and John providing fact after fascinating fact about paw prints (the wolf's is five to six inches, the coyote's only four to four and a half), length of stride (the wolf's is five to six feet, the coyote's forty-two to forty-eight inches), scat size (six inches to four, though young wolves can produce confusion on this point of measurement), and scat texture (there are major differences arising from the greater likelihood of the coyote consuming not only vegetable matter but the hair and/or feathers of his prey). The parents of this pair swelled with interest and with visible pride at the "conversational" talents of their offspring. The rest of us either sat attentively or played in desultory and furtive fashion with our mixed green salad. This was a performance, unrehearsed to be sure, and there was agreement among others at the table that any interruption would be rude. We all knew, at least dimly and intuitively, that we had been cast in the role of audience at a TV talk show that was being presented to us without intercession of cameras, monitors, producers, or unions. At the end of the exchange John, his performance over, fell into a silence that lasted the rest of the evening, though his sister persisted in attempting to "talk show" several others at the table. She was foiled by the centrifugal character of the seating arrangement.

That dialogue was a textbook case of Life imitating Art, in short a third stage phenomenon in the Art-Life relationship. Within any genre, such a relationship is likely to develop through four stages; this book might be considered a manifestation of Stage IV. In Stage I, in original genres such as drama or epic, the province of Life and the province of Art are separate, connected only through a presentational (as opposed to representational) nexus: for example, medieval mystery plays or Homeric epic or classical Greek tragedy. (A tragedy is an imitation of an action, said Aristotle, and the imitation was oblique.) In grafted or secondary genres, such as formal printed language (grafted onto the rhetoric of formal speech) or TV drama (grafted onto radio drama), Stage I may be marked by the genre's retention of certain useless features of its rootstock. For example, formal English prose in print retained the syndetic signals of oratory long after Gutenberg had launched Europe into print culture. In English, it was not until the early 1700s that such signals, unnecessary in print, were sharply curtailed by Addison and Steele.[5] Similarly, early *Perry Mason* scripts for TV unnecessarily retained the nominatives of address that had been essential to the show in radio format:

Perry: Della, get me Paul Drake right away.

Della: Right, Perry. (Dials phone) Hello, Paul? This is Della. Perry wants a word with you.

Perry: (Picks up the phone): Hello Paul, this is Perry.

In Stage II, the grafted and secondary genres drop the obsolete signaling systems. In both original and grafted genres, Art becomes more self-consciously mimetic of Life, as in the development of realistic techniques of pictorial representation in the fourteenth and fifteenth centuries, and in the development of more "conversational" styles of writing in English beginning with the age of Dryden (1660 ff.).

In Stage III, the process is reversed, and Life begins to imitate Art. Addison becomes the paradigm for polite English prose; Delacroix provides the youth of France expressions of agony and heroism suitable for death in battle; Young Werther serves as a role-model for those who would like to experiment with Romantic *angst*; James Dean teaches a generation of young American males how to lean on the motorcycle, curl the defiant lip and at what angle to droop the cigarette from the corner of the mouth. Not long after, Jack Parr will be teaching slightly older Americans to raise one eyebrow, to say "I kid you not," and to use the demonstrative pronoun "this" in lieu of "that"—for example, to someone's statement that his mother has died, "This is a very great shame."

In Stage IV, Art returns, sometimes in the form of criticism, to give reflective consideration (often playful in character) to the question of what Art does to Life when Life imitates Art. Most obvious manifestations of this stage are the fictions of Pirandello, Calvino, Borges, and Berger, and the brief epidemic of movies occupied with the Life/Art question in the late 1970s and early 1980s (*Stunt Man*, *The French Lieutenant's Woman*, *All That Jazz*, and *My Dinner With André*). More recent filmic explorations of the question have tended to forsake the larger philosophical concerns of the four films just named in order to explore the Life-Art nexus on a media-centered way with radio and TV (*King of Comedy*, *Broadcast News*, *Talk Radio*).

RHETORIC: DISPLACEMENT

In the case of the TV interview and its immediate predecessor the radio interview, we are confronted with Stages II, III, and IV running concurrently. The movement of history has accelerated, and this fact has made reflection difficult. It therefore may be useful to consider some of the rhetorical features of the genre, using as an occasional paradigm the Willa-John exchange in the second part of this article. That conversation has the form of a dialogue, but only to the extent that it consists of two people taking turns talking. What in fact we were audience to was a monologue, or lecture, by John: the content of the conversation was entirely his. The style, on the other hand, was Willa's. John's facts were interesting enough, but the most memorable formal features of the conversation lay in the verve of his interrogator and in the practiced slickness of her manner of leading him on.

It is thus with all the great radio and TV "personalities" who do interviews: what tends to stay with us over the long run is not the content (interviewee) but the style (interviewer), especially that part of style which consists of mannerisms. Recollect briefly the work of any of these people: Buckley[6] (the rolling eyes, the "weeeeeell," the eruditely interrogative, sometimes prosecutorial approach, the antiquated turns of English phrasing), Cavett ("That reminds me of a story about me ... "), Parr (the affectations described a few paragraphs above), Winfrey (the owner of more different ways of suggesting empathy than are at the disposal of the entire psychiatric staff of Columbia Presbyterian Hospital), and even—nearly three decades back—the hardy aboriginal David Susskind (the heavy handedness of his ironies, the ironic asides and leering glances at the camera, the drooling sycophancy of his manner with people he liked or admired such as Adlai Stevenson). Take a fragment of the style of any of these people, and most who had seen them would recognize who was involved. But how much of the content that appeared on their shows would we recognize or recollect? Far less, I dare say.[7] And why?

The reason is simple. Content is accidental; style is recursive and systematic. In Art as in Life, style tends to be more memorable than content (we recognize voices on the phone saying things we have never heard them say before), and nowhere is this proposition more true than in the visual media. How many people who saw the particular Winfrey show will long remember much from the discourse of the ladies who had been three-time losers as battered wives, beyond the fact that the ministrations of a therapist had been of some use to them? One, two, three years from now, the bulk of the audience will remember very little of the detail in their accounts, but there will be strong recollection of Ms. Winfrey's sympathetic handling of her guests and her way of bringing to her task all the manifold apparatus of sisterhood, friendship, and solidarity.

Nevertheless, withal, something is wrong. However much we may admire the erudite urbanity of Buckley, the ability of Cavett to make an interview look like a genuine conversation between two real people, or the richness and variety of Winfrey's visible empathy, the physical extrusion of the style of a piece of discourse from its content presents us with a displacement probably unprecedented in the history of human communication. It is certainly unprecedented as a pervasive element in our lives. The implications of this displacement, which we shall return to later, may be disturbing.

There is also another kind of rhetorical displacement in these dialogues. In the classical model of rhetoric and in its progeny, a rhetorical situation comprises four elements: speaker, subject, audience, and occasion. In the interview, the speaker's traditional functions and attributes are divided, as we have seen, between interviewer and interviewee. There is a similar division in those of the audience. The nominal speaker is the interviewee and the nominal audience is the interviewer; indeed, it is sometimes clear from body language, eye contact, and other paralinguistic aspects of an interviewee's behavior that he believes himself to be addressing the program host. But the real audience is in the studio and out there beyond the cameras. The host always knows this fact, and the best kind of interviewee will know it, too, and play to it as John did with Willa.[8]

The displacement that consists in the extrusion of nominal audience from real audience has a more extensive and richer body of precedent than that involving style and content, and the reason is simple: utterance intended to be overheard is probably almost as old as discourse itself. We have all encountered it in our daily lives. Though it is sometimes mainly for display (e.g., certain loud conversations in restaurants), its usual context—indeed, its true native context—is the power play. Sometimes the power plays are intrafamilial: one sibling will shout at the other, "Ronnie stop hitting me!" knowing full well that Mother, two rooms away, is the true audience. Spouse versus spouse arguments are often staged for the benefit of the neighbors or the children (who can get whom on whose side?). Other plays of this sort are likely to be institutional rather than domestic in their settings—military organizations or schools. When the sergeant shouts at the raw recruit in front of all hands, "Hold the fuckin' rifle like that again, soldier, and your ass is guava jelly!" he knows that his powers of edification are being expended on a more numerous audience than the one recruit and that the real message has more to it than how not to hold a rifle. Similarly, the teacher will often isolate an aberrant member of a class for public dialogue for the benefit of the third parties present, especially in grades six through nine. The habitual context of this particular displacement does not have felicitous associations.

I believe this last to be an important fact. Context-defined vocabulary carries with it strong association. For example, "charges," "accused," "prosecutor," and other members of that lexical set produce instantaneous associations of adversary proceedings, courtrooms, and the like. Formal settings—contexts that are content-defined—will do the same thing: the psychiatrist's couch, the negotiating table, the judge's bench and witness box, the altar, and the pulpit. Rhetorical modes likewise can have strong suggestive power.[9] When the guest participates in the charade that is the dialogue intended to be overheard, does the host somewhere in the deep structure of the transaction become the authority figure in whose hand lies the continuous threat of humiliation before the multitude?

RHETORIC: CLOSURE AND CONNECTEDNESS

"A speaker ready to give up his role employs signals through multiple channels: content, syntax, intonation contour, paralinguistic behavior, and bodily gesture.''[10] These are the signals of closure, or readiness to sign off. On the talk show it is common for the host not to attend upon them. Often the failure to wait for the signals of closure is part of a gag, as in the following exchanges. Carson, at the top of the show, asks his straight man, 'Did you have a nice Thanksgiving?'-

"Yeah, wonderful. We had this terrific turkey."

"Who cooked the turkey?"

"I did. It's a special family recipe. We use Courvoisier in the stuffing."

"I get it. You drink the stuffing and throw out the turkey."

(Roar of laughter from the studio audience). CUT. Similarly, the Carson figure in *King of Comedy*, Jerry Langford (played by Jerry Lewis), asks his straight man Ed Herlihy how he's feeling tonight, and Herlihy replies, "Wonderful."

"Wonderful," Jerry says, "Sorry to wake you."

(Roar of laughter from the studio audience). CUT.

The two examples above are mere warmer-uppers for the audience. Such encounters are usually placed at the beginning of a show, and they are too brief in any case to warrant the apparatus of closure signals, even though the termination is abrupt and turns the straight man into the butt of the joke. In longer encounters, the host often not only does not wait for visible closure but interrupts in the face of a guest's obvious desire to continue. Morton Shulman, the ex-coroner whose show was on CTV in Toronto for what seemed an eternity, was a past master at this latter trick. Things would routinely come out like "Why should I let you continue? You've talked twice already and everybody can see you're being totally inconsistent." The other Morton (Downey, Jr.) does likewise: as the vegetarian is expositing her abstention from all things animal including clothes, Downey interrupts, "I eat raw hamburger. I eat raw fish. I smoke four packs of cigarettes a day; I have about four drinks. I'm fifty-five years old, and I look as good as you do!" CUT. In the cases of the two Mortons, and of David Letterman, the naive belief that the normal rules of human interchange will be respected often makes the guest an easy target for the host, who has right of utter disregard of those rules, a right not extended to the guest.

This difference in status is often magnified by dissociative apparatus in the physical arrangements of the show—most commonly by the fact that the guest must be stationary while the host is relatively free to roam. The host thus becomes the teacher-figure, able to invert in Art the advantage that in Life genius or even distinctiveness will often have over mediocrity.

Not all talk show hosts cherish eye contact in the manner of Willa. On the *Tonight Show*, both host and guest sit on chairs that face the audience at an angle of sixty to seventy-five degrees, so that in order to make eye contact both must turn their bodies. Thus not only is such contact inhibited, but further opportunities are created for the host to disrupt the interchange and play to the studio audience. I can recall a memorable and paradigmatic exchange on another show in similar format that occurred shortly after the 1984 Olympics. A young female competitor in track was being interviewed.

Host: What got you into track? Was it at school?

Athlete: Well, when I was thirteen, I noticed I could run faster than all the boys, so I joined a track club, got me a coach, and started running regular and pumping weights.

Host: Couldn't you have run for the team at school?

Athlete: I could've run for the boy's team but I didn't want to do that, so I ran at the club. School didn't have a girl's team. That school still don't have a girl's team.

Host: And you in the Olympics. How do you feel about that?

Athlete: I think the denial of opportunity to female athletes in our schools and colleges in this country is a national disgrace.

Host (Squeezing her bicep): But you were still able to develop all those muscles over at the club . . .

Athlete (Confused): Yeah. Oh yeah.

Host (Turning away from the athlete and grinning at the audience): I'm sure glad I didn't have to be your brother!

(Roar of laughter). CUT. Commercial.

Indeed, one often suspects—especially in cases like Shulman, Downey, Letterman and Rivera—that it is interactional insensitivity that lands someone his job as a program host, or at least an ability to disregard the norms of interaction without feeling uncomfortable in the process. Such insensitivity was the principal qualification that turned Dallas suit salesman Barry Golden (Eric Bogosian cast as a visual dead ringer for Tiny Tim) into radio phone show host Barry Champlain in *Talk Radio*. ''You're my joker, Barry,'' says his station head, Dan, ''You hang up on people.'' And his highly developed talent for ignoring, misinterpreting, and walking roughshod over the signals of others seems totally unconscious, even though it pervades his private life as well. His producer-mistress, Laura, complains, ''When I approach you as your producer you treat me like a girlfriend, and when I approach you as a girlfriend you treat me like a wife.'' For the prattling host, displacement is a way of life.

STAGE IV: ART RECONSIDERS LIFE IMITATING ART

In *Broadcast News*, Life (news) is not good enough if it does not imitate Art (soap opera). The William Hurt character, an airhead with a telegenic front, understands this fact, and is able to manufacture tears, especially generated and videotaped, in a news interview on date rape. His eventual promotion to national news anchor of his network and his triumph over his more scrupulous, more intelligent, more morally sensitive colleagues is a media parable for our times.

Broadcast News has but partial relevance here, though it makes a persuasive presentation of television's insistent tendency to improve upon reality.[11] More directly relevant to the decorums of the talk show is *King of Comedy*, a DeNiro-Scorsese collaboration about a New York nobody named Rupert Pupkin (played by DeNiro).

Pupkin and his sidekick Masha (Sandra Bernhard), a slightly deranged rich kid from Manhattan, have focused all their energies on celebrity, notably on New York talk show host Jerry Langford. Masha's interest is largely devotional, but Rupert's interest in Jerry not only includes but transcends devotion: he wants to do a comic monologue on Jerry's show. One night Rupert and Masha contrive a situation at the studio exit in which, in the confusion of a mob scene, Rupert gets to drive away with Jerry in Jerry's chauffeured car. He presses Jerry for an audition, and Jerry tells him (to get rid of him) to drop a tape of his work off at the office of the Langford show. At the entrance to Jerry's Manhattan apartment building and a day later, at Jerry's office, Rupert shows himself a hard man to get rid of; signals of closure, even when reinforced by the security staff, are wasted on him.

Rupert's brief encounter with Jerry drives him into three fantasy sequences: (1) In his basement, which incidentally is set up as a talk show studio with lifesize cardboard figures of celebrities like Liza Minelli waiting to be "interviewed," he fantasizes that Jerry is asking him to take the show for six weeks; (2) he fantasizes that Jerry invites him for the weekend to the Langford estate in the exurbs of New York, to work on Rupert's material; (3) he imagines a ceremony, presided over by his former high school principal, in which he marries a former classmate, the darkly handsome Rita, now a Manhattan barmaid. Victor Borge plays the wedding march. It is all on national TV.

Next Saturday morning, acting on Jerry's fantasy-invitation, Rupert takes Rita to Jerry's place, reaching their destination by train and taxi. Jerry is out playing golf, but they make themselves at home and wait. Johno, the Japanese houseman, gets hold of Jerry on the phone to give him the news. When he does come in, golf club in hand, he is momentarily flummoxed, but on recovering his composure he throws out the two uninvited guests. The following week, frustrated by being continually stonewalled at Jerry's home and office, Rupert, assisted by Masha and Masha's family Mercedes, kidnaps Jerry on his way to work and takes him to the posh townhouse of Masha's absent parents. The payoff for her is to be a candlelit dinner with Jerry; for Rupert, a fifteen minute appearance on *The Jerry Langford Show*.

Each gets the desired payoff. But at the candlelit dinner, after Masha strips down to her bra and step-ins, Jerry—strapped into a chair, immobilized with adhesive tape—asks her to cut him loose, which she does. He then knocks her down and flees the house, but not in time to stop Rupert from appearing as "The New King of Comedy" on the *Jerry Langford Show*, guest-hosted by Tony Randall. After going to Rita's bar to view the previously taped show, Rupert surrenders to the two FBI men who have been his constant companions since he appeared at the TV station for taping early in the evening. He is sentenced to a tour at Allenwood Penitentiary, where he writes a best-selling autobiography, *King for a Night*. He also acquires an agent. After all, his monologue had ultimately been seen by a record eighty-seven million viewers, and his kidnap caper had been given feature coverage by every single nationally distributed magazine. When he is released from Allenwood at age thirty-seven, he is made host of his own talk show.

Rupert is the perfect creature, the ultimate product of the age of telegenic colloquy. Life (reality) and Art (fantasy) in Rupert's mind are merged and indistinguishable from one another.[12] His immunity to signals of closure is so total as to be almost autistic, his lust for self-display exceeds even Jerry Langford's, and the kidnaping caper reveals a genuine talent for the exotic and sensational. When he is given his own show at the end of the film, it is only a matter of justice prevailing. He has demonstrated beyond a doubt that he has, to an exceptional degree, the qualifications for the job.

ENVOI: MR. HOST, HAVEN'T WE MET YOU SOMEWHERE BEFORE?

Through the use of visual tropes, Scorsese makes a few telling points on the style-content question. For example, the "guests" in the fantasy studio in Rupert's basement are life-size photographs mounted on rigid board—pure material, total content.[13] Jerry's function as total style is emphasized in a number of ways. His life is unfurnished; the interiors are white and bare as a hospital, and the one picture we are allowed to see is of him. He has no friends or companions; the only humanity in his life is Johno, whose purpose is largely summed up in Jerry's command to him after Rupert and Rita are dismissed: "Johno, lock that door!" Jerry's trademark is a single-line profile drawing of him, starting at the back of the head and moving forward past the nose and chin to the throat: the smiling face with nothing behind it, the personification of geniality but only as a style without content.

Our style—the style of each of us—is the distinctive sum of the elements of constant form that distinguishes each of us from everyone else. Who has the right to have a style? Constitutionally each of us does, provided our style does not include blowing up city hall or committing certain antisocial acts against our fellow citizens. But the decorums of the TV talk show suggest otherwise, for it is the host alone who possesses that right.

In the Berlin of the late 1930s, at the mass rallies organized on Hitler's behalf by Mr. Goebbels and his colleagues, Hitler would come down the avenue approaching the speaker's podium surrounded by ten thousand goose-stepping soldiers. But Hitler would walk, and his different gait would make him the most conspicuous thing there, even in the midst of the marching soldiery.[14] It was unto him alone, the incarnation of the *Volksgeist*, that style—the deviance that consisted in his natural gait—was vouchsafed.

It is similar with the host of the talk show. He, too, is the incarnation of the *Volksgeist*. The painter or sculptor in this society who lets his work hang or stand on public exhibit runs a high risk of having that work trashed and vandalized as recompense for the public display of the deviance that lies in his genius. Our host, on the other hand, with his waist-high sensibility, his appearance of utter averageness, and his absolute freedom from meaningful content or achievement, will be applauded for whatever he wants to be applauded for.[15] There is a strong possibility that, in the manner of the conversation books of the seventeenth and eighteenth centuries, he is going to be the paradigm for our social relations in the 1990s and on into the indefinite future. And even if he is not to be that paradigm, what is it in us and in our culture that accounts for the thralldom in which he holds us?

It is, of course, difficult to formulate a simple answer to a question of such rich and layered complexity, but I can make a suggestion. Over a century and a half ago, in *Democracy in America*, Alexis de Tocqueville formulated his famous paradox: that in its Constitution and laws the United States had conferred upon its citizens more liberty, more vested right to deviance, than any other polity in history, but that in its actual social behavior American society has a similarly high and equally unprecedented level of conformity.

As a general truth about American culture, de Tocqueville's paradox has had a remarkable longevity, and as a brief formulation of what we are it may to this day have had no peer. Surely many of the tensions and contradictions in American life take place along the axis of conformity and deviance, mediocrity and genius, and the collective and the individual. The American talk show gathers up the poles between which these tensions operate. On behalf of our collective selves it brings deviance, genius, and individuality into the mainstream—sometimes by humiliating them, sometimes merely by putting them on display. It is the ultimate melting pot device, whoever the host, whoever the guest. When Morton Downey, Jr. brings that vegetarian to her knees, he does more than might be done by fifty advertisements from General Foods to reassure us that the national dietary and sartorial habits are humane, healthy, and environmentally sound. When Oprah gets Donald Trump to make a few modest disclosures about his French military jet helicopter, the allegorical process that is set in motion ("He got a good deal like me with my Ford Tempo") does more to make Trump like the rest of us than might be done by a century of highly progressive taxation. Is it not possible that the talk show's practitioners have developed over the years an instrument of the collective will more subtle than the law, more visible than the police, and indeed as powerful as democracy itself?

NOTES

1. Northrop Frye, "The Mythos of Spring," *Anatomy of Criticism* (Princeton, 1957), 160ff.

2. It is interesting that Donohue used cross-dressing instead of transvestitism: the terminology indicates implicit approval of the activity by the transfer from a classical name to an English one. The strictly verboten sexual intercourse of my teenage years (the late 1940s) was transmuted about twenty years ago into the original English monosyllable coincident with its general acceptance by the North American single population.

3. *CBC Journal*, the nightly magazine show of the Canadian Broadcasting Company, did a study of trash and tabloid TV in November of 1988. Ms. Raphael's words are from an interview on that show. I am much indebted to Dr. Kimberly Echlin, cultural affairs producer for *Journal*, for letting me see the file tape.

4. There are two kinds of quotation used in this article: verbatim, transcribed from a videotape; and reconstructed, taken from memory and notes. Verbatim quotation is signaled by double quote marks (''). Reconstructed quotation is signaled by single quotes (').

5. Robert Cluett, *Prose Style and Critical Reading* (New York, 1976), chap. 9.

6. Buckley is an exception to the talk show type in two respects: formidable intelligence and genuine achievement. But *Firing Line* was a weekly rather than a daily show, and it was aired on PBS rather than on a major commercial network.

7. There are exceptions to this rule too. A glittering one here is a talk show appearance of Zsa Zsa Gabor several years ago (10? 15?). I cannot remember who the host was. Her trick was to ignore all the normal constraints on the guest role and thereby to produce an inverted transaction.

8. Northrop Frye, cited in note 1, was a cardinal instance of a bad guest, refusing to believe in the reality either of his interviewer or of the TV audience. Once at CBC, when retaping for the second time an interview of Frye by Eli Mandel, the frustrated producer stopped everything and pleaded, ''Please, Mr. Frye, you must do a better job of looking interested in Eli.'' Frye's reply: ''I'm not interested in Eli. I'm interested in what he's saying.''

9. Nobody in our time has had a keener appreciation of context defined language than Martin Luther King, Jr. His ability to couch social issues in the language of The Psalms was a master stroke of rhetoric and, it seems to me, a key ingredient in his remarkable success.

10. Erving Goffman, *Relations in Public* (New York, 1972), 4.

11. The most notorious case of ''improved'' news, or at least the one given the greatest attention, was during the Vietnam War, when the news department of a major network edited and recut the tape of an interview with a high-ranking officer in the U.S. Army, so that the intent of his utterances was warped.

12. The only reality to intrude upon Rupert's life is his mother, played with delicious irony by the mother of the film's director. But we never see her; she is only a voice that rasps from upstairs ''Rooo-pert!'' to disrupt his fantasies in the basement ''studio.''

13. Reification of the interviewee is not confined to the talk show. My CBC informant, Dr. Echlin, tells me that news reporters speak of a potential interviewee as ''my interview.''

14. This information comes from two conversations I had in 1952–53 in the New York Athletic Club with a man introduced to me as Colonel James Cosgrove, who claimed to have been a military attaché at the American Embassy in Berlin in 1936–37. I have not been able to verify his claim, nor have I been able to see film footage of Hitler calling attention to himself in the fashion described. The colonel's report, nevertheless, has a very high degree of plausibility, given the propaganda talents of those around Hitler.

15. A fine instance of the lowest-common-denominator occurred on the *Tonight Show* during Christmas week, 1988, with Jay Leno as host: 'Arafat is spending Christmas with Hitler.' (Pause) (Scattered laughter). 'They were gonna make it a foursome, but Kadaffi

and Khomeni couldn't make it.' (Roar of laughter from audience). The assumption underneath this joke is clear: It is OK to be a bigot about a race, religion, or a movement for national independence so long as the butt of your joke is currently unfashionable. No doubt the great bulk of regular viewers and regular members of the studio audience would agree. Let's face it, there is one thing the talk show guys are really good at: they know who their people are.

2

Television Intimacy: Paradoxes of Trust and Romance

Judith Kegan Gardiner

Television is at once the most intimate and the most public of contemporary cultural forms; it shapes our images of both intimacy and community. We rely on it for news and entertainment, yet we distrust the medium. While this knowing distrust colors our responses to everything we watch, it is especially pronounced in the case of sentimental or romantic programs. The daytime program *Love Connection* begins with an enthusiastic male voice telling us that here "modern technology meets old-fashioned romance." Dedicated to ensuring that boy meets girl three times each half hour and to involving its audience in the rituals of the "dating game," *Love Connection* (and similar daytime programs) epitomize the contradictions of contemporary society concerning heterosexuality and intimacy, "modern" television and "old-fashioned" trust. Increasingly, adults in our society want and expect rewarding, even blissful personal relationships, yet distrust trust, fear being known, and don't have time for lifetime commitments.

Prime time television aims to entertain a broader range of viewers with a broader range of fare. The evening melodramas set in exciting workplaces like hospitals, police stations, and law offices provide immediate action, humor, and violence, but they also solicit their viewers' long-term identification with their central characters, especially with their romantic attachments. Leisurely courtships between romantic couples on screen parallel the medium's courtship of its consumer viewers. In *Moonlighting*, one of the self-conscious prime time serials, the prolonged romantic impasse between the glamorous main characters illustrates the contemporary crisis of trust in heterosexual relations and attracts us through its very ambivalence.

INTIMACY AND POPULAR CULTURE

The combination of "technology" and "romance" defines American television, which is both slickly beautiful and motivated by marketing. We are accustomed to commercials that shed the aura of romance over products we are being taught to desire, commercials that show couples hugging on wind-swept beaches, their hair luminously shampooed or skin protected or thirst quenched by appropriate products. Moreover, commercials establish the format for the rest of television programming, so that news, science, and religion appear as parables of fulfilled desire, and women on screen, whether reading news or turning quiz answers, stand lusciously packaged to evoke female envy and male lust.[1] Easy as it is to condemn the prostitution of romance to sales, more radical critics question the very nature of television romance.

To the demystifier, romance is always a trap. Masculinist lore warns men not to fall prey to female domestication; feminist critics blame romance for luring women into the male-dominated institution of marriage. The first feminist television critics decried the stereotypes to which women were relegated, stereotypes organized around the pole of male desire, so that lovely dumb ingenues fled men sought by vicious vamps. These critics found such stereotypes demeaning and also outdated. In the last decade, women have achieved better representation on television. There are fewer housewives and more female heroes who are working or single or divorced, and women are interested in and attractive to men as young teenagers and as wisecracking grannies. The ditzy housewife of *I Love Lucy* is replaced by Mary Tyler Moore, responsible if beleaguered professional, and she, in turn, by the career and child-juggling yuppies of *thirtysomething*. The demographics of representation may be less interesting, however, than the paradoxes of desire, as television persuades us what we men and women want.

Traditionally, women's culture has been built upon desires inscribed within the culture as a whole. Insofar as women inhabited the "separate sphere" of domestic life, literature by and for women could explore the range of opportunities available within that sphere.[2] Many cherished English and American novels from the eighteenth century through the twentieth celebrate courtship leading to marriage, often to the point that this seemed women's only plot. Jane Austen and her followers showed young women defining themselves through their choice of men, learning caution against handsome seducers and reverence for rich, mature, moral men like Fitzwilliam Darcy or Mr. Knightley. If romances like *Wuthering Heights* thrilled women by repossessing their right to passion, more frequently the novel warned women against foolish or hasty marriage choices, assuming that marriage was the most crucial decision of a woman's life, her vocation and the irrevocable source of her later misery or happiness. Social constraints on decorous behavior and financial incentives for marriage meant that courtship was a time of potential camouflage and persiflage as much as of self revelation. Courtship did not necessarily bring knowledge of the other, true intimacy, or trust, and the courtship novel had to stage trials of faith so that we and the heroine could discern her rightful soulmate.

From the beginnings of the contemporary women's movement, feminist critics assailed romance as a root of women's oppression and popular culture marketed to women as its poisonous fruit. Germaine Greer excoriated the "middle class myth of love and marriage" in English literature from Shakespeare to modern women's magazines: supposedly transcendent romance corrals people into monogamous heterosexual couples made up of male breadwinners and female childbearers.[3] Today's popular culture, critics say, has the same pernicious effects, especially on women. Tania Modleski analyzes the psychology of patriarchy embedded in popular romances and soap operas, whereas Janice Radway upholds the woman romance reader's right to escape her real circumstances within the locked space of addictive popular fiction.[4] Looking at the most recent romances, in which women can be freely sexual, Carol Thurston finds women's popular culture becoming more progressive.[5]

The current "revolutions" in U.S. social relations are interlinked. Most American women are in the paid labor force most of their lives, even when their fewer children are young, and the role of full-time homemaker is no longer the dominant one. Although job segregation by sex and the differential between male and female wages remain high, women are now better represented than formerly in a number of high prestige occupations. The radical 1960s goal of smashing monogamy now appears equivocally fulfilled in the increasing number of divorces, single mothers, and reshuffled families. People experience greater sexual access than in former generations and expect to spend less of their lives in monogamous unions.

As with other "revolutionary" situations, we may have a crisis of rising expectations about personal relations at the same time that the real relations are changing in unexpected ways. Women have higher expectations for their autonomy, career advancement, and sexual fulfillment, and at the same time greater fears about poverty and male violence to women. The 1950s' "war between the sexes," which depended on stable but potentially antagonistic social roles for men and women, has been replaced by "tales from the front," the anarchic battlefield of new sexual mores.

The old courtship novel assumed that it was difficult to know the other during courtship, but necessary because knowledge after commitment to an irrevocable institution would arrive too late. Contemporary circumstances would seem to have erased this problem by creating a ready market of social availability in which single persons are encouraged to meet, mingle, and, until the recent sexual diseases scare, become sexually intimate before making long-term commitments. Recent movies highlight the psychology of fear about the sexual intimacy that precedes trust. Casual sex with a woman exposes a man to horrifying peril in *Fatal Attraction*, and intimacy leads to betrayal—and betrayal to intimacy—in David Mamet's *House of Games*. Such plots raise questions of epistemology as well as of morals. The terror of these films is not simply that sex can kill, but also that one does not know the people one seems to know most intimately. Intimacy remains illusive and desired, though the desire may be sexually asymmetrical: women yearn for intimacy and understanding which men do not provide, even men who are their lovers or husbands, whereas much male literature remains "homosocial," dependent on men's bonds with one another and their distrust of women.[6]

According to current studies, American women seek more intimacy than they feel they get, especially in heterosexual relationships. Nancy Chodorow describes a cycle whereby girls raised by women develop capacities for intimacy and empathy; boys, who are also raised by women, form their identities by differentiation and hence need autonomy. Such boys grow into men who fear reengulfment in the feminine and so distance their female lovers.[7] In *Intimate Strangers*, Lillian Rubin spells out the sociology of this dilemma. Men she interviewed sought independence and feared intimacy, while women longed for intimacy with men that approximated their ties to their mothers and to female friends.[8] Women associate self-disclosure with affection and isolation with danger, whereas men feel threatened by intimacy.[9] Scholars studying supermarket romances and television soap operas see women as addicted to literary forms that both provoke and assuage their anxieties about heterosexual attachments. By its domestic form, television incites anxieties about intimacy versus isolation, anxieties which are particularly evident in romantic plots.

Television is a perverse and paradoxical medium with respect to intimacy. Most people watch it in intimate settings—either when they are alone, like women doing housework, or with lovers or family members at home.[10] It is usually off limits to workers, even in workplaces with sets, and it is considered rude to leave a set on when entertaining formally. In a sense, with its private setting and narrow range, television is always intimate, murmuring semi-heeded throughout the waking hours. In some households, televisions stay on in children's rooms all night, so that they will know when to get up and go to school. But if television is intimate in its reception, it is nonetheless public—providing our access to the world at large, our chief source of information about public affairs, sports, fashions, and products, as well as entertainment. Television gives every American stories and characters with which to identify, and it focuses social discourse. I know young lawyers, for example, who rush home to watch *L. A. Law* in the evening so that they can discuss it at the office the following morning.

Jerzy Kozinsky did an experiment with school children in which he asked them embarrassing questions like whether they masturbated or stole. The children were reluctant to reply. However, when he told them he was making a television documentary which their family and teachers might see, the same children confidently confessed their misdeeds to an invisible but implied public.[11] The television form invited disclosure; the familiar, yet faceless television medium inspired trust. Since what makes someone a television celebrity is being on television, anyone can imagine being a television celebrity, and the children imitated their television models with ease and poise.

Daytime television programs often play on this imaginary democracy of the medium, inviting "real people" to participate with whom the audience can identify. In programs like *The Dating Game*, the ironies of identification and intimacy are complex. As in Kozinsky's experiment, familiarity with television inspires viewers to stage themselves as celebrities in view, even in a context where they are ostensibly seeking intimacy, individuality, and Mr. or Ms. Right, their unique romantic complement.

LOVE CONNECTIONS

Whereas the traditional English novel made courtship its entire plot, "dating game" television programs truncate traditional narratives into capsule versions of erotic attraction, choice, satisfaction, and disillusionment. *Love Connection's* opening voiceover promises that here "you hear all the intimate details." Such shows star "real people," not fictional characters, who engage in an abbreviated courtship in which the audience gets to participate. The cartoon that accompanies the credits promises that people's lives can follow the carefree pattern of cartoons—though its childish form makes us skeptical. On the *Love Connection*, both male and female contestants pick one of three people after viewing video-tapes in which the potential dates describe themselves. The original contestant then dates the chosen applicant, and both report their adventures on the air. The private video contest that the candidate watches is thus not identical to the show that we see. For us and the studio audience, it is as though the couple meets for the first time when the audience meets them, since past and present conflate into a single ten minute segment for each couple.

The format of the program parodies the American political process in that the studio audience votes along with the person on stage to determine which of the three candidates would make the best date. As in politics or market research, the three candidates have been strictly preselected. Matches are proposed only for persons of the same race and approximately similar age, with the men often a few years older than the women. The contestants are similar in class background as well; lower middle class occupations like legal assistant or travel agent predominate. A number of people seem to have come to California because they aspire to careers in entertainment. They describe themselves as part-time models, actors, or musicians. Implicitly, their goal is less to find a date than to be seen on television. The contestants also match one another in levels of conventional attractiveness—an ungainly man chooses among three ordinary looking women, whereas a female model picks among three men who could be models as well.

As in American politics, the videotaped speeches are presumably much more informative than the few-second clips we see. In these clips, the candidates list their likes and dislikes, condensing their personalities into a few quirks of taste.

For example, one woman says her worst first date was a man who said he'd lost his wallet and expected her to pay. A man states he's really attracted to redheads but can't stand women with clammy hands. Another man says he likes eating hotdogs at ballgames, then dancing all night.

From buttons on their chairs, the studio audience votes for the most suitable match. This apparently democratic choice is irrelevant, however, since the contestant has already chosen and met his or her date, and both members of the couple appear to give their versions of what happened and to tell us what they think of one another. The screen then flashes the percentage of the audience who voted for each, so that we may compare our choices with theirs. Usually the audience seems to vote simply for the most conventionally attractive person, that is, the one already most closely approximating the television ideal.

Again, it is appearances that matter most. A woman is "really disappointed" because her date wore bell-bottomed jeans; the man disliked the woman's appearance as well, saying "she looked like a pretty witch with all that eye makeup." High marks go to those who master the rituals of courtship. A man who bought a rose for each of his date's roommates plus a dozen for her gets an encouraging sigh from the audience, and the crowd titters when a woman says she drank only soft drinks in order not to get too friendly with an unappealing date. Another woman reports that she and her date "had a good conversation." The camera moves from the young woman's face to the host's as he asks her whether there was "any spark" between the couple. She felt the "love connection," the woman replies, but the man, whom the camera now captures, wanted to take things more slowly.

Everyone is assumed to start each date ready for romance with a clean slate, with preferences but without a history. Even in the few cases where potentially divisive issues surface, they are rapidly submerged. A thirty-one-year old medical equipment salesman with two children says he wants a woman who likes kids, but that is the end of the matter. There is no further discussion of his former marriage, divorce, or custody arrangements, and his children are thus simply another predilection, like New Wave music. As the participants describe their dates, the host wisecracks, gleefully embarrassing the participants and teasing their remarks for unintended erotic innuendoes.

The material for an entire courtship novel is here condensed into before and after anecdotes. The studio audience is flattered by the illusion of participation in this process, but the real pleasures offered it are the same as those offered the audience at home, the pleasures of eavesdropping and voyeurism fostered by the television medium. We can feel we are insiders, even matchmakers, enjoying an endless stream of gossip about who likes whom and who did what with whom. More frankly than many of our friends, the contestants tell us what they thought of each other and why.

Congruent with computer dating and personal ads as ways of marketing the self, the *Love Connection* allows the at-home audience to enjoy watching "real" people produce their own romantic stories, choose their partners, and plot their encounters. As in personal ads, people describe themselves through only a few tags; character is reduced to matters of taste, of brands of people who go with other brands. People stage themselves as potential catches; romance becomes a matter of consumption; and despite the higher official value accorded long term relationships, the format rewards instant attraction. Intimacy remains an implicit goal, but it is achieved through illusions of self-presentation. The program responds to the distrust the audience may feel both about everyday dating and about television dating by acting as chaperone and surrogate community for the new couple, judging their progress, oohing their happiness, snickering at their embarrassment, and envying their rewards.

If *Love Connection* miniaturizes courtship romances, the *Newlywed Game* abbreviates the marital situation comedy into a perpetual squabble between husbands and wives. With a proprietary air, the male host urges the audience to "meet my couples." As the program's paterfamilias, he incites rivalries among the young couples, who are like siblings competing for attention. "Your wives have been secluded safely offstage," the host assures the men, as if the women's temporary purdah releases the men into male camaraderie. On one show he asks the men, "what is a bad word in your house—'sex,' 'mom,' or 'marriage'?"

When the women emerge onstage in order to guess what their husbands said, the couples hug when they get the right answers. However, the show's enthusiasm ignites at disagreements and blazes with the airing of dirty linen. The retaliatory turnabout reverses the situation. It sequesters the husbands so that the wives can answer silly questions, but the questions are not random. They continually hover about sexual euphemisms, like where does your husband like to "make whoopee," and they plumb the trials of lower middle class family life, assuming that traditional sex roles should still be in force. What would your husband say you can't cook, the host asks the wives, and what can't your husband repair around the house. The more humiliating the anecdotes the better, as the wives remember their husbands caught under sinks or dirtied by broken vacuum cleaners. Recasting themselves as Dagwood and Blondie, a wife complains, "you always say I'm so stupid." The couples argue, "how could you say that?" "I thought our marriage was fine," a woman quavers, but her husband says things are "rocky." If they agree with one another and thus win points, they hug with elation, even if their agreement confirms bad news about their marriage, like the fact that both have recently considered separation.

As John Fiske and John Hartley note, the *Newlywed Game* is of interest in our time of high divorce.[12] It buttresses traditional ideas about marriage as a team effort while defusing incompatibility into Punch and Judy comedy that never questions the marital boundary. The program expresses more pervasive anxieties, however, not only about marriage but more generally about the meaning of knowing oneself through another person. In the *Newlywed Game*, intimacy is two-edged and dangerous. You win prizes if you are intimate enough to know what the other person will say, and teamwork consists in this congruence of perceptions. On the other hand, the other person knows your secrets and can reveal your personal identity as it is exemplified through your habits, like leaving dirty socks on the floor, or your history, like why you left your old lovers, or your idiosyncracies, like what vegetables you can't stand. This knowledge gives the knower power to humiliate the partner and betray the other's trust in the sanctity of shared secrets. Flush with the pleasures of publicity, one mate may ridicule the other on screen and form an alliance, instead, with the host and audience as intimate if temporary confidants.

PRIME CONTRADICTIONS

To turn from daytime dating games to prime time melodrama is to burst into the big time, with the rich, elegantly produced programs on which a network's popularity and profits ride. Romance in prime time is more complicated than earlier in the day. Daytime soap operas languidly explore character in decapitated triangles in which two people talk about a third.[13] As we have seen, the dating games triangulate the contestant's irritations with and desires for the other person through us, the judging audience. Intimacy is a goal and a danger for both sexes on these programs, though the predominantly female daytime audience may be thought especially interested in intimacy. In order to assess the roles of intimacy and trust in prime time, I looked in particular at a few of the programs being touted for their responsiveness to a changing society and especially to women's new positions and needs.

Many current evening series use an intertwined story line, a structure that solves some problems of both the soaps and the older prime time situation comedies. On the soaps, stories never conclude, and action is attenuated for the sake of the habitual if intermittent viewer. The classic sitcoms like *I Love Lucy* or *The Honeymooners* featured characters who could not change themselves or their allegiances. Marriage was their permanent and primary relationship, whether the couple fulfilled or transgressed traditional stereotypes. Lucy could be wilder than Ricky, Ralph more pompous than Alice, but they must be endlessly fooled by one another and endlessing trusting. More recent situation comedies expand the family and deflect its follies. Archie Bunker's racism was crude but charming, available for conservative corroboration and liberal rebuke, yet relevant to the family dynamics chiefly insofar as it proved father didn't know best. Father did know best on *The Cosby Show* in the conservative 1980s, but the family comedy remains essentially the same. Even in the reshuffled families with grandparents, adopted children, stepparents, and single parents, family members continue to resolve silly problems by the end of the half hour without learning from experience or growing up.

Prime time melodramas solve these structural problems by combining continuing heroes capable of change, with whom the audience can identify, with two-dimensional subordinates and dispensable antagonists. The work settings often resemble families. The wise police chiefs of *Hill Street Blues* and *Miami Vice* father their lively crews, and in such settings working women may be dutiful daughters or office wives, the "heart of the workplace" as Todd Gitlin commented about Mary Tyler Moore.[14] These prime time melodramas are set in workplaces that promise action, adventure, and new roles for women.

Such work settings correspond to the viewers' experience of meeting more people at work than at home, but this realism is minor in comparison with the vicarious excitements associated with crime, violence, and authority. For the viewer who delights in character more than action, such settings further our knowledge of how the characters respond to threats, dangers, and seductions. In these police stations, hospitals, and law offices, romances spring up both among the co-workers and between the central cast and guest stars. It is largely through these love plots, in fact, that programs create a sense of continuing and developing characters with internal depth. The habitual viewer follows these central characters and their affairs. A colleague, for example, explained to me in some detail Furillo's marital difficulties on *Hill Street Blues*. The central characters' love stories thus endow them with a private self broader than that displayed in their weekly solutions of crimes.

Heterosexual plots on prime time act as romantic glue. Often such romantic interest is used to attract more women viewers and to balance conventionally male-oriented violence. Despite the usefulness of romantic plots, the state of heterosexual relations represented on such programs is troubled in interesting ways. Of course, part of this apparent trouble is structural. In the old sitcoms the married had to stay married; in the new prime time melodramas, most of the unmarried have to stay available.

The obvious case of an explicitly liberal feminist television series is *Cagney and Lacey*. Conceived as a result of the second wave of the American women's movement in 1974 and written by feminists Barbara Avedon and Barbara Corday, the program was not aired until 1982. Its opening course was rocky, with ratings wavering though the critics were enthusiastic. After remodeling the characters to seem less lesbian and after glamorizing Christine Cagney, the series settled into a steady run, tackling a wide range of controversial issues from job discrimination to abortion.[15] *Cagney and Lacey* attempted to balance male dominance on prime time action programming with a show of interest to women, and it defied earlier conventions for presenting women on television. The popular action series of the 1970s, *Charlie's Angels*, featured strong, beautiful women who operated safely under remote male control.[16] In contrast, the female stars of *Cagney and Lacey* have all the advantages of their male counterparts on other police shows. The women are well-developed and autonomous actors who succeed as a team of complementary buddies.

Given the network's fear of implying a lesbian relationship between the two women, their heterosexual ties are manifest. Mary Beth Lacey (Tyne Daly) has a supportive, ordinary-looking husband and three children—two teenaged sons and an infant daughter born during the series. Although her family sometimes produce conflicts like those on situation comedies, conflicts between a politically conservative son and his liberal parents, for example, these issues are rarely central to the program. The series portrays the single Cagney (Sharon Gless) as a woman with a deep need for autonomy. Her romantic relationships with men break off, and she is curing herself of dependencies—most obviously on alcohol, but also on her devotion to her alcoholic police officer father, now deceased, and to the coercive bonhomie of the men at the station house.

A program on date rape, in which Cagney herself, not a guest star, was the victim, highlights the single woman's desires for a fulfilling heterosexual relationship in a society where men may be dangerous to women. Through such controversial topics, the liberal show hopes to attract ratings while educating its viewers. The film *Broadcast News*, in contrast, played the handsome anchorman's lachrymose television special on date rape as the sign of his moral triviality. As an issue, date rape spotlights our society's ambivalence about sexuality. It apparently validates the conservative view that all extramarital sex is dangerous and that women should keep to traditional roles. It is often considered as the inevitable, not too serious, result of the liberal sexual revolution and at the same time as a crime uniquely destructive and humiliating to the victim, since it involves betraying trust and forcing physical intimacy.

The program's opening sequence shows Cagney and Lacey at firing practice, tough, professional, even phallic. Then Cagney meets an attractive, well-to-do professional man who invites her on a date, over which she flutters in happy anticipation. At the end of the evening she bids him goodnight, gives him a light farewell kiss, and tells him that she had a nice time but wants to take things slowly. The sequence ends with her closed door, and the scene switches to the married Laceys snuggling at home in bed. A telephone call from Cagney interrupts this quotidian idyll with her report that "he raped me." Lacey rushes over to her friend's house and hears the story. We do not see it dramatized. We believe Cagney, as we might not believe a supposed victim played by a guest star, because the series has already established Cagney's integrity.

According to Cagney, her date returned to her apartment by inventing an excuse to need her telephone. Although he had no weapon, he threatened to kill her, and Cagney shudders at the hatred in the man's eyes. Lacey acts as the perfect supporter. She praises her partner's courage under assault and reassures her that she could not have responded differently than she did. "I'd do anything to make it this didn't happen," Lacey assures Cagney and hugs her. Lacey's intimacy with Cagney is unquestioning and maternal, and Cagney responds like a daughter growing up in a dangerous world: "I have to learn to be safe here by myself." Lacey accompanies Cagney to the hospital and backs her in the effort to charge and convict the rapist.

Many of the men at the station house blame Cagney. "I guess you couldn't get your gun fast enough," says her boss, implying that a woman who can get raped may not be man enough to be a police officer. But not all men on the show are villains. Cagney's old boyfriend is concerned and responsive. "Thank God you weren't hurt," he breathes warmly, and she replies, "I am hurt. I was raped." The prosecutor assigned to her case warns her that the rapist is an upstanding Mr. Clean who will be hard to convict. Alleging that their intercourse was voluntary, the rapist charges that Cagney was too drunk to remember what happened that night. Since she took a blood test that will show she had not been drinking, the program ends with the presumption that her virtue, not merely her victimization, will ensure that justice is done.

One critic of the series complains that Lacey's marriage has become increasingly central to the program, marginalizing Cagney's single status.[17] However, if the program shows companionate marriage as preferable to romance, it is because it has debunked romance. Romance is no longer the gilded trap that lures women into patriarchal marriage; romance is no longer even attractive. Instead, marriage is the safe haven to which women can flee from the predatory dangers of heterosexual sexuality.

The perfect "marriage" on the program, however, is not the Laceys' but rather the relationship between Cagney and Lacey, a loyal and deep friendship that involves mutual support and common adventure. Despite demurrals from the more restrained Cagney, the two women are intimate, open, and trusting with one another. The episode on date rape illustrates the dangers single women face in assessing whom to trust and contrasts Cagney's trauma both with Lacey's supportive marriage and with her own supportive relationship with Lacey. Even outside the extreme of rape, the program does not show extramarital sex as lastingly romantic or fully satisfying; nor is marriage romantic, though it is sometimes satisfying. Instead, the trust and intimacy between the two women develops within the romanticized context of their professionalism. Their joint police work offers danger, adventure, physical excitement, and immediate intellectual gratifications, and their co-workers value them as a team. The special romance of police work, however, may be a synecdoche for the romance that professionalism itself still holds for women.

Another show that dramatized the dangers and pleasures of heterosexuality through a sensational plot involving rape also contrasted the rape with a marriage between program regulars. In this episode of *L. A. Law*, an accusation of rape is made against the good-hearted but retarded mailroom clerk Benny (Larry Drake). Police pick him up, and he admits that he's done something "bad"; having visited a girly show for the first time, he feels so guilty he does not defend himself against the rape charge and must be rescued by his lawyer employers. Like the program about date rape, this one has a liberal and didactic point: we should not fear the mentally handicapped as criminals. Despite the primary sympathy directed at the retarded man, the program also treats Benny's accuser sympathetically. She is not malicious but traumatized; her false accusation springs from her desperate need that her attacker be safely incarcerated. Since the plot clears the innocent man without finding the criminal, it leaves the viewer with the sense that sexual menace endangers women. More interesting, perhaps, is the writers' choice to counterpoise this rape plot against the long-awaited marriage between two of the show's star lawyers.

The courtship between Ann Kelsey (Jill Eikenberry) and Stuart Markowitz

(Michael Tucker) involves constant squabbles that accompany the bride's preparations for the wedding and continue into the ceremony itself. Bickering right up to the altar, the bride then stops and apologizes to her groom for being a "bitch." She tells him he is the only person who has ever understood her, who loves her for herself and not her looks: "you love me for me." They pledge their vows. Loving marriage, this episode implies, is only possible when intimacy has established trust—trust, that is, in the partner's willingness to use knowledge of the other only for good, not for harm, in contrast to the philandering judge's wife who punctuates the wedding ceremony with sarcastic remarks. The wedding couple's moment of liberatory intimacy and self-revelation occurs in the romantic context of a wedding, but also in the comic context of embarrassing dialogue that is overheard by outsiders. Whatever the slow inner evolution of the character's feelings, they are crystallized at the public ceremony. The wedding couple thus resemble the children in Kozinsky's experiment who admitted misbehavior only when they thought they were televised. The implication is that private life is not fully authentic if it stays entirely private. A wedding is a spectacle performed before an audience, as television is. In this episode of *L. A. Law*, private emotions require public witnesses to exist fully, and distrust of the other's power to hurt one through intimacy dissolves only momentarily, in the wedding show.

MOONLIGHTING MADNESS AND METHOD

A sustained example of ambiguities in prime time romance is the dalliance between the principals on *Moonlighting*, a beautiful upper-class female boss and her earthier male associate. The program's detective agency setting indicates the characters' fears about committing themselves to traditional sex roles. By making its stars a heterosexual couple rather than the same-sex buddy teams of most cop shows, including *Cagney and Lacey*, the program seems to solve problems of courtship and intimacy: slow trust can develop between comrades through common adventures. But both Maddie Hayes (played by Cybill Shepherd) and David Addison (Bruce Willis) are by turns emotionally irresponsible and confused. In their all-tolerant and ambiguous world, no clear guidelines assure them of the other's trust or intentions, not even a sexual relationship. Since the characters don't know their own minds, viewers may feel that they know the characters better than the characters know each other or themselves.

Changes in attitudes toward desire in recent years lead to changes in the representations of trust, issues which can be seen more clearly in this self-consciously postmodern series than in more traditionally "realistic" and conventional programs. By prolonging their romantic impasse, these characters both adhere to the narrative conventions of their genre and dramatize the contemporary crisis of trust in heterosexual relations.

In her famous definition of poetry, Marianne Moore wrote that its imaginary gardens displayed real toads. On television, imaginary moonlight illumines real contradictions. The very name *Moonlighting* captures some of the program's ambivalence about work and romance, the prohibited and the enjoined. The term "moonlighting" refers to work outside one's main job, something shady, yet it is also romantic, evoking the mad and secret transformations of the night. The pilot program's opening credits showed the actors' first and last names moving toward each other from opposite sides of the screen until they met and passed above and below one another. That is, the very credits present people as self-divided and dramatize the question of how the characters would meet. The program's theme song, too, croons of "strangers who met on the way," alluding to today's singles' anxiety about the uncertain free market in romance.

The opening scene of the pilot program shows a man arising from his marital bed and going out jogging: he meets a speedy demise. His death is part of a plot about smuggled Nazi diamonds that the stars will eventually solve. Given his irrelevance as a character, however, the decision to open the program with a vignette that goes from married intimacy to instant death casts its shadow on the coming romantic meeting between the principals. Our introduction to the show's leading female character, Maddie Hayes, plays on actress Cybill Shepherd's celebrity status, showing "Maddie" as a cover girl model whose business managers have stolen all her money. Seeking to recoup her fortunes, she visits one of her few remaining assets, a money-losing detective agency run by co-star Bruce Willis playing the character David Addison. Caught dribbling a basketball in the office, he is all suave self-assurance. "I have always loved you. Nothing personal," he tells her as she fires him. Such glib pseudoemotion will be one of the prime movers of the series. Can two such narcissists connect with one another? When love is a matter of the right line, "nothing personal," how can anything personal ever take place?

David aggressively chases Maddie as they are both chased by criminals looking for the lost Nazi diamonds. Abducted by evil businessmen who "will do anything to protect that bottom line," they escape through David's bravado, though Maddie pitches into the fight scenes as well. As the plot progresses, he continues to sweet-talk her, telling her, "you have to trust me." She tries to call the police, but 911 puts her on hold. Clearly there is no help from the constituted authorities; the principals will have to rely on each other. Maddie alternates between anger and admiration at David. "You need me to live. . . . When's the last time you had any fun?" David goads Maddie. Later she admits that chasing criminals is great "fun." On ladders extended from an office tower high over the city, David and Maddie throw diamonds back and forth over a greedy old man who falls to his death—a criminalized bad daddy the kids can enjoy surviving. Bonded by danger, hugging with joy at their safety, Maddie is ready once again for David's soft soap. "We make a terrific team," he tells her; "this case has been a real growth experience for me." One does not lie to or pressure one's partners, he tells her, while conning her once again.

The program establishes that its characters are trustworthy by having their plots succeed and their adversaries perish, but it also makes untrustworthiness, the "bull" of a male "line," essential to male charm and danger for women.

Her attractiveness as a beautiful woman is simply a given, and his desire for her as sexual object and meal ticket is explicit. It is his honesty beneath the hype that will keep her coming back for more.

The program's sexism seems apparent, yet there are changes within the traditional formulae. Shepherd is a former model playing a former model, and throughout the program she continues to model, wearing lavish clothing with many low-cut evening gowns. Yet she is also an independent working woman and a man's boss. The show adapts 1930s screwball film comedy to television a half century later. The late 1980s, with declining standards of living and increasingly materialistic private values, seem attracted by the themes of depression comedies. The work ethic is dull; *You Can't Take It With You*; and, as in *Holiday* or *Bringing Up Baby*, one member of a couple must teach the other "how to live," which means treating social norms irreverently before fulfilling them.

As *Moonlighting* settled into a successful run, it featured a knowing, self-conscious style about its medium. The actors, especially Bruce Willis, addressed the audience with asides about being on television, and the investigative plots were often subordinated to comic chases. Maddie and David make the perfect contemporary romantic couple: they work together; they've been through a lot together; they're both beautiful and sophisticated people in an exciting, apparently upscale job. Though inept regarding money, both live extravagantly, surrounded by luxurious consumer goods. Throughout most of the series' life, they orbit around one another in a feuding and agreeing, push and pull sort of dance. Their own relationship remains static but turbulent, with arguments and slamming doors followed by erotic glances. Their characters polarize around a few attributes that are relevant to work styles—spontaneous versus reliable, intuitive versus planned, tidy versus sloppy. Although she values her planning skills, orderliness, and control, she is vague and indecisive. David is a ladies' man with a drinking problem, yet loyal to Maddie and effective.

Unlike the police shows, *Moonlighting* has no reliable father figure, and its office does not recreate a whole nuclear family. As in Shakespearean comedy, romantic leads are underscored by more broadly humorous sidekicks who also form a couple—Herbert Viola the bumbling accountant (Curtis Armstrong) and Agnes DiPesto the rhyming receptionist (Alyce Beasley). The crew of other office workers act as a chorus for the principals. Though the program has a work setting, its characters model clothing and leisure activities for us, inviting us to consumption rather than production.

The program stresses the fragility of bonds between people rather than the reverse. Usually only the two main characters investigate crimes; they hide their feelings and often even their interpretation of the plots from each other. In an amusing article in *TV Guide*, Dr. Ruth Westheimer chastised David and Maddie for their infantile behavior. They lie to themselves and each other, don't say what they want, and act to hurt and thwart one another. To improve things, Dr. Ruth deadpans the humanistic psychological panacea of better communication, though of course this transformation of the characters into real, improved people would defeat the program's humor.

Unlike the old sitcoms, this program does not work on the premise that one character gets into a mess which the other must clean up. Instead, each partner's antithetical style creates irritations for the other in spite of which they successfully conclude their investigations. Although it polarizes its characters, *Moonlighting* defuses the hierarchical implications of such polarizations in comparison with older sitcoms by aligning them both with and against traditional gender stereotypes.

Moonlighting's underlying ideology about heterosexual relations shows clearly in an episode entitled "Atomic Shakespeare" that is isolated from the developing relationship between Maddie and David; it remakes Shakespeare's *The Taming of the Shrew* by way of Zeffirelli's film. The television program's irreverent postmodernisms aim cozily at everyone who studied the bard in high school. Burt complains he gets "stuck with all the exposition," for example, and crowds chant "wrong play" when Bruce Willis as Petruchio in sunglasses starts intoning "To be or not to be." Despite this modern gloss, the remake turns *Taming* into a liberal parable.

"If you're a man you're going to love the sixteenth century," Petruchio addresses the audience before embarking on a slapstick courtship full of sexual innuendo. At the wedding, Cybill Shepherd as Kate is tied and gagged at the altar, and Petruchio quips, "how well she doth look in bondage." In contrast to Shakespeare, this Petruchio threatens Kate with sex rather than with with- holding it; she resists, obdurately bopping him until he changes his ways. Then she stops snarling and begins cooing in humanistic "psychologese." "I believe in our marriage," she tells him; "I have changed. Now you change too. . . . I ask you to retreat from your role as a chauvinist and respect me as thy wife and partner." As incentive, she will share his bed if he shapes up, becoming a Doris Day rather than a Shakespearean heroine. Cockcrow finds four feet in bed and an affectionate pair of lovers. "We are kindred souls, Kate. I saw thee in me," Petruchio says, underlining the premise of the series as a whole that Maddie and David's antagonisms mirror one another and thus indicate compatibility. After reasserting the pleasures of humiliating a woman, the program humbles its male lead briefly before trying, finally, to represent a liberal and egalitarian hetero- sexual partnership.

The characters David and Maddie are shadowed by their pseudo-Shakespearean counterparts, but there is no explicit connection between this episode and the rest of *Moonlighting*. Therefore, the Shakespearean program can be unusually explicit about its own ideology; compatibility requires equality, and equality is sameness despite apparent difference. As in the Latin epigram about the couple who agree to disagree, the characters' fears about commitment and their pug- naciousness prove their sameness. In the format of the isolated Shakespearean episode, closure is possible, as it is not in a continuing series, so the characters' transformations may be complete and the moral about equality underlined. Covertly, even this program may indicate that women have to pay for equality by undergoing humiliation, but at least trust, so difficult to achieve in the series as a whole, is here magically posited by Shakespeare's plot.

As the romance form has always implied, pursuit may be more satisfying than consummation. If David and Maddie stay circling around one another in the sequence as a whole, they need not face mundane issues of domestic existence. Trying to change this static formula produces problems. The program entered a crisis about commitment that was precipitated by actress Cybill Shepherd's pregnancy and leave of absence. Pregnancy raises a whole new set of issues, and it makes explicit Dr. Ruth's demand that the characters "grow up," even though the series ignores the equally obvious pregnancy of Alyce Beasley as Agnes. Though permanence is still considered desirable in heterosexual unions, people do not believe in it, and today parenthood may be the only commitment that people recognize as lasting.

This anomie about relationships is one of the things the program is about, one of the persistent anxieties upon which its comedy plays. In one early show, for example, Maddie is grouchy, and David asks her what's going on. She answers, "the arms race, disease, apartheid." Her unease is more personal than global, however, as soon becomes clear, when she wails, "Nothing makes sense. What's happened to all the rules—love, marriage, romance? What's happened?" David replies, "This is the 1980s. Take your romance where you can get it."

"Romance where you can get it" is clearly unsatisfactory, exactly because impermanence precludes trust and intimacy. The series dramatizes these issues by having Maddie get pregnant after having slept with two men. She is not treated as a wicked woman for this situation but rather as a confused person in a confusing world. While she is deciding what to do, and while the actress is on leave, the character goes home to her parents, a retreat that underscores the adolescent dynamics of these issues although the characters are people in their thirties. Such a retreat also underscores the underlying dependency still attributed to women, even career women. Appropriately for the age of narcissism, the characters experience no problems with desire or sexual pleasure, only with commitment. Both sexes, not just the man, fear intimacy and distrust trust. Although they can attract and be attracted, they don't know what these sexual feelings mean to their larger selves. Normally the two characters' opposing personalities work toward the solution of a crime. The messes they create in their personal relationships, on the other hand, are their own and can't be solved by or with the other person. In fact, change or improvement in either character exacerbates the ambivalence of the other.

Maddie and David's mating game is dualistic and solipsistic but not triangular; all obstacles to their intimacy are internal to each character. The outside world merely provides props and adventures that bring them together. When the writers try to invent romantic rivals for David and Maddie, the attempt fails and collapses back into internal ambivalence within the characters. Instead, jealous triangles are endemic to the greed, lust, and generally destructive passions of each week's criminal plots.

When Maddie is pregnant and debating what she should do, she dreams of a reformed David as a complete bore, a "model husband" and father who ignores her even when she flaunts herself before him in black lingerie. Sorrowfully she admits that this good citizen is everything she "asked for." Then her old, sexy leather-jacketed partner appears at her window to ask "which David do you want—me or that jar of mayonnaise?" Maddies wakes and editorializes, "I'm not sure I want him. No, I want him; I just can't stand him." Lewd, loud, exasperating, David is still her "best friend. He keeps the spark alive." Back at the office, she announces that she's married. Her husband, a nice wimp named Walter, is simply the personification of the "perfect husband" David that she's already dreamed and rejected. The choice between David and Walter is not a contest between two men but within her wavering desires. The choral office staff rejects the husband and wants the romantic leads back together again. We the audience are assumed to agree, having invested our intimacy and romantic expectations in the two main characters for several seasons.

The situation is far different in the crime plots, which are triangular and destructive. In them intimacy corrodes, and the people one should trust least are one's lovers or spouse. In one program, for example, a woman wants the detectives to save her marriage by paying her husband's mistress to relocate. The mistress claims she "gets the best" of her married lover and accepts him without possessiveness. Apparently, both women are happy with their man. As the plot unravels, however, it turns out that the two women have united in antagonism against the husband: they kill him and try to profit from his wealth.

In another episode, a man seeks to track down his business partner's obsessive secret love, known only through a passionate coded diary. "You're all I have that's real, and I have nothing of you except these words," the diary addresses its anonymous beloved. But his inamorata turns out to be the first partner's wife. The married partner wants to kill his rival, but his wife shoots her husband first. Marriage is murderous, and desire is voyeuristic, mediated, and indirect. Such plots—and television as a medium—valorize voyeurism and fantasy as safe sex, potentially more satisfying eroticism than that between two people fully engaged with one another. Such plots also justify ambivalence about marriage and about trust. Maddie tells Agnes that she couldn't marry David because "he would try to reinvent himself into a perfect husband and father but he'd be miserable," whereas single and free, "at least he'd still be David and being David is like a first kiss all the time."

As soon as Maddie's ill-fated marriage is annulled, she boasts she's "free as a bird" and available. Freedom seems an advantage over commitment because a new romance is always possible and because the old romance stays new. Although the principals now ought to get together, they continue their approach and avoidance dance. Simultaneously in voiceover, Maddie and David "think" the same doubts about commitment: "some people are better at arm's length"; "red hot tempers may not settle over white picket fences." The trouble is, "things are different now but they're still the same." Maddie says they can be different people, forget their past differences and change. David tells her he wants to stop talking about feeling and commitment, despite his commitment to her. The freedoms of the present have left both partners confused and ambivalent. When David tells the wife who murdered her husband not to kill herself but to stay alive for the partner, he assures her that "two people can make it if they try; the future is all that counts." Maddie kisses him. Yet if the future is all that matters and the past can change, on what is their commitment based? What bases exist for trust or intimacy?

Sex does not equal commitment and may even work against it. The sexual diseases epidemic, especially AIDS, heightens the distrust of intimacy. Sleeping with someone means sleeping with all of their former sexual partners, we are told, as personal history becomes epidemiology. Thus sexual relations become an involuntary commitment potentially so grave it frightens away voluntary commitment. The incestuous dangers of free sexuality are indicated by a program in which David's father marries a younger woman with whom David himself once had a brief fling. The woman is a recovered alcoholic who does not even remember David, and this amnesia, this meaninglessness of sexual experience, may be even more frightening than the idea of sharing a woman with one's father.

In the context of widespread fear of commitment, the characters' constant bickering indicates a new kind of intimacy. Knowing each other's weak points, each can both help and harm the other. Knowledge does not necessarily bring trust. The new social rules don't assume any end point; sexual intercourse, pregnancy, and marriage are all temporary, and there is no extrinsic reason for trust. The traditional complementarities of active and passive or rational and emotional no longer work to consolidate a couple through mutual dependence, yet at the same time people fear collapsing into narcissism, into a mirroring sameness in which the other is as untrustworthy as the fickle self. There is difficulty, too, in imagining any joint enterprise other than chasing someone else. Raising a child seems the only alternative, and the statistics on broken families render that too, unsure.

If the characters have difficulty attaining trust and intimacy with one another, we the audience can mediate that trust and intimacy with them. The narcissistic personality, we're told, needs an empathic mirrorer in order to connect with others.[18] We the audience simulate such a mirroring, watching, empathic presence. Safely on our side of the screen, we can trust the infallibility of fictional conventions to drive plots toward romantic conclusions. But we also assure the characters' safety. When each voices ambivalence about the other in unison voiceover, for example, we know the characters are identical and therefore suited for one another, even though they do not reveal to each other what they reveal to us. We think the characters know one another because we think we know them. The program teaches us how to read the characters as we are taught to read real people, yet our intimacy with them can be more intense, our trust in their constancy greater. "We all feel let down," Agnes tells Maddie when she seems to have forsaken David: "there isn't much in this world that's real . . . but you two—I've loved it, when you fight and when you make up. I just thought it was realer than that, and I feel let down."

The idea that television people are "realer" than we, "realer than that," is part of our intense and conflicted connection with television. Day and night, the medium invites us to the safest of sex, a voyeuristic intimacy we can enjoy in isolation and on which we can always rely. Nonetheless, popular television reflects a contemporary crisis of trust; it provokes tensions in heterosexual relations and assuages them through romantic couplings that resist closure, repeating the cycle and involving the viewer. The issue of trust is not merely a theme introduced into the television story lines; rather, it is intrinsic to the intimate and ambivalent relationship between the viewer and the medium itself.

ACKNOWLEDGMENTS

For their comments and suggestions, I thank Kathie Henderson, Noel Barker, Virginia Wexman, Carita Gardiner, Viveca Gardiner, and Linda Williams.

NOTES

1. See Neil Postman, *Amusing Ourselves to Death: Public Discourse in the Age of Show Business* (New York: Penguin Books, 1986); and John Berger, *Ways of Seeing* (London and Harmondsworth: British Broadcasting Corporation and Penguin Books, 1977).

2. See Nina Baym, *Woman's Fiction: A Guide to Novels by and about Women in America, 1820–1870* (Ithaca and London: Cornell University Press, 1978).

3. Germaine Greer, *The Female Eunuch* (New York: Bantam Books, 1983), 209.

4. Tania Modleski, *Loving with a Vengeance: Mass-Produced Fantasies for Women* (Hamden, Conn.: Archon, 1982); Janice Radway, *Reading the Romance: Women, Patriarchy, and Popular Literature* (Chapel Hill: University of North Carolina Press, 1984).

5. Carol Thurston, *The Romance Revolution: Erotic Novels for Women and the Quest for a New Sexual Identity* (Urbana and Chicago: University of Illinois Press, 1987).

6. The term is Eve Sedgwick's, *Between Men* (New York: Columbia University Press, 1985).

7. Nancy Chodorow, *The Reproduction of Mothering: Psychoanalysis and the Sociology of Gender* (Berkeley: University of California Press, 1978).

8. Lillian Rubin, *Intimate Strangers: Men and Women Together* (New York: Harper & Row, 1983).

9. Carol Gilligan, "On *In a Different Voice*: An Interdisciplinary Forum," *Signs* 11.2 (1986): 304–9; Catherine Greeno and Eleanor Maccoby, "How Different is the 'Different Voice?' " *Signs* 11.2 (1986): 310–16.

10. John Fiske and John Hartley, *Reading Television* (London: Methuen, 1978).

11. Quoted by David Sohn, "A Nation of Videots," in *Television: The Critical View*, ed. Horace Newcomb, 3d ed. (New York and Oxford: Oxford University Press, 1982), 358.

12. Fiske and Hartley, 151.

13. Bernard Timberg, "The Rhetoric of the Camera in Television Soap Opera," in *Television: The Critical View*, ed. Horace Newcomb, 142.

14. Todd Gitlin, *Inside Prime Time* (New York: Pantheon Books, 1983).

15. Julie D'Acci, "The Case of Cagney and Lacey," in *Boxed In: Women and Television*, ed. Helen Baehr and Gillian Dyer (New York and London: Pandora Press, 1987).

16. Gitlin, 73.

17. D'Acci.

18. Heinz Kohut, *The Analysis of the Self* (New York: International Universities Press, 1971).

3

Field and Screen: Baseball and Television

Michael Seidel

INTIMACIES

Television can make the instantaneous memorable. Who can forget the startling sequence just after Carlton Fisk's climactic, and barely fair, home run in the sixth game of the 1975 World Series? The camera zoomed to close-up on Fisk's deliberate and somewhat perpendicular movement along the base line, capturing a slow private flamenco as, hands imploring, he waved his high fly fair around the foul pole. Fisk's image has become a large part of the way we remember the dramatic '75 Series; television made the image and, in a technical way, made history.

Or consider the indelible television image of George Brett of the Kansas City A's right after the infamous pine tar incident in 1983 at Yankee Stadium. Brett had just found out that a potentially game-winning homer against the Yanks has been declared null and void by the umpire because the pine tar he rubbed on his bat went too far up the handle. The close-up was at the right spot at the right time. Brett was beyond himself, in agony, a man possessed. He came so furiously and so fast out of the dugout that another umpire had to grab him from behind before he annihilated the home plate ump by mere force of impact. Brett by then was bright red, jumping and pumping like Rumpelstiltskin, gesticulating wildly as if his air supply had been cut off. He was so forcefully held by the second umpire that both their bodies moved in a curious up-down and sidewards morris about the plate and batter's box. In silent close-up, Brett's face had the bizarre look of a suffocating man through a diver's mask. Boom mikes on the field that might have picked up the shouting were discreetly off—the FCC would have come down on the station like locusts upon the Pharaoh—but the all-purpose "read my lips" sufficed.

On television, the loosed Brett was a phenomenon: *Hercules Furens*. His charge occurred again and again, in replay, in slow motion, then on the evening news. It was encapsulated, framed, and never to be given back to the field on which it took place nor to the flow of the game it interrupted. Like the fury that generated it, the scene fed on itself, and television refused to let it rest. I still cannot get the image of Brett's exploding face out of my mind. It was, as my young son is wont to say, INTENSE! Of course, the networks ran the sequence several more times on the evening news. One local announcer, after screening for the umpteenth time the tape of an enraged Brett, signed off with a sardonically sweetened, "This goes to prove once again that baseball is, and always has been, just a kid's game played for fun."

I have begun with two powerful scenes that television has brought to baseball because in the balance of this essay I will focus on some of the things it takes from baseball. But before I get to the subject, in all its phases, that truly interests me—game watching—I want to supply a few rudimentary bits of information about television, baseball history, and the greenness of money. I feel a responsibility to set the television scene with some raw facts, if only to suggest that I am not fooled into thinking that my interests in television baseball have any real connection to the reasons baseball is on television in the first place. Whatever I have to say about the ball park versus the screen, baseball and television are inextricably linked by finances. Broadcast contracts, sponsors, and market shares are paramount stories in the history of the sport and the medium. That is the long and short of it.

Let's set the stakes. In 1947 Gillette paid $65,000 for sponsorship of the World Series broadcast locally in New York to a total viewing audience of under 300,000. In 1988 CBS negotiated a contract to pay $1.1 billion for four years for the right to televise twelve regular season games a year beginning 1990, plus a package of All-Star, League Playoffs, and World Series games. That is, the network shelled out over a thousand million dollars for at most a total of 136 and at least a total of 100 games, depending upon the duration of the playoffs and World Series in those years. With the advent of cable contracts, the majors are selling shares in their television image in huge chunks. To take the most aggressive example, the New York Yankees will share in the CBS deal to the tune of $10 million a year (the cut of each major league team) plus $4 or $5 million each for major league cable rights, plus $40 million a year for local cable rights. In 1990, before any of his quondam pitchers toes the rubber and chucks his first hanging curve, Mr. George Steinbrenner will have put $55 million in the bank from television. That gives him a nice cushion for chintzing out on Dave Winfield's charities.

It did not take the American business mind long in the early years of baseball television to grasp exactly what a piece of the picture meant. Having spent

$65,000 for their first World Series broadcast, Gillette almost tripled their ante in 1949, paying $200,000 for rights to the Series, a figure that ballooned to $800,000 in 1950. The All-Star game, a bargain for Gillette at $2500 in 1948, went for $50,000 in 1950. It was only natural that Gillette should parlay its World Series broadcasts into the long-standing NBC Game of the Week contract where the best of the early broadcasters, Dizzy Dean and Buddy Blattner, looked sharp and were sharp.

It is no surprise that technological advances in broadcasting marched in step with the revenues that sponsors and networks could expect to generate from the medium. Early efforts at televising ball games were sorry competitors to the aural excitement of radio, which held sway in America from the 1922 Grantland Rice call of the Giant-Yankee World Series to the omnipresent Gillette's dominance of World Series radio sponsorship in the 1930s. Experiments in telecasting Dodger games took place in the late 1930s and early 1940s within a limited broadcast range to an equally limited number of monitors, sometimes only several hundred. From all accounts, the broadcasts were dismal. The only effective pictures were from stationary cameras; the result was an almost instantaneous loss of the ball's flight and the runner's progress. Fickle outside lighting conditions proved a greater challenge than the camera was able to master. Whatever the weather, near invisibility seemed the order of the day for television coverage, clouded by limitations of technology and, finally, interrupted by our entry into World War II.

Later, after the war, refinements in televising baseball made the enterprise a paying affair. Many more monitors picked up local broadcasts, the panning camera served the interests of continuity, and lighting techniques improved dramatically, so much so that on a sunny day the sun was in fact seen to shine. Television began to pursue with fervor the inherent appeal of America's national sport. In the early days of regular season television, the radio networks with team rights would participate in the television broadcasts by working out arrangements with capable production facilities. Mr. Wrigley of the Cubs even began by giving away television rights gratis in 1949 to his radio broadcasters as a source of advertising exposure for his team, but he cured himself of this beneficence soon enough when he realized the independent draw of the medium.

The World Series was for television the biggest show on earth. But viewing habits were very different in 1947 and 1948 from now. Most of the monitors were in bars and taverns, and the owners of these watering holes were in competition with each other for the sports locals who could, without finagling for a seat at the park, wander in for a look-see. Tavern owners, of course, complained that the baseball crowd was not exactly the same as the drinking crowd and that revenues per occupied seat tended to be less with a cheering occupant than with a regular drinker. That much stood to reason. Yet the economics of baseball and television emerged just as clearly: there were many more folk in the bar occupying those seats when the ball game was beamed in.

The 1948 Series between the Braves and the Indians was the first to split broadcasts region to region. Local stations throughout the Midwest, as well as the East coast, broadcast games played in the viewing areas. It was estimated that nearly 400,000 monitors were receiving signals, and that some 7 million fans viewed the games in one place or another. Boston enjoyed the unusual sight of a hundred mounted portable monitors ringing the historic Commons, with hundreds of local fans ringing each of the monitors. This was hardly the beer guzzling, chip chomping fan of today's panelled family room, but it would do in 1948 for baseball hungry Boston cheering for a team that hadn't won a pennant since 1914.

Television entered the world of regular season play and the minor leagues with a vengeance when controversies of all sorts were headlined in the *Sporting News* during the '48, '49, and '50 seasons. Attendance, and the threat to it, became an issue. Those shrewd enough or affected enough recognized early that the ready availability of major league ball to television audiences could hasten the decline of the minor leagues. On May 18, 1948, for example, a television broadcast of a New York Giants night game emptied the stands of the club's local affiliate, the Jersey City Little Giants, on a traditionally strong Saturday night date. Only a few hundred sat in the minor league stadium while thousands poured into Jersey City taverns to watch the parent club. This was a harbinger of things to come.

In 1950, with California leading the nation in purchase of television monitors (some 25,000 sets a month in Los Angeles and environs), attendance was off at the local ball parks by significant margins, almost half in the case of the Hollywood Stars, who televised home and away games over KLAC. League President, Clarence Rowland, insisted on immediate cuts in telecasts, but the Stars refused to oblige. Television contracts would make the club more money than the modest click of the turnstiles. Taking the long view, the Stars also hoped that television would make them more fans by expanding the demographic pool of those who might, at one time or another, actually purchase a ticket for a game at their park, Gilmore Field.

A year later in the majors, controversy brewed over how teams could capitalize on the burgeoning regular season television venture, a question baseball has been asking ever since. The Phillies and Dodgers got into a brief dispute in 1951 when the Phils wanted a share of the television revenues at Ebbets Field. Branch Rickey bristled that it was Brooklyn's field and Brooklyn's money; he accused the Phillies of more than creeping socialism: "What is this, Russia?" The Phils have grown more subtle over the years. When they signed Pete Rose in 1979 for a million dollars, they renegotiated their lapsed television contract on the same day for a far greater sum than they paid Rose. Television, in effect, subsidized salary inflation.[1]

All of this is to say that television baseball is now as much a phenomenon, and as important to those who experience the game, as a day or night at the park. As a fan who attends more games than his schedule really permits and who watches more on television than his sanity ought to allow, I will now try to describe my reactions to the spaces and images of field and screen, to stadium sounds and television voices.

"I GASPED AT THE PERFECT GREENNESS OF IT"[2]

Two elements essential to viewing most sports, and baseball in particular, are missing in televised games: depth and spatial range. At the park you see in three dimensions and, depending upon your seat, you can take in a large percentage of the field with the slightest turn of the head. The television image is not even a simulacrum of the field; it is a distortion that flattens one dimension and parcels out the whole of the image in frames. Flatness on television is a negative condition. E. M. Forster tells us that in novels flat characters perform a service but not much more. To have depth is to have a kind of inner form, a relational life. From these obvious facts derive some not necessarily obvious conclusions.

Let me pause over the implications here because it gets to the gist of the matter. In honoring only the flat and the fragmentary, the television screen image scants the single most important judgmental factor on a ball field: depth perception. Everything is keyed to that perception—speed, direction, instinctive reflex, in essence the entire available repertoire of moves on the mound, in the field, at the plate. To say that television does not have depth is, for the time being at least, a descriptive and not a judgmental observation. Nor can television, save from the Goodyear Blimp or the rooftop at Fenway Park, provide anything like the panoramic view of the field possessed even by the forlorn fan seated behind the legendary posts in Detroit's Briggs Stadium.

Think about what happens when you watch even a common event such as a batted ball on television. You have to learn to conjure a new physical reality from the images offered. The television screen gives far fewer clues than you would think. Many of its images are cut shots, camera switches, split-second improvisations on reality. You see bat contact and think you're following the flight of the ball, but you're not; you are plotting the track of a ghost. I do not mean all this to sound more mystical than it ought, but the likely destination of a batted ball viewed from the television screen is a sublimely schooled guess. The ball leaves the field of vision too soon, does so without any comparative sense of range, and even its direction is variable to a greater degree than the image conveys.

Those fans who have watched little television baseball, and there are probably precious few left, would have great difficulty making the game they see on the screen jibe with the one they know from the field. The accomplished television fan, on the other hand, can tell with some degree of accuracy how hard a ball is hit, what its probable trajectory will be, and the likelihood of it remaining in the park. There is no inherent reason why the practiced viewer should be able to do so, given the severe limitations and outright distortions of the screen image, but, having seen thousands upon thousands of balls leave the screen off the bat, the viewer builds an internal computer of sorts for spatial projections. He or she is conditioned to replay a fragmented sequence of images into a greater space, each image insufficient in itself, but each with enough information so that the whole becomes hinted at in the sequence of parts. Moreover, the sense of what it all ought to look like if viewed at the park in full spatial array, with full depth perception, is also at work; the mind replaces the missing parts and puts them in some kind of remembered pattern. One of the renewing and refreshing things about going to a ball game in person after months of watching on television is the ease with which you let go of the secondary visual clues and compensatory phenomena for making simple judgments about the direction and velocity of batted balls.

You quickly realize when watching ballplayers work from the stands rather than seeing them on the screen that a ball travelling 380 feet off the bat or 280 feet on a line throw from right has a very different look to it. The image on television gives you little sense of true speed and even less sense of speed in relation to other activities on the field. The sheer beauty and full movement of the most graceful sequences in baseball are lost. To chart a ball slammed to right and to calculate the outfielder's chances to nab a runner, then heading full tilt around second, by gunning a throw to third base is to experience several actions vital to the game that cannot be fully appreciated during telecasts. Here's what is lost: the true sound of bat contact, the full flight of the ball in time, the image of the runner adjusting to the speed and location of the hit, the image of the fielder adjusting to the hit and to the positioning of the runner, the throw overtaking the runner, and the look of the whole at the moment of execution and resolution.

There is nothing like the game in its fullness, nothing like its expansive array of sights and sounds at the park. Television cannot even replicate the first crack of the bat during batting practice as you walk early into a mostly empty baseball stadium for a day game. The sound of the bat on the ball is slightly odd. It is indeed a crack, but there are after tones as well, a kind of echo. The ball is in flight before you really hear the impact. Sound doesn't travel that fast. You see and hear the ball hit twice, something like the singer's lips moving a millisecond before you hear the strains of the national anthem. The experience is at once invigorating and slightly unsettling, as if the sound is unreal, yet doubly confirmed. The emptier the park the more complicated the overtones.

Standing deep in the outfield, the player shagging flies hears the same sound as the fan in the bleachers or high in general admission. And he hears it almost as late, though habit has probably melded the swing and crack into one sound. He makes a subtle and instinctual adjustment: watching, listening, judging distance, depth, velocity, angle. He sees, hears, and tracks the whole of the play, swing to catch. So can you in the stands. Sportswriter Tom Boswell insists that "all baseball fans can be divided into two groups, those who come to batting practice and the others. Only those in the first category have much chance of amounting to anything."[3] To sit in the stands and watch batting practice, even intermittently, is to adapt the mind and eye to the timing, range, relational spaces of baseball. Batting practice is an abundant version of the *agon* between batter and pitcher, in which the batter is extended the privilege of getting the edge on every pitch. Meanwhile, infielders and outfielders are not only moving to shag batted balls, but are often taking supplemental grounders and flies between each swing. The field is abuzz with want. Everyone gets what he wants and does what he would want to do in the game, should the struggle be contoured only by the shape of desire. After watching batting and fielding practice, the fan at the game can measure the difference between relaxed and tense competition, between natural talent and game-time difficulty, between the panorama of practice and the panorama of play. These are fine measures.

Television arrives too late for all this. Even if a camera crew were to show up for batting practice, it would transmit its images with park sounds silenced, with one less dimension than necessary, with severely limited scopic vision. But this is all moot: Television simply does not *do* batting practice in the way that much domestic help doesn't do windows. Neither does television do what each fan has done by merely arriving at the park, an experience so satisfying that it diminishes the very notion of coming upon a baseball game any other way. Television can present the reduced image of the ball field, but it cannot approximate the quickened march through the turnstiles into the suffused green light of day. That paradise is lost on television. On the screen, we are far from what baseball's former commissioner, Bart Giamatti, called the *hortus conclusus* or enclosed garden of the ball field. The screen is a transmitted illusion; it emits an image, but not one by any stretch of the imagination you would want to walk into. For reasons that are part technological and part cultural, television's spaces are not compelling, even in the way a large movie screen or a rotogravure spread in a magazine is compelling. Television's spaces are miniaturizing, restrictive, and harsh in their geometry and electronics.

The park is gloriously compelling, a locus of almost physical, multisensory desire: the smells of beer and popcorn and peanuts and ice cream, the aroma of grilled and steamed hot dogs, the sounds of the crowd, the vendors. Its expanse is a ready place, ready for a sequence of actions that, as in every sport, are drawn from a repertoire of the familiar but can never be repeated exactly the same way. That first view is both a survey and a template for the game. The cynosure of a green park, which in landscape art connotes both an expanse and a place of proprietorship, typically beautiful and owned by somebody, has a special oxymoronic feel to it; a privatized openness. And being there is tangible: the feel of the concrete, the grasp of the rail, the bright hot sun of the bleachers, the creaking hinge of your seat. That baseball demands an entry price adds something to the feel of walking in, an impression that amounts to a kind of entry pride. A ticket is as much an invitation as a purchase.

Upon physically entering the park, you have experienced something like stadium time, an interlude hard to grasp but impressive in the way impression means pressed or printed on the brain. An afternoon or evening at the park is not compassed by the mere ludic action of the game, but by all the time between and around the game's action. Interlude means between play, and much of the feel of baseball, much of its witnessing, is based on those paced intricacies of inbetweenness where nothing overt seems to be happening. This is what televised baseball misses. On television there is always a press for something to take place. Free and timeless ruminations at the park before the game, between innings, pitches, plays are impossible. Television time runs counter to the notion of free time precisely because someone else has purchased it. Commentators must fill time with features, with banter, with precooked and canned observations.

To televise a game is not to bring you the interlude but to interrupt the idyll. From the anthem of baseball, "Take Me Out to the Ball Game," we learn a number of things, not the least of which is the persistent sense of the game as a hole or lapse in real time—"I don't care if I never get back." For a host of reasons, it is easier and more natural to televise sporting events that count on the clock as part of their design and shape. Playing the clock is what television does every hour, every day. No medium is more aware of itself as belonging to time. Other time sequences intrude from the moment the telecast begins: commercial time, station break time, updates, and previews. There is the relatively new phenomenon of breaking in with minisnippets from other ongoing games, one game time interrupting another, which is not an extension of the baseball interlude but its penetration. Worse, television time assumes the viewer's attention span is limited; the very temptations of the channel dial on the set encourage such a notion. As Roy Eisenhardt, owner of the Oakland A's, put it during a conversation with Roger Angell: "If the other team scores four runs in the first inning, we go *clicko*, else we flip the dial and watch Burt Reynolds."[4]

To be at the park and to watch a game whole, to watch it from chosen perspectives, perspectives that you choose, is one of the real pleasures of being a fan. The eye at the park makes its own camera angles, determines focus, duration, range. Many things go on at the same time over a defined space. You can watch for a few innings or a few minutes and see more than possible in an hour of television time. With just a little bit of fan initiative a ball game is rarely boring at the park. On television it may only seem so. Viewers simply do not see enough. What is more, if they could see enough, they still wouldn't control the looking, which is just as limiting. You need time to see and you need patience and you need to generate the points of interest. Baseball is a game of most subtle ritual. Television catches, or wishes to catch, these rituals intermittently, but the fun of the game is to catch them accretively, to watch them happen again and again, to see the habitual in action.

If you are at the park early and stand at the rim of the bleacher seats, you see the roster pitchers play an outfield game they have played from time immemorial. Pitchers hate to run, but they must do so daily. So they line up to go out for what appear to be passes, thrown by a coach standing in short center field. As the coach remains in place, pitchers run along the contours of the outfield from two directions flipping balls to the coach as they run past and catching ones thrown by the coach over their heads and shoulders as they accelerate. While waiting in line for their turn, they will gesture and kibitz with the fans lining the bleachers, especially the young kids, and chat incessantly with each other. They become, in their way, familiar. Kids love listening to and talking with the pitchers; it is even better if, later during the game, one of them, not necessarily a front-line star, enters in relief. The young fans have a special stake in his performance. On television, he's just another number.

Take another ritual. I do not imagine that any network or local station would contemplate televising the seemingly irrelevant readying of the field by the groundskeepers before the game, but I can barely imagine watching a game in which I have not attended to it. The sequence is so immensely and immediately gratifying; a field made picture perfect in a pattern that never varies. I remember one exception, though, which the television cameras would have done well to record. It was a game at Candlestick Park in San Francisco when the Giants were playing the Dodgers. The variance in the ritual of preparing the field provided the edge in the ball game. Los Angeles had Maury Wills, a brilliant and unforgettable base runner, whose forte was a jump from first that could humble a kangaroo. After watching their fellow groundskeepers drag the field, those hovering at first base did not move in their usual snake walk, hose in hand, in order to wet the base baths and limit dust. Instead they soaked the area around first base with long, continuous streams from the hose. I remember my friends in the stands assuming at first a labor-management dispute, then suddenly thinking of Wills. We were Dodger fans in San Francisco and aroused the locals with our shouts of sabotage, outrage, conspiracy. No luck. Of course, after the game began, and Wills led off with a single, he couldn't get any kind of a jump out of the mud to steal a base. The Dodgers protested and the groundskeepers had to haul out absorbent sand. Wills, if my memory serves me, was then picked off. At the park, observant fans were aware of this story while the local broadcast station back in Los Angeles, KTTV, was still warming its tubes.

The subtleties of action on the ball field encourage the ranging eye and the nuanced look. Once, at a game in New York, a companion asked how the fielders knew who was taking a throw at second base on a steal. That's easy—because with a runner on first the second baseman and shortstop signal to each other before every pitch, every pitch in every inning of every game from the time I can remember seeing games and, no doubt, decades before that. Either the shortstop or second baseman waits until the moment before the pitcher stretches and quickly puts his glove up to hide his face and presents to his mate an open or closed mouth. Open can mean "I'm taking the throw," and closed, pursed lips, "You take it." Who covers the base is crucial for the hit-and-run play and makes for a tense little game of nerves and odds that is, for the most part, hidden to all but the fan seated strategically at the park with a pair of binocs. The idle, supposedly inactive, time between pitches when nothing seemed to be happening on the field now teemed with concentrated activity. This was a new bit of information and my friend was newly fascinated. Next inning we began to steal pick-off signs.

Television sometimes zooms in for these sorts of close-ups, but only occasionally. The fun at the park is not in the one time sighting; rather in the habitual rhythm. Zoom lenses and close-ups on television, however, do have their virtues. In the rush to analyze what television loses for baseball we ought not forget just what television manages to bring to it. To watch a game well requires both scopic and concentrated vision. Television cannot provide the first, though it does much better at providing the second. In some instances, television supplements the action we see only once at the park. We get a temporally displayed version of spatial action. Cameras go back and pick up in sequence what the watching eye could not see in detail. Moreover, just as there are impulses for revision that only replays can satisfy, there are moments of intimacy that only the camera can do justice.

Over the years, television has been getting better at the game's intimacies, perhaps because it will never really master its range. The major innovations in televising all sports have to do with variations on camera angles and kinds of camera shots: split screen, slow motion, replay, isolation, wide angle, reverse angle, and hand-held cameras. For baseball, at least, there are two camera shots of abiding interest: the shot from behind home plate and the telescopic one from centerfield. In both, the viewer sees what is an impossible angle for most ball park viewers; and, in the case of the center field camera, for all viewers at the park. In addition to being unique, and potentially revealing, these television angles are also the most distorting in flattening the field and foreshortening the image. Variations on them get gimmicky. In the 1988 World Series, NBC produced one of the worst of all. On José Canseco's bases-loaded home run in the first game of the Series, a blow recorded and replayed from a close-up ground level camera head on, you saw only a mighty set of heavily muscled arms swinging the bat and nothing else. For all you knew, the pitcher could have been ten feet away and Canseco could have lined to short. The result of the swing had to be taken as a matter of faith.

As I watched the replay—NBC never did show a normal version—it occurred to me that I might get better at reading this shot if I saw it a few thousand times. After all, it's hard to tell exactly where the ball is going from the standard center field shot as well, but the eye and mind have a better basis of comparison for that one. I detested the Canseco television angle mostly because it was framed and fragmented in a different way from those I had learned to gauge. In its more practiced close-up shots, television can produce remarkable images of the hitter at work, better framed and much more coherent. You can see the detailed business of the at-bat ritual and pre- and post-pitch ritual. The close-up of Reggie Jackson's classic at-bat and strikeout against Bob Welch to end the third game of the 1981 World Series is a case in point. With a power pitcher against a clutch power hitter at a crucial moment, the camera not only recorded the tension of the at-bat but helped produce it. Before Jackson finally struck out after working the count full by fouling off pitches, taking his time and taking it dramatically, the camera was everywhere; inside Welch's glove, gripping Jackson's bat, mopping both brows, grimacing. It was a brilliant piece of work.

Matters get more complicated for television once it leaves the confines of home plate. Some opportunities and many more pitfalls await. I remember being at the park in Yankee Stadium and witnessing a deep drive to the outfield and a complicated baserunning play that required every bit of spatial cunning to comprehend. A ball was driven deep by a Yankee, perhaps Lou Pinella, on the fly to left center. The man on second planned to tag if the ball were caught, and hence only lingered off the base. The man on first was hellbent on scoring should the ball roll to the fence. The two runners ended up virtually on top of each other when the ball sailed between the outfielders. At this point they ran like baggage car and caboose around third. But the runner in front tripped just before the base and took a header. The man behind slowed until the first man scrambled to his feet and resumed running. Two men were heading to the plate within a step of each other. By this time the ball was making its way via a system of relays home, arriving at about the same time as the first runner. The catcher swept and tagged that man out and then looked up to see the second runner coming right at him. Gotcha. Double play, and one of the strangest ever.

During the course of the few seconds that it took the play to form and build, the excitement was immense. What were the runners doing? Where was the ball? What happened? "He's down! My God, the ball's coming in. They're going to get him! They're going to get both of them! Unbelievable!" When the play was over thousands of individual hands slapped thousands of individual foreheads. Everyone was talking to everyone else. "Ever seen anything like it?" "Never! Never in all the time I've seen ball games. Nothing like this, ever!"

The television version of the play, the videotape of which I saw next day on the news, came only in a jumble of sequences. There were two cameras, perhaps three, on the play, and each covered a different set of circumstances and a different cast of characters. The flight of the ball was separate from the adventure of the runners. The confusion and tumble on the base paths registered on one camera was independent from the realization of the ball falling safely on the other. The play at the plate was recorded before the episode of the lead runner falling, which was not telecast in proper sequence on the first run-through. Only on the replay was the falling runner and the fiasco around third base shuffled into the action in proper order. Apparently, it required some frenzied replay choices in the booth (and again in the sports news editing room) to make some sense of how best to recreate this bizarre play for television.

This is not all bad. In truth, it was fascinating to see the play broken down and resequenced by the camera. At the game in the park, I wished the scoreboard television would show the play again, but close plays at the plate are barred because the fans might literally kill the umpire if the image proves him as blind as most assume. Nonetheless, the television version the next day was for me a radically different experience from watching it all develop whole, with the momentum and tension building in sequence, with the assessment of distance, depth, chances of tagging with the progress of the outfield relays timed to the movements of the runners, with the likelihood of scoring all right there in front of me. On television the play had to be lost before it was found.

"DON'T FAIL TO MISS TOMORROW'S GAME" (DIZZY DEAN)

I am not certain whether the Marshall McLuhan theory of television as a cooler medium than most suffices to explain anything about the effect of watching baseball on the tube; if it does not, there are other means to gauge effect, almost all of them having to do with the tendency for the sense organ that is most bombarded with stimuli to take over when the opportunity exists. In the case of television, the viewing soul is always counting on the viewing eye that relies on miniaturized, flattened, angled images.

Radio does not allow the eye to contravene the ear. The voice becomes the memory. Mention Red Barber's or Mel Allen's voices and fans grow misty. It is obvious why this is so. The intense moments of baseball on the radio are inevitably vicarious; those on television are, even if fragmented, at least seen. The great voices of the radio booth are the stimuli of the imagination; the auxiliary presences in the television booth are the corroborators of images. We may remember the colorful natures of Dizzy Dean, Joe Garagiola, and even Bob Uecker, from television, but their relation to the game, their connection to the immediacy of its action is negligible no matter how extensive their bag of tricks, no matter how considerable their innate wit.

An announcer I consider superb on radio and mediocre on television, Vin Scully, focuses the difference between the media. Scully succeeds on radio and does not fully register on television because his voice is dramatic and almost exquisitely paced, whereas his eye for the game is not as shrewd as it seems when its televised images are right in front of you. Scully does time portraits with his voice—he is brilliant at it—and no one in the game has ever done so well with words the tension and strain of that struggle between batter and pitcher. To hear his radio call of the last inning of a Koufax no-hitter or of Drysdale's fifty-nine scoreless innings is as scintillating a baseball experience as any. Scully was so good that he would even do simultaneous play by play on radio and television so the Dodger audience wouldn't miss any of him. I have a memory of Scully's voice doing the classic last inning of the 1959 Dodger-White Sox Series, but I do not remember if it was a simulcast or not. In any case, his voice carries most authority when it is the record of what the eye must imagine from what the ear hears. Those tones of surprise, shock, awe, veneration, and sheer excitement work far less well when the image is a rival for sensory priority.

The finest announcers on television bring something else to the game—a reactive, analytical, lag-time or after-the-fact fervor. Some are good at it, and only an absolute purist can resist the lure of broadcasts by Tim McCarver or

Jim Palmer, whose analyses of plays are intricate and brilliant. They are unfailingly provocative about the exigencies, choices, strategies, and complexities of the game. When responding to any phenomenon in aesthetics or culture, be it symphonic music, politics, or baseball, the power of analysis, even the redundancies of analysis, prolong, widen, and expand the pleasure in pursuing it. The best television commentators understand this even if they would never say it quite this way.

Commentators doing television analysis actually watch two games, the big one on the field and the one produced for them on the monitor by the selection of framed camera shots. The experience of looking at two versions of the same game often results in revaluations of what has just been seen. This process makes up the bulk of television broadcasting. Never is this more dramatic than on close calls at the bases, and never is this more apparent than on such things as the checked swing, which, no matter how it looks the first time around, almost always looks unchecked when replayed in slow motion. But herein lies an interesting fact about baseball judgment for which the checked swing serves as a representative instance. Announcers watching both the game on the field and on the monitor in the booth will debate the matter of the checked swing into silly submission. The umpire, who probably knows what slow motion usually proves, that a good swing is hard to check, also knows that he will generally give the batter the benefit of doubt. There is no slow motion analysis on the field to prove him wrong. Furthermore, slow motion does not call the pitch; the umpire, who recognizes the necessity of a batter's cranking up on virtually every delivery, does. Some of the shrewder broadcasters, who use the monitor with abandon, come to understand how its images are not the ones that determine the way the game is perceived on the field, nor ought they be.

The primary role of announcers on television is to comment on the game's images; they also have an implicit responsibility to compensate for the restricted flat space of the television viewing surface without embarrassing their employers by calling attention to the limitations of their medium. Because the camera, at any one time, sees so little of the field, the viewer is rewarded by hearing more palaver than is strictly necessary. But the best commentators know that there is a balance between useful and useless talk. If you listen closely to a broadcast game on television, you will learn quickly that the announcers tell you things you ought to know as if you are not paying attention and things that you cannot know as if you were. They subtly help make the kinds of judgments about plays that players make on the field or fans make in the stands.

Take a simple call of a ground ball, heard a thousand times: "It's deep in the hole to his right. He'll have to plant to throw. It's going to be close. Nipped him." This is so common it is almost a sort of lingua franca. But none of this can be certain for the television viewer no matter what picture he or she sees on screen. The commentator provides depth-of-field. He is also giving us the implicit judgment about the play opening up before him and seen by us only in fragments from several angles. We do not see exactly where the ball goes when it leaves the bat; we have only a trained sense of its velocity; we can't tell whether the shortstop appears to be in range; we don't have the dimensional sense of what "deep" means in relation to the impending velocity of the throw or in relation to the speed and positioning of the runner; we don't know if it's going to be close until it is close. The seemingly simple description by the television announcer sounds as if he's echoing our eyes, but what we really get is a vision of the play as we might project it, in which the commentator's voice is a means of corroborative judgment.

Television broadcasts have a kind of rhythm, orienting patois followed by analytical commentary. Occasionally, the broadcast director allows a shot of his announcers at work in the booth. Sleeves rolled up, pacing, smoking (maybe), shuffling papers—these are the voices that we see. Their job is never to fall completely silent, but never to do sustained play-by-play as on radio. If we hear less on television during the actual moment of play, we hear far more after it. The verbal replay is as much a phenomenon of television as the instant replay. Every situation in baseball comes equipped with a dozen situational clichés attached to it, and the television announcer's job is to seize the time between events we see and fill it with sequenced variations. Dozens of times a game and hundreds of times a season we hear discourses on the "knockdown" or "brush-back" pitch, on "working the corners," on "pitching behind in the count." There are other workhorse subjects that help account for the bulk of air time: holding runners on base, outfield cutoff throws, signs from the bench, bullpen rituals, bunting, and base running. On the social side: salaries, free agency, team owners, trade rumors, minor-league talent.

At the stadium, I like to think about the game with the buzz of the crowd in the background. The more indistinct the better. On television, I like well-placed and well-paced articulate chatter. Silence is eerie on television, even for a fan who pretends to a detailed knowledge of the game—baseball or any sport. Just how eerie was discovered several years back when one of the networks tried a silent broadcast of a professional football game from Miami. It was a media disaster. Someone got the bright idea (or, more likely, wanted to disabuse viewers of the bright idea) that announcers are intrusive. They might well be; but the medium demands it. Announcers are guides and corroborators; their relation to listeners is in many respects like that of the seeing eye dog to the sight impaired.

Commentators are singly responsible for another feature of television base-ball—and television sports generally—that makes watching a game on television altogether different from attending a game (attending one, that is, without the bloke in front of you carrying a portable television, which is becoming more and more common). The announcers must provide substitute sounds for those that come naturally at the park: the crowd noise, the wind, the airplanes, the vendors. Announcers talk because the game on the screen would appear largely a silent movie if they did not. The talk of television commentators is the missing sound of the live action, a more or less blatant sound, given the style of those who do the game.

There have been some over the years who make wonderful television noise. Dizzy Dean and Buddy Blattner broadcast the game of the week on NBC during the golden age of television in the 1950s. They were superb even at a low-tech time when Dizzy's "he shoulda slud" was the closest television got to instant replay.[5] Later duos on NBC, Kubek and Garagiola, were no match for Dean and Blattner, though they were good together. Today's Scully and Garagiola are not that good together. Both fly solo even if they seem to occupy the same cockpit. They simply do not respond well to each other's points or to each other's style. Resistance is a form of insult.

One reason that Dean and Blattner, Kubek and Garagiola, even Phil Rizzuto and Bill White, locally in New York, are good on television is that they recognize the kitsch of the medium in which they perform. They play to each other and play on each other the way comic partner routines used to work in vaudeville and comic couple routines still work in situation comedies: The day's plot is modulated by the season's themes and foibles. A look, a gesture, a remark can recall the way things have gone before. There's a "Say goodnight, Gracie" quality to it all.

When the Earl Weaver-managed Baltimore Orioles used to come into New York you knew within a couple of innings that Bill White in the Yankee booth, who agreed with Weaver's big inning theory of run production in baseball, would begin to taunt Rizzuto, who believed in Joe McCarthy's theory of never missing the opportunity to advance men and score them one at a time. Part of the fun of listening to the game was to overhear the ingenious, and always amusing, ways White worked Rizzuto into a lather over this issue. A clever director in the booth would pan to a live shot of the two just as White was readying for the final Rizzuto rib, the moment when Rizzuto knew that he was the subject of a slow-building put-on. Perhaps radio announcers could do something like this, but there is rarely enough dead air time and never the chance for a visual flourish or coda.

Special moments that test the mettle of announcers as vaudevillians can come during a game delay, when television would rather be elsewhere but has to hang around on spec. Baseball good will can turn to desperation as the rain lingers, until, finally, the local network provides relief, a sports feature, a rerun, anything to get the announcers off the hook and the station back on schedule. But I remember an occasion during a Yankee rain delay in which White and Rizzuto had come upon a book of famous bloopers, spoonerisms, and verbal tangles spoken by baseball announcers. They simply began reading the entries while waiting for the rain to stop, having no intent at first of perusing more than a few. Eventually, they read nearly the whole book. The foul-ups and tongue twisters on air had a peculiar fascination for the two broadcasters. Rizzuto's own classic screw-ups were even in the book. With the long delay, the pressure of filling time, and the increasingly madcap citation of bloopers, Rizzuto and White began to lose control.

Nothing is funnier on air than a pair of increasingly hysterical announcers.

All White had to do was begin to cite something from the book and Rizzuto would break up at the first syllable. It didn't matter anymore what the mistake was. The laughter was infectious and riotous. Through the rest of the game, when it finally resumed, Rizzuto and White, without even mentioning the exact citations read earlier, began recalling bits and pieces of them. The game now had a set of running, extratemporal and extraterritorial motifs. Whenever something in the game recalled one of the announcing gaffes the laughter would recur. A new perspective existed for the viewer and listener, and full robust laughter made the experience of that game memorable on television the way it could not have been at the park.

Though the palaver in the booth can, in some instances, be a cloying nuisance, there are these moments of almost transcendent amusement. I recall another bit of television dialogue between Rizzuto and White that a season ticket could never purchase. White: "Say, Phil, I've often wondered about the ads you do for that New Jersey finance concern, the Money, what is it . . . ?" Phil: "Oh, oh, don't say it, White. I know what you're thinkin.' " White: "No, Phil, tell me. By the way, what happens, I wonder, if you don't pay these fellows back?" Phil: "I ah . . . ah. What d'ya mean? What d'ya mean?" White: "Well, gee Scooter, what do they do to you if you don't pay them? I heard they break your knees?" Phil: "Oh, my God, White, don't say that. Please, White, please don't say that."

There is something about the pacing of baseball that allows for such banter in the broadcast box. The announcers are a part of a kind of parallel show that compensates, as television must, for moments of ennui or inaction on the field (at the park there is always something to look at and think about). They are cast as friends, friends presumably of each other but friends also in the wider sense of all those who tune in on a regular basis. Sometimes there are guests in the booth, like guests in your home or on your stage, and the result is pure baseball shtick. When Bob Uecker used to show up for NBC Game of the Week with Kubek and Garagiola, the invariable result was a frenzied routine. About his notoriously poor hitting: "Hey, I used to level dozens of drives off the St. Louis fences. Why, before the game I'd go out there in deep left and hit balls off the wall with a fungo bat." Uecker's bit exists in two worlds, the stand-up routine of the booth and, quite possibly, the real memorial and folkloric world of pregame baseball. In other words, the fan of mid–1960s, out early at a Cardinal game, may well have seen the irrepressible Uecker as player actually peppering the wall with fungo line drives from twenty feet away. It might have been funnier at the park than in the booth. But you had to be there.

Some announcers on television could not manage such interludes; they can barely do the game. Inadequate announcing, like so many inadequacies, is more telling in the breach than in the performance. I have listened to broadcasts recently in which I was unfamiliar with the commentators. Ted Turner's Atlanta Braves find themselves piped into living rooms all over the nation on cable with homogenized dullness at the microphone, but the best of the worst, as W. C. Fields well knew, originates in Philadelphia. I have always gotten the Phillie games where I live, which is no blessing. Their commentators are soporific, including the great former center fielder, Richie Ashburn. It is almost as if the Phils' announcers rest content to let television's images do most of the work, which is to say they fail to grasp the nature of the work the images actually do. Lag time is one thing on television; drag time another. My own kids, who are baseball addicts, can't bear the silences and bored voices of the Phillie television announcers. When their bedtime nears I insist they watch an inning. It usually does the trick.

If announcers are to be successful on television, they must perform services that go beyond analysis and amusement; they must, after a fashion, console. A real fan knows that things can go wrong for a team and they can do so quickly. There is no solace in the silence of others. After a sudden turn of events, a loss on a ninth inning homer, say, a suffering local television fan finds immediate sympathy in the voice of the announcer. This is less so on radio because the announcers themselves convey the bad news. I remember radio games in which I could hear in the announcer's voice the home run that he knew was out of the park before he could finish his sentence: "There's a long blast to left; it's deep; it's outta here." By "There's" I could tell I was in trouble, and by "long," I knew I was in for some profound suffering. My first impulse was to blame the voice for the action.

Television is very different. You learn, though it's not easy, to recognize disaster from the look of a swing. The voice of the announcer is only a form of instant commiseration. After a game-losing hit against your team, you long for the familiar voice of the broadcaster to hint, even if merely by the soothing assurance of the terms of his employment, that tomorrow is another day, that sponsors, camera crews, directors, and producers, all intend to be there. The station has slotted a time period for the game and advertisers have already paid for the broadcast. These workaday realities rest in the mind as potential revenge. They are not small consolations when your team has just been annihilated. Anyone who has been at the park and felt the violation of a loss with nowhere to turn but to the backward turning turnstiles, knows how much easier it is for television to lapse back into the regular rhythms of reality. The interlude is less painfully over when Curt Gowdy or Ralph Kiner or Bill White put on their "it's another day" faces and sign off the air.

There is a final aspect to baseball announcing, a sometimes subtle and sometimes none-too-subtle injection of politics into the game during the broadcast. Having entered this essay with a few words on baseball and money, I exit with a few words on baseball and politics. Neither of these inevitable combos is a subject of consuming interest to me, but neither can be ignored. It's merely obvious with what dogs some commentators lie down, and what fleas they end up scratching. Joe Garagiola is most blatant about this; his politics are worn on his sleeve, and the deeper structure of baseball plays out his conservative myth of America. The owner, management, player complex is a triad for power relations, all supposedly conducted in the name of sports and fun. The players are coddled; they are the loafing, greedy, malingering labor force to the benevolent owners who suffer so to put on a show everyone loves and who earn a modest buck for their efforts. The players almost, but not quite, ruin the game. For Garagiola, baseball in its modern-day incarnation falls just short of being played by a collection of clown princes with mediocre talent and lots of chutzpah, who are lucky to be indulged in the activity they ought to love.

Howard Cosell, nearing the other side of the political spectrum but never quite reaching it, believes in conspiracies; and conspiracies are never conducted by the simple rube trying to earn a living hitting .260, but by those who for one reason or another have either accumulated or think they might accumulate power for the express purpose of abusing it. To listen to Cosell do a ball game or a spot on baseball is to search for unsavory motives. He likes to crawl under rocks and, gloomily, stay there. Good baseball announcers have either a sense of irony, as do McCarver, Scully, Jim Palmer, or a sense of fun, as do Harry Caray, Phil Rizzuto, or Dizzy Dean. Since Cosell has little irony and probably no fun, he casts a pall over the game. He was trained as a lawyer and his broadcasts are less commentaries than they are depositions. A joyless man, he takes the spirit out of the game and makes even neutral things litigious. For Cosell baseball is a harsh and chicanery-ridden business. Its most exciting feature, because it looked like—and indeed probably was—a mass conspiracy, was the reserve clause.

My own favorite television commentator is Tim McCarver, who broadcasts locally in New York for the Mets and nationally whenever his contract allows. His vision of the game is socially democratic in every sense. The ballplayer for McCarver is neither lumpen nor conspiratorial. Instead he's middle management. There are better and worse ways to do a job that, to an extent, involves the same adjustment between individual and group interests that energizes American political and social life. McCarver is about as probing as they come in assessing the game. Listening to him is like reading de Toqueville or Henry Adams.

I remember McCarver once citing George Santayana's "they who are ignorant of history are condemned to repeat it." Ralph Kiner was stunned. "That's amazing. Did you think of that?" McCarver: "Well, no, not exactly." Kiner: "Who said it?" McCarver: "Somebody. Somebody else." A few minutes later the broadcast booth had several telegrams with the answer. McCarver, a history buff, began talking about this, that, and the other thing concerning history and historical mistakes. It became a motif for the game, and the conversation became increasingly animated. Ralph Kiner played straight man, a properly baffled one, no doubt, but at the same time McCarver chatted on about history he also knew that Kiner, blissfully ignorant of so many things, was in himself baseball history, one of the game's most powerful home run hitters. In other words, it was still baseball and baseball history that was the subtext of the other conversation no matter what highbrow shape it seemed to be taking for one of its participants. This is something that television encourages in its best announcers, often to entertaining and engrossing effect. And this was a moment I was glad to be watching baseball on the tube.

NOTES

1. *The Sporting News*, lovingly described as "baseball's Bible," took to television with particular fervor in the late 1940s and early 1950s. The information in the preceding section was gleaned from this weekly journal, and anyone with a historical interest in the financial side of baseball would do well to peruse the almost weekly feature in *The Sporting News* during these years.

2. Walking through the tunnel of Yankee Stadium and confronting the field is the subject of my epigraph for this section from Leslie Hazelton's reprint of a "Hers" column from *The New York Times* in *Diamonds are Forever* (San Francisco: Chronicle Books, 1987), 14.

3. Tom Boswell, "How Life Imitates the World Series," in *Diamonds Are Forever*, 127.

4. Roger Angell, *Season Ticket: A Baseball Companion* (Boston: Houghton Mifflin, 1988), 92.

5. Dean's bouts with the English language during the 1940s on radio had, of course, raised the ire of America's schoolmarms, not only with the baffling injunction I used as an epigraph for this section, "Don't fail to miss tomorrow's game," but with such wondrous redundancies as, "The score is nuthin' to nuthin' and nobody's winnin'."

4

Not Such a Long Way, Baby: Women and Televised Myth

Harriet Blodgett

Television honors the current myths of American culture, but its mythic affinities are even more extensive. When Diane of *Cheers*, whose own characterization owes something to goddess Artemis-Diana, taunts her jealous boss Sam that his brother and rival is "just a guy like any other guy in Greek myth,"[1] she reminds one that classical mythology and more widespread archetypes also live on in television imagination. Indeed, myth and television are intimately related, although women have not necessarily benefited from the connection. The mythology of Western culture in its traditional tales—comprising not only tales of gods and heroes, but also folklore and fairy tale and the images, motifs, and symbols thereof—may provide a distinguished ancestry or source for television narrative. But unfortunately, like the currently viable myths of American culture, it is also inescapably patriarchal as a consequence of its own male-dominant sources.

Television can claim mythic ancestors because it is a purveyor of narrative, that is, story, told by the "intangible narrating presence" of the camera;[2] and narrative is the descendant of myth in the form of the sacred and traditional stories of early human culture devised to interpret and order the mysterious and chaotic aspects of existence, within the psyche and without, in nature. Not only have mimetic forms ultimately developed out of such myth, but myth has persisted even in realistic narrative. As Robert Scholes and Robert Kellogg long ago pointed out in discussing the heritage of the novel as a form, "the unrationalized plots and motifs of sacred myth" are "always a fruitful source of narrative structure, even in highly rational narrative traditions. Mythic archetypes . . . appeal powerfully to even the most empirically oriented audiences through their manifestation of universal psychic patterns."[3] Had they not been speaking in 1966, before literary critics were contemplating television too, they might have said the same about its sources. Others have, in the critical field of narrative theory founded by Vladimir Propp's path-breaking study in 1928 of Russian fairy tales, *Morphology of the Folktale*, and by Russian formalist critics. Subsequently swelled by the work of diverse other critics who worked out the formulaic implications of Propp's work, more recent narrative theory has pointed out the affinities between myth and other forms of popular imaginative expression, such as television. As Sarah Ruth Kozloff puts it, "American television is remarkably like Russian fairy tales . . . certain motifs, situations and stock characters may have a nearly universal psychological/sociological appeal and thus appear again and again in popular cultural forms." Roger Silverstone, who rightly contends that television "is the preserver of tradition and that novelty is a thin disguise," uses structuralist theories to relate television elaborately to myth to demonstrate that "the possibility for effective, ideological communication is dependent on the presence and pre-existence of other, perhaps universal, forms of communication."[4]

The myths of early culture apparently were not originally male dominant; Near and Middle Eastern paleolithic and neolithic societies have left strong evidence of worshipping a supreme Great Mother Goddess of nature and fertility. But, even as the Goddess in time gave way to a male deity, Western mythology became patriarchal.[5] The folk and fairy tales that later emerged from myth are notorious for their patriarchal bias. The major heroines in the tales collected by Hans Christian Anderson, for example, as Jennifer Waelti-Walters has pointed out, are incapacitated—imprisoned, lamed, or shoeless—and a recurrent symbol in the Grimm brothers' collection is a girl incarcerated or forced to wear a mask or obliged to play dead. Fairy tales, in fact, are gendering devices that, as Marcia Leiberman has demonstrated in copious and careful detail, "serve to acculturate women to traditional social roles." In Andrea Dworkin's unequivocal terms, they largely teach an unmistakable patriarchal lesson that

Men and women are different, absolute opposites. . . . Where he is erect, she is supine. Where he is awake, she is asleep. Where he is active, she is passive. Where she is erect, or awake, or active, she is evil and must be destroyed.[6]

Myths, however, are as instrumental as folk and fairy tales in their gendering messages, even if less transparent.

All such narratives share, ultimately, a biological provenance for their female images. Behind those images lie myths of the Great Mother Goddess of nature that reflect not only love for the giver of life but fear of the death that her gift entails. Thus woman in traditional Western mythology and its folk derivatives is source both of good and of evil, of pleasure and of pain: both a Mary who comforts and a Pandora who pours out human woes. But whether woman is praised or damned, she is confined. To be seen primarily in her biological role as the mysterious source of life—whether as goddess or as mother, wife, mistress—is for woman to be seen in her role-relationship to man rather than as an autonomous being. She is the necessary Other, against whom, as Simone de Beauvoir has demonstrated at length, man defines his transcendence of nature, not only in his life but in the representations of his literature and mythology. "Representation of the world," as Beauvoir puts it, "like the world itself, is the work of men; they describe it from their own point of view, which they confuse with absolute truth." Typical of what they describe is their own power over nature:

on earth as on Olympus it is the male principle that is truly creative: from it came form, number, movement; grain grows and multiplies through Demeter's care, but the origin of the grain and its verity lie in Zeus; woman's fecundity is regarded as only a passive quality.[7]

With a few exceptions, Zeus remains more active in television mythology too than Demeter, even if she is no longer merely a field hand.

Archetypal theories underscore the patriarchal bent of most Western mythology, for such theories find their basal pattern in the preponderance of hero myths. In Northrop Frye's schema, for example, according to which myth has spawned literature while becoming increasingly displaced towards mimesis of the ordinary in place of fabulae about the gods, "Myth constructs a central narrative around a figure who is partly the sun, partly vegetative fertility and partly a god or archetypal human being." The archetypal story of all literature is the myth of this hero whose life cycle follows the rhythm of the sun and the seasons. For Joseph Campbell too, but one hero prevails, wearing a thousand faces. Campbell weaves "one composite adventure" out of "tales of the world's symbolic carriers of the destiny of Everyman"; the monomyth is contained within the formula of the rites of passage: separation, initiation, return. Campbell's syncretism draws heavily on Jungian archetypal concepts. C. G. Jung's theory of a collective unconscious indeed renders myth inescapable in the imaginative process by endowing all psyches with a predisposition to the archetypal images embedded in myths, a sameness of imaginings even if the details are determined by the particular culture that an individual inhabits. Myths themselves are "original revelations of the preconscious psyche, involuntary statements about unconscious psychic happenings" first laid down as the species developed into consciousness but recapitulated in each individual's heroic task of psychic growth as the "symbolic expressions of the inner unconscious drama of the psyche which becomes accessible to man's consciousness by way of projection."[8] Jungian theory foregrounds the myth of a hero who projects this inner drama of personal, as well as racial individuation. The hero dominates current television programming as well, despite any changes inspired by the renascent women's movement, or perhaps because of them.

Like the myths culturally or possibly psychologically inherited, televised myths largely preserve and reconstitute the gendered status quo throughout all change, by way of their characterizations and situations and plots. Through the images that are the televised language of the narrative, viewers are instructed or reinstructed in the supposed nature and the existential status of males and females. Why? The answer is essentially the same for television as for the myths that were its precursors. In Silverstone's words, "The mythic dimension of culture contains traditional stories and actions whose source is the persistent need to deny chaos and create order." To create order, then, by preserving gender distinctions, the function which, Soviet semiotician Jurij Lotman has proposed, mythic narrative originally fulfilled. According to Lotman as feminist film critic Teresa de Lauretis discusses him, narrative endlessly reconstructs the world as a "two-character drama in which the human person creates and recreates *himself* out of an abstract or purely symbolic other—the womb, the earth, the grave, the woman." In the earliest myths, the primary distinction is sexual difference and the central actor, male:

the hero, the mythical subject, is constructed as human being and as male; he is the active principle of culture, the establisher of distinction, the creator of differences. Female is what is not susceptible to transformation, to life or death; she (it) is an element of plot-space, a topos, a resistance, matrix and matter. . . . [T]he mythical mechanism produces the human being as man and everything else as, not even "woman," but non-man, an absolute abstraction (and this has been so since the beginning of time, since the origin of plot at the origin of culture . . .).

Less flattering than Beauvoir's conception of the "Other" but akin to it, such semiotic-narrative theory again reduces the female, in her difference, to a very secondary sex. It also explains how her reality is constituted by her culture. For the work of narrative, de Lauretis continues, is to map difference, especially sexual difference, into each text and by accumulation into the "universe of meaning, fiction, and history, represented by the literary-artistic tradition and all the texts of culture."[9] Television has secured its place in that (gendering) tradition.

The presence of myth in television bears threefold discussion. Television narratives, first of all, may take their characters, situations, and/or plots directly from particular known traditional myths (including folk and fairy tales) or mythic motifs. Second, in so doing, they utilize archetypal patterns and symbolic images such as are found universally or at least widely in myths. Third, and again in so doing, television valorizes the myths of its own culture, here comprehending myth as Martin Esslin has so concisely defined it: "Fictions . . . which embody the essential, lived reality of a culture and society."[10] Esslin demonstrates that the TV commercial, like Greek tragedy, deals with the basic myths of a culture. Commercials aside—not, certainly, that they are innocent—under whichever aspect the presence of myth in television programs is observed, television proves still remiss in its portrayals of women. Feminists had hoped for better than television of the eighties has yielded, for it continues to reinforce the gender distinctions and patriarchal hierarchy still central to American culture. The prime time television programs of 1988–89 (new and rerun) drawn on for the following discussion are indicative.

The presence of well-known myths in television is evidenced by programs that employ the physical metamorphosis motif of myth. (Actually, even plots which show radical nonphysical transformation in their protagonists are indebted to the metamorphosis motif.) The Narcissus myth, for example, furnished an episode of *Twilight Zone*. Narcissus is the tale of a youth who so admires his own reflected image in a pool that he drowns in it, though he is reborn as the flower named for him. *Twilight Zone* translated aging movie actress Barbara Jean Trenton into the celluloid image of her beautiful youthful self, which is the only reality she can accept. Offered a part as a mother, whereas her sense of herself is as a love goddess, and shocked to find that her romantic leading man of twenty years past has become a common grocer, Barbara Jean wills herself into the screen on which she has so often fondly gazed. Presumably, as evidenced not only by her pragmatic male counterpart but also by the good friend who has arranged the offer of the despised movie role, men can better accept their mutability and the mundaneness of things than can women.

Another, more elaborate tale impelled by a physical transformation was *The Love Goddess*, which gave quiz show flunky Vanna White her first dramatic role as Venus—the Venus (or Greek Aphrodite) of the Pygmalion myth who is generous to lovers. As the original story goes, after Pygmalion, King of Cyprus, prays to Aphrodite for a wife resembling a statue he has fallen in love with, she instead brings it to life for him and they marry. Ovid in his *Metamorphoses* elaborated on the myth in a version that has become far better known and presumably inspired the televised fiction. As Ovid retells the story, Pygmalion is a bachelor who, shocked by women's vices, has not married, but instead sculpted himself an ivory statue of a virgin and fallen in love with his own workmanship. Venus brings his statue to life under his touch because she has comprehended his unstated wish for a wife like unto his ivory girl:

> and Pygmalion came
> Back where the maiden lay, and lay beside her,
> And kissed her, and she seemed to glow, and kissed her,
> And stroked her breast, and felt the ivory soften
> Under his fingers, as wax grows soft in sunshine,
> Made pliable by handling.[11]

A paradigmatic myth of masculinist culture, "Pygmalion" becomes, in fact, a myth of how man molds woman to his own desires. The woman is an object who gains her humanity only through her sexuality for him. "Pygmalion," moreover, embodies the archetypal sleeping beauty motif, for the female awakens to life only through a male's impassioned love for her. The myth, in short, valorizes the male lover. In the televised version, it does so as well.

Ted Beckman, a hair stylist rather than a sculptor, on the eve of his wedding carelessly puts the wedding ring he has been carrying on a statue of Venus, whereupon she is brought to life, and desiring him for herself, jeopardizes his intended marriage, though finally granting him the force of his love for his intended and releasing him to marry. Like Pygmalion the young man is a true lover; he has refused bachelor party promptings to illicit dalliance before his wedding; he has refused the love goddess herself; Venus honors true lovers. Of course, she is given no choice but to do so, for the young man is as adamant in his fidelity as Venus is unfixed in her marble—and her longings. Proving stronger even than the goddess, Ted molds Venus to *his* desires: not only awakening desire in her but quelling it.

Though it involves no shape change, the dramatic series *Beauty and the Beast* also draws on the metamorphosis motif, now of fairy tale, by borrowing its "beauty" and "beast" from the story first written down in the eighteenth century by Mme Le Prince de Beaumont. Her tale tells of a beautiful and virtuous young girl who, to save her father's life after he has trespassed on the domain of a beast and stolen a rose, agrees to live with the Beast. Learning that the Beast has sickened for her while she is away on a visit to her father, she returns to the Beast to save his life and acknowledges that she has come to love him. Upon her kiss, the beast not only becomes well, he becomes human and they marry. While this tale might seem to be the female answer to Pygmalion/Sleeping Beauty myths, attesting to the power of female love, in fact it is no such thing. Rather, it is a maturation myth whose subtext valorizes patriarchal culture in which females do not so much grow up as change their masters, going from their fathers to their mates, having translated their aversion for sex into romantic attachment. Young Beauty has an Oedipal problem; excessively devoted to her father, she refuses suitors so that she may cling to her father; she even offers her life to save his. The Beast's ugliness embodies the adolescent's anxieties about masculine desires that she transcends, however, as she comes to know and cherish the gentle Beast, and she is therefore rewarded with marriage to a handsome prince. As Karen E. Rowe observes, the tale embodies conformity. "Beast's transformation rewards Beauty for embracing traditional female virtues. . . . She trades her independent selfhood for subordination."[12]

The prevailing assumptions of the television version are likewise patriarchal, and it is no longer a female maturation tale. A more accurate title for the television series would be The Beast and His Beauty, for the tale has been refocused on him. He, Vincent ("the conqueror") is a hero figure who is cherished by the secret underground community where he has been reared ever since being found in a trash heap behind St. Vincent's Church as an infant swaddled in rags (unusual circumstances typically attend the infancy of the mythical hero). Beneath the streets of New York, in abandoned subway tunnels plus chambers they have excavated, live these exiles from the harsh and corrupt world above, in a vaguely medieval setting apparently intended, like their garb, to recall typical illustrations in fairy tale collections. The middle-aged doctor who is leader of the colony, known as Father, and Vincent are revered for their wisdom, gentleness, love of their kind; viewers often see Vincent serving as savior of the unhappy and downtrodden.

Of Vincent's beloved Beauty, Catherine, the lawyer who provides the colony's major contact with the outside world, his introductory voice-over often asserts that he knew she would change his life. This Beauty, however, is beyond adolescent crises and, the episode "Ozymandias" points out, a year ago left her wealthy father's law firm to work in the district attorney's office. There she can do more public good. In the same episode, like her precursor, she offers to sacrifice herself for the sake of her beloved, only now it is for Vincent's colony. She is ready to marry the developer Burch whose proposed tower requires foundations so deep they will annihilate the colony's home, if that will stop him from building (fortunately, the law stops him first). Besides serving as Vincent's inspiration and love, Catherine also functions as Vincent's helper, carrying out his research work and occasionally referring new candidates to the colony.

She cannot be his bride, however much they adore each other, for Vincent is the Beast; a human being with an unfortunate resemblance to a lion in his facial features, a huge and hairy frame, clawed hands (but with thumbs), and an ability to snarl like a big cat (conventional illustrations for Beaumont's stories depict the Beast as leonine). But Vincent and Catherine are tied, as Catherine's voice-over proclaims at the start of episodes, by spiritual bonds so that "though we cannot be together we will never ever be apart"[13]—and though they fondle affectionately, they never exactly kiss. It saddens Catherine that she can never have a child, even frustrates her. Yearningly she intimates to Vincent in "A Child Is Born" how fortunate he has been even to hold a newborn child in his arms. Catherine, however (appropriately named after a fourth century A.D. virgin martyr of Alexandria), sublimates her sexuality. For Vincent, in turn, Catherine is a spiritual force, an asexual being affirmed by his adoring gaze and a voice-over in which he declares his love for her goodness. The reverent manner in which he quotes Byron's "She walks in beauty like the night" during the "Chamber Music" episode confirms the platonic quality of his love.

The underground setting not only implies unconscious ramifications, but as in Jungian psychology proves to be the locus of rebirth, itself an archetypal theme. There, Vincent succored Catherine, at the beginning of the series, after he found her in the upper world the battered victim of a rape. Not only was her health restored, but her desire to live and her love of her kind—and of Vincent, whose goodness, as in the original tale, she recognized despite his shaggy exterior. There too, Lena, a despairing and very pregnant prostitute in "A Child is Born," rediscovers her faith in life and self-respect after Catherine has rescued her from the streets and introduced her into the colony to bear her child. (It will afterwards be named Catherine too, in tribute to her agency.) Lena is spiritually renewed but lapses because she is physically attracted to the Beast; when he rejects her, she runs away to prostitution again. Catherine, however, seeks her out, whereupon Lena, who has recognized how good the communal life will be for her and cares more about that than her desire for Vincent, agrees to return. Thus the underground community might be said to save females from their sexuality, one way or another—scarcely the intent of the original tale.

That it saves Vincent too from his carnality is no saving grace, but the program has apparently set its sights on a message of the need for a greater love. "We have a bond stronger than friendship or love," intones Catherine's voice-over in the introduction to the various episodes, presumably meaning that each serves as the guiding inspiration for the other to lead a life made meaningful through service to the human community, whatever self-abnegation is required. In "Remember Love," Vincent reconfirms that message for himself, after an access of despair in the course of which Catherine is projected before him like a Jungian anima image. The Jungian anima is a female image which, in its positive function, serves as mediator between the ego and the unconscious center of personality, the self. A precipitate of all human experience pertaining to women, at its highest stage of development the anima has transcended all sexual elements to become a capacity for spiritual devotion. It enables the limited individual to transform his loyalties from his bounded self to a larger community. As the story goes, enraged that he cannot accompany Catherine on an above-world outing because it would be too dangerous—the community might lose him—and shattered by a surge of romantic desire, Vincent breaks down, longs for death, dreams and sees the Catherine within himself projected onto a female wraith. She, having helped out the viewer by explaining herself as Vincent's inner Catherine,[14] now leads Vincent through projections of unconscious terrors—including a confrontation with the alchemist Paracelsus, useful for viewers who know that alchemy plays a role in Jungian theorizing about symbols of transformation. Vincent's ordeals bring the hero finally to a reaffirmation of his worth to the world he serves and to Catherine. Having seen what a lesser place the world would be had he died at birth, he is now reborn, renewed. At the end, he is reminded to "remember love" as his talisman against future despair. Meanwhile, the portrayal of Catherine as the perfectly good female of male idealization ironically duplicates in its very asexuality the patriarchal nature of the original tale designed to promote sexuality. Beauty continues to serve male needs.

Television has such difficulty escaping its gendered assumptions that even when the ostensible intention of a program is to validate women's inherent rights, the depiction may create a contrary impression. That image and plot may be at variance in their implications, plot favoring female selfhood while image renders it a fearsome thing, is demonstrated by yet another version of the metamorphosis motif that appeared in an episode of *The Twilight Zone*. In it Louise Simmons, an abused wife, finally acknowledges her anger against her philandering and abusive husband and vents it through the agency of a ceramic doberman, a gift from her sister, which transforms into a vicious attack dog. The dog, which she quickly recognizes as a projection of her emotions, is about to kill the man and has plentifully bloodied him when she calls it off; she cannot bear to kill. Yet the timid, self-deprecatory, and inhibited Louise is changed. It does not matter that the statue has broken and the dog disappeared. As a voice-over announces, driven into her inner recesses, Louise has discovered her inner power. She commandeers the family pickup to leave her husband. When he threatens her as she is leaving, she challenges him and the dog reappears, growling savagely beside her. She drives off, triumphant; the camera switches to him, bleeding and consternated. The viewer should simply rejoice in Louise's victory over manifest evil. Instead she has become the image of a fearsome thing: witchlike, though her familiar is not a cat but a dog; a Hecate, dread goddess of the realm of the dead, whose principal animal is the dog. Apparently those who composed the episode felt obliged to reintroduce the dog to say (by the logic of the program) that Louise would forever be protected, not by her new found self-respect, but by anger—Beware!

But they had archetypal sanction for doing so. As the final image of frightening Louise implies, television draws often on the archetypal symbols embedded in particular myths and motifs. Moreover, as Beast implies, favorite among them is the prominent archetype of the hero. In Jungian terms, he is the ever-forming, individuating self, emerging into consciousness, reintegrating with the unconscious in symbolic projections of just such unconscious encounters such as Beast experiences. But whether or not one accepts the Jungian explanation of his provenance and function, his various manifestations can be summarized as the monomythic hero that Joseph Campbell describes, who comes triumphantly through his trials to the betterment of himself and/or the land. In the nuclear unit of Campbell's composite myth, the "hero ventures forth from the world of common day into a region of supernatural wonder: fabulous forces are there encountered and a decisive victory won: the hero comes back from this mysterious adventure with the power to bestow boons on his fellow man."[15] He may have female helpers along the way or secure a female as a prize. He may confront female figures as obstacles. But he does not share his title role or his glory with women.

He still dominates prime time television, as *21 Jump Street* can illustrate. It chronicles the adventures of a group of young plainclothes police agents, three of whom are male and one, Hoffs, female (the numbers are already a statement). In two successive weeks the episodes included, first, a segment in which Hoffs infiltrates a problematical situation, and then one in which the males apprehend criminals. Hoffs gets a female problem to deal with: befriending a high school senior who needs an abortion and attends a counseling clinic, under siege by right-to-lifers, that her boyfriend bombs. Hoffs, who provides a shoulder for the girl to lean on, meanwhile reveals that she herself had once had an abortion. She had never told her mother about it, but in the final frame she calls her to do so. The male agents play a far more active and heroic role in their episode. Disguised as pledges, two of them infiltrate a fraternity house where there has allegedly been a rape, and therefore they must undergo the ritual trials demanded of pledges—and of archetypal heroes. Not only do they save lives in the process, but they flush out the rapists in the end. Hoffs's role in apprehending criminals is slight, and her triumphs personal; theirs are crucial and their triumphs communal.

The television movie *Glory Days* presented yet another version of heroic male ordeals leading to good. Its fifty-two year-old protagonist has returned to college, desiring not only to complete his education but to play football. As he is in excellent physical shape and is willing to give his all, he passes successfully through the visible ordeals of tryout and training and makes the squad. There, he knows a brief period of glory as an outstanding player, though he alienates his wife and children in the process. However, not only does he refuse the temptations of a coed's advances; in the midst of the big game he steps aside to let a younger player make the significant touchdown and returns to his wife and family as husband and father. He and his wife embrace like two young lovers, for the hero has matured into adulthood and (re)gained his bride—whose active role, needless to say, has been limited to pointing out to him the error of his excesses. But she has provided a touchstone against which he can be tested for really being a (good) man.

Like myths of the hero, mythic archetypes of the female are quasi-universal imaginings expressive of communal emotions and ideals as well as of psychological stages. Moreover, a prominent characteristic of female archetypes has traditionally been the splitting up of women into discrete images of favored and feared beings. Five symbolic constructs fragmenting female wholeness are acknowledged as common: (1) the frightening female (the powerful or evil goddess, the monster, the witch or crone, the wicked stepmother, etc.); (2) the venerated female (the self-sacrificing madonna or pure maiden) and generous fairy godmother; (3) the sex object (the seductress, the whore, the prey, the "chick"); (4) the earth mother (fertile, nurturing, "natural"); (5) the misbegotten man (the asexual single woman, the too aggressive woman).[16] Long the source of stereotypes for popular literature, such characterizations fit readily into the type casting of television narrative even if literal goddesses are few, and single women no longer automatically condemned. Furthermore, not only characterizations utilize such archetypes. Discrete images and plots also perpetuate them, as evidenced, for example, by the preliminary shot of barely covered female breasts that always introduces *Miami Vice* in a reassurance that this program will (dis)honor woman as sex object. Likewise, even an episode of *Designing Women* unfortunately turned on the issue of the overly ample breasts of a Danish *au pair* girl, Ursula, whom the title women hired; Mary Jo has found that one cup of Ursula's bra fits Mary Jo's head. Ursula's amplitude steals the designers' boyfriends' affections away until Suzanne tells her to take her too big bosom elsewhere.

A prominent instance of the splitting up of the female image occurs on the popular program *Cheers*, whose central cast consists, among others, of Sam, the womanizing owner of the Cheers bar in Boston; and two waitresses: Carla, the earth-mother type who has eight children and sometimes is even shown on screen as pregnant; and, more dominant, Sam's sparring partner, the clever

Diane, the "maiden" type appositely named for the powerful goddess of the hunt, Diana (the Greek Artemis). Artemis-Diana, as classicist Sarah B. Pomeroy says, never marries; "her lack of a permanent connection to a male figure in a monogamous relationship is the keystone of her independence."[17] Many men try, but no man captures chaste-minded Diane, who regularly is shown rebuffing Sam's tries at sexual intimacy. Earthy Carla is blunt and unashamed of her sexuality; upper class, intellectual Diane prefers analyzing emotions. Though often shown to be pretentious, she serves as a spiritual force within the bar by reminding others of their higher duties, whether to self or to principle. In an indicative episode, Sam, formerly a baseball player, is menaced by a female publicity agent who deals in ex-athletes; attracted to him she arranges for him to perform on a television commercial, with promise even of a national series of spots afterwards. But she is also woman the seductress, complete with a lascivious leer, who exacts her pound of flesh from him so that, while he is thrilled at the promise of a career in television, he feels debased by having to purchase it with his body. Diane persuades him that he must break with the agent, and he does so. In the climactic, nearly closing lines of the episode, he tells her that she has taught him what morality is.

Midnight Caller provided a variant illustration of splitting the female image in subjecting its main character, Killian, in the opening episode, to two women who serve respectively as promise and threat to him. The segment is peppered with mythological motifs, especially those of the great goddess in her maleficent and beneficent aspects. Killian is introduced as a San Francisco police officer who is so demoralized by accidentally killing his partner while on duty that he quits the force and takes to drink. But he is rescued from his decline by "Ms." Devon King (an interesting choice of surname), who owns radio station KJCM. She persuades him to become a nightly telephone talk show host. Devon is his good angel or fairy godmother who restores him to a life of active virtue and prestige. The talk show, as she points out after a few months, has served as his "rite of passage" in becoming an "urban folk hero"[18] who has done more good on the air than he did as a cop. A caller who identifies herself only as "Angel" plays the antagonist. This prostitute and serial killer of males, who has goddesslike delusions of grandeur, papers her walls with a reproduction of Michelangelo's Sistine Chapel *Creation of Man*—God reaching out his hand to humankind—an image over which the camera lingers. She lures Killian (instructed to wear a wedding ring, for he is to play consort to the great goddess who destroys her lovers) to her place to kill him. But he shoots her first—blasts her out the window, in fact, so that her "angelic" image, garbed in flowing white, drops to earth where it belongs. Powerful women are acceptable if they use their power to help men; otherwise, they must be destroyed.

With or without drawing on such archetypal categories of female image, television narrative promulgates archetypes in the many myths it persists in telling that embody patriarchal assumptions still viable in American culture. The soaps of course are infamous for doing so. As Tania Modleski says, "patriarchal myths and institutions are . . . wholeheartedly embraced'' by soap operas. That men make the world turn has not lost its force for the prime time soaps such as *Dynasty* and *Dallas*, where nothing much has changed since Ellen Seiter described them in 1983 as revolving around "masculine competition and intrigue in the business world. While women were affected by and sometimes embroiled in these financial matters, they existed largely as appendages to the men. Often women were prizes to be won by men, rewards for shrewdness and material success." Alternatively, they are menacing sirens or, like Angela Channing of *Falcon Crest*, dragon ladies to beware of. As late as 1987, N. D. Batra had reason to describe *Dallas* as a "collective," "male" fantasy of an America that never existed but "which is being lost daily to feminism, Jerry Falwell, Japan. . . . ''[19] Also embedded in the soaps but extending well beyond them, as *The Equalizer* regularly demonstrates, is the classic assumption (sanctified by myths of the hero) that the (active) male is the defender and rescuer of the (passive) female, whom he protects from harm. He may be assisted by a female in so doing, but she only provides backup or companionship; the achievement is his.

In a possibly desperate endeavor to offset the gains in equality brought by the women's movement, programs will insist on a woman's need for male protection, and like the Virginia Slims commercial that assures her of her progress while labeling her "baby" to keep her in her proper place, use *au courant* touches to obscure *au fond* traditionalism. Programs may even proselyte for it, as evidenced by an episode of *Night Heat* which began with a shot of women who have been attending a Ladies' Night display of male strippers. A serial rapist-killer of women is on the loose, who kills one of them and then menaces Prosecutor Elaine Jeffers. Having been used by the police as a stalking horse—much to her distress the killer phones her to gloat over his activities and she is instructed to encourage his calls—she is finally more directly at his mercy, a knife at her breast, when the policemen rush in to save her. "He took control of my life," she laments to the police captain. "No one can truly control a liberated woman," this fatherly figure reassures her, meanwhile inviting her to spend the night with him and his wife. When she demurs, he orders her to come (for her own good), and so she assents. For "Sometimes it's not so bad not being in control."[20]

A founding principle of crime shows, the archetype of the male protector/savior remains true even when the damsel in distress has been granted the nominal autonomy of being a police agent herself and is allowed to use a gun. A gun is a symbol that American culture so strongly identifies with masculinity that until the mid-seventies, the few women who made their way into crime and adventure tales had to operate without firearms; they were limited to martial arts or feminine wiles (persuasion and deception) to disarm criminals.[21] By the late eighties, westerns with their gun-toting males are out and crime shows in which women may shoot for themselves are in. Yet femininity remains assured. Women's shooting comes with qualifiers even when the women ostensibly do not need protectors. In an episode of *Hooperman*, for example, the widowed female police captain, Captain Stern, who is a good shot as well as a strict boss, is demeaningly obliged to hire an escort to squire her to a banquet for a councilman held in a Chinese restaurant. Her escort proves to be a moonlighting cop, Pritzker, the chauvinist whom she has had to recommend for transfer because of his intransigent refusal to accept a female superior (surely his name too is not casual). When assailants suddenly open fire in the restaurant, Stern whips out a pistol and routs them. Not only does Pritzker then present her with the bill for his services. Though he compliments her shooting, he also sells her his silence about the escorting in exchange for cancelling his transfer. So much for her show of strength, contained within the boundaries of male power.

When other policewomen use guns, they prove like any ordinary women to need protector/saviors. On *Hunter*, for example, Connie Chin, a brave cop, is shot while she investigates an apparent robbery; because it appears that she has meanwhile shot a man to death, she comes up for disciplinary review. But Hunter comes to the rescue while Connie lies wounded and inert in a hospital bed (a veritable sleeping beauty) and proves that a pawnbroker with underworld connections was the actual murderer. Climaxing this patriarchal salvation, Connie's father (who had never approved of her being on the force) accepts her back in his love as well. On *Midnight Caller*, Killian comes to the rescue of a policewoman who, along with two other cops, has been shot by a waiter while staked out in a hotel room. She alone survives yet cannot recall the assailant's face. The killer menaces her as she too lies inert in a hospital, so Killian hides her in his apartment. Finally she realizes who the killer was and leaves the apartment to apprehend him, determined upon a, so to speak, man-to-man shootout. However, she loses her moment of glory to Killian, for he has followed her, and when she is on the point of being killed by the desperate criminal, saves her again. The motif of paternal love in conjunction with a patriarchal-style savior returns on *Mission Impossible*. East German communists kidnap a diplomat's seventeen year-old daughter prior to an East-West summit and put another sleeping beauty into an induced coma, but male Mission agents rescue and awaken her, once again to return her to her father's embrace, as the episode ends.

Father-daughter love and protection is a given of television, which is much less assured of mother-daughter affection. On successive nights, *Growing Pains* and *Too Close for Comfort* told stories that vindicated paternal protective love with remarkably similar plots about daughters who have (misguidedly) attempted to flee from it. On *Growing Pains*, a runaway girl whom the youngest child has brought home is urged by Dr. Seivers, the protective-savior father of the happy family in whose midst she has come, to call home to reassure her parents that she is alive. She refuses but in the final frame capitulates; the viewer leaves her affectionately talking to her father on the phone (Why did her mother not answer the rings?). On *Too Close for Comfort*, after Monroe shelters "Sam" (Samantha), a Florida runaway, in the Rush home in San Francisco, Mr. Rush, who lectures her on the nature of paternal love, likewise insists she at least call home to reassure her father (there is no mother, in this case) that she is safe. She too is receiving and returning his declarations of love as the program nears its end. The title of *Empty Nest* is ironic because its widower main character, Dr. Harry Weston, may have two daughters who are old enough to be on their own, but they have moved back home so that, with mutually reciprocated affection and much fatherly wisdom, he is still perpetually involved in their lives. On *Raising Miranda*, a father nurtures his teenage daughter by himself.

Patriarchal mythology focuses on opposite-sex relationships. About same-sex female relationships—those of mother and daughter, close friends, lesbian lovers—such mythology has little to say and often belittles, so that it provides a distorted picture of the range and complexity of female attachments. Television still subscribes to that distortion even though the women's movement has disseminated more accurate knowledge of women's ties. The mother-daughter relation provides a case in point. According to the conventional myths of patriarchy, Oedipal and otherwise, mother is a rival and a repressive force on daughter, not a friend or confidante. Thus *Kate and Allie* may be able to conceive of a close tie between its title characters, but certainly not any rapport between mother and daughter. When Allie is to reenter the patriarchal domain by marrying, the episode harps on her antagonism to her uptight mother who criticizes and "chills" her daughter—and the viewer, for when Mother talks to Allie she is indeed a shrew. Yet Mother, to Allie's chagrin, is a great success at the wedding reception (which Allie accordingly vacates); the final ignominy (and closing line) is a male guest's praise of Mother's charm. On *Mama's Family*, Mother's stereotypically stuffy Victorian influence and domineering ways have kept Mama Thelma conventional. Yet it is not too late for her to conduct an adversarial dialogue with her mother's waspish image and exorcise it from her mind—a liberation she celebrates (and trivializes) by planning to buy her first designer jeans. On *Golden Girls*, Dorothy's mother Sophia destroys daughter's budding affair with an attractive man by tagging along on their dates, though daughter also foolishly allows herself to be imposed upon, despite her resentment, because she has too keen a sense of being responsible for her mother. Kathryn Weibel remarks of the medical programs popular in the television world of the sixties and seventies that children were often shown as the victims of their mothers' overprotectiveness and inability to face facts. She instances an episode of *Marcus Welby* in which a mother refuses an essential operation for her deaf daughter, but "kind, paternalistic" Welby finally persuades a "weak and possessive woman to do what is best for her child."[22] He plays exactly the same role in *A Holiday Affair*, a made-for television movie shown in 1988, albeit now the child is a blinded young ballerina whom her foster mother has refused to tell that her condition is permanent. Fathers on television may be something for daughters to come home to, but mothers too often are a burden to endure, lighten, or discard.

Heterosexual love, moreover, remains the archetype for television, though in an endeavor to appear timely, television mythology has managed to give a grudging but increasing assent to the possibility of male homosexuality. Occasional programs endeavor to validate it. An episode of *Cheers* allowed an old buddy of Sam's to make a public declaration of his homosexuality which Sam (after some prompting from Diane) accepted; and the Cheers' regulars were rendered foolish for their fears about gays taking over the bar. An episode of *Golden Girls* likewise presented Blanche's brother as a gay man revealing his propensities to a disbelieving sister who finally accepts his right to difference. *Thirtysomething* without comment allowed a self-declared gay to enact a role in its depiction of eighties' lifestyles. Yet while asexual female pairings have finally, in a few programs, come into their own, lesbianism remains almost entirely taboo on prime time television, doubtless because it poses too great a threat to male hegemony.

In 1986–87 *Golden Girls*, a program about four women who share a home in Florida, did dare an episode in which a lesbian visits the "girls" and consternates one of them, Rose, by declaring an attraction, though the two part as friends anyway. But the show's format dares not allow for lesbians among its regular cast. *HeartBeat* did include an avowedly lesbian couple (nurse practitioner Marilyn and chef Patty) among its main cast of characters before the 1988–89 season. But when the show returned to the air in January of 1989, no new viewer could have known that any of the women at the Women's Medical Arts clinic were gay. The now defunct *Cagney and Lacey*, one of the few programs to give a fair portrayal of female friendship, almost foundered early in its career because of the network's fear that its title characters might be construed as lesbians. According to an unidentified CBS programmer in *TV Guide* for 12–18 June 1982, CBS found the characters "too tough, too hard, not feminine" and perceived them as "dykes." Fears that the program might therefore become associated with lesbianism gave the network a focus for its objections to the nonconventional representations of women. Its characters had to be redesigned to be more "feminine."[23]

According to patriarchal mythology, women are not even supposed to be close friends or loyal to their gender, for their identifications and emotional energies should be directed towards men. It is only men, presumably, who have a sense of solidarity with their kind. Television programming has acknowledged the contrary about female comradeship with the supportive pals and sisters of *Roseanne* and with friendship series such as *Kate and Allie*, *Designing Women*, and *Golden Girls*; it has even allowed the wife on *Newhart* to develop feelings of sisterhood with the seventeenth century "witch" buried in the basement of the Newharts' colonial inn. Meanwhile, however, an episode of *Mama's Family* could take its humor from allowing the title character Thelma to accidentally ruin, without the least remorse, the quilt her neighbor Iola has spend days cross-stitching, by shrinking it to the size of a table mat. Mama subscribes to a patriarchal estimate of the value of women's time and handicrafts even in post-Judy Chicago days.[24]

Television apparently still finds it hard to transcend the assumption that women are so male-directed that they will put men first in their loyalties. The manifestations may be blatant, as when Mallory Keaton, the daughter on *Family Ties*, has her heart broken by a sorority girl who ostensibly courts her for membership in the group but actually only has designs on brother Alex. Or on the TV movie *Marked for Murder*, for love of a handsome young man, the main character's assistant dupes her boss into the marriage intended to kill her. The manifestations may, however, be more subtle. On *TV101*, for example, overzealous student reporter Penny has broadcast a secret told her by her girlfriend, Craig's girl, that Student Watch member Craig has been planting incriminating evidence in the lockers of school bad boys. Whereas Craig forgives Penny for ruining his reputation and endangering him with the school bullies, Craig's girlfriend refuses ever to talk to her again for doing so. The program soon ends, now, with an exchange between one of the school's athletes and a wimp who has been trying to improve his image by practicing his batting. The athlete who had always ragged the wimp now compliments him for his courage and his improved technique. Harmony has been restored to the high school—at least among the males.

Another cultural myth dictates that as woman ages, she becomes a disprized object. Summarizing studies done on age-roles in television through the early 1980s, Nancy Signorielli observes that "Old women are often presented as eccentric and foolish. Though still underrepresented, old men are portrayed in a more flattering light than [old] women. Many elderly men are active in their careers and might even be romantically involved."[25] The romantic involvement is more latterly allowed to a woman over fifty too, provided it not be with a younger man (in *Marked for Murder*, even a woman in her forties was punished for taking that liberty, as the title implies). But otherwise, Signorielli's conclusions describe late 1980s television too. A striking illustration is provided by *Golden Girls* (with its insulting title, despite its social consciousness) and *Empty Nest*, televised back to back so that the difference in their valuations becomes all the more evident. The two half-hour programs in effect constitute a single hour program for viewers, who even find characters from the one show appearing on the other. The fifty-to-sixtyish golden "girls" Blanche, Rose, and Dorothy, plus, Sophia, the seventyish mother of Dorothy, like children, have only to divert themselves in their Florida setting, whereas the pediatrician of *Empty Nest*, who is their neighbor on the block, still practices his profession with aplomb. They are foolish females—drawling Blanche is narcissistically vain about her allure; naive Rose is nostalgically obtuse about her St. Olaf's, Minnesota, home; even the more sensible Dorothy is too sentimentally bound to her mother Sophia, who fantasizes ridiculous past affairs—but Dr. Harry Weston is judiciously wise. The same night that saw Dorothy mired in the unhealthy dependence on her mother's affections which cost her a lover, saw him refuse to succumb to a destructive nostalgia for his dead wife. He was saved by a self-awareness denied to Dorothy even as he is regularly portrayed with a basic dignity denied to all the girls. Granted, they are more impressive than the fatuously blustering leading-role grandmother, Thelma, of the comic *Mama's Family*, or the would-be siren supporting-role grandmother, Mona, of *Who's the Boss*. It is a rare event for a program to do as an episode of *Annie McGuire* did in allowing a sixty-five-year-old a straight, honorific role. Annie's elderly friend Francie taught Annie (middle-aged and unglamorized) not only integrity, but courage and determination to succeed when Francie sought out her black vaudeville partner of fifty years past to apologize for having wronged him.

All this is not to gainsay that television programming of the late 1980s has progressed in what sense of women it projects through its prime time programs, but rather to propose that it tends to take back with one hand what it yields with the other. Even Francie played her part with a puckish manner as if brave old ladies have to be cute too. The predisposition to temporizing is marked with respect to women's careers. Maybe, as Gillian Dyer rightly observed in 1987, "The 'new woman' has become the new media cliché, overtaking the traditional domestic image of the 1950s";[26] nonetheless, the old domestic image still thrives. Another cultural myth television perpetuates, despite its many career women, is that the home and family constitute the center of reality for women, which is to say that they are sexual beings.

Because conventionally they are—or should be—biologically determined, the title character of *Murphy Brown* is not just portrayed as a successful, independent-minded anchor. She is a strikingly glamorous career woman whose looks belie the forty years with which she is credited and on whose shapely legs the camera lingers lovingly. What critic Lillian Robinson argued in 1976 continues to be true; namely, that for women,

The overriding message it [television] sends out is that their sex is its [television's] most important component; her identity as a female informs every aspect of a woman's working life, so that it appears as if she does not so much hold a job as play a role—one of whose facets is expressed through whatever the job happens to be. Although television intervenes in the lives of all working people, regardless of sex, its principal function in defining the working woman is to add yet another layer to the myths that define woman herself.[27]

Thus Elyse Keaton, the mother on *Family Ties*, is a successful architect, but only as an adjunct to her career as wife-mother; rarely do we see her interacting with co-workers but perpetually with family. In one episode that does display her on the job, her major efforts go into tactfully fending off a young co-worker besmitten with her charms. Claire Huxtable, mother on *The Cosby Show*, is a lawyer with the same domestic agenda. The only time viewers see her performing in court she is arguing a case for her own daughter, who has been cheated on car repairs. The medical personnel of *HeartBeat*, conversely, are shown at work, in exchange for which they are shown in domestic roles only very peripherally. That is, viewers are privy, for example, to some of the fluctuations of the precarious love affair between doctors Joanne and Leo. Dr. Cory arrives at work late when her housekeeper quits; Cory has had to chauffeur her children to school. Where are the programs that follow women's dual lives, with full respect for both, as *Empty Nest* does for Dr. Harry Weston? Among major programs, only *LA Law* regularly remembers that both matter.

Married women's narratives have ousted the single career-woman situation comedy that David Marc designated "the staple" of seventies "telemythology,"[28] but women do continue to work for pay on television. Policewomen aside, most women who do so on prime time television in 1988–89 are lawyers. As has always been true, white collar professions are overrepresented, though many bit parts go to doctors' receptionists. The title character of *Roseanne* atypically is blue collar, though she too is rarely seen involved in her outside work. The factory is, rather, where she interacts with her sister and friends, an unobjectionable arrangement since Roseanne (who refers to herself as a "domestic goddess") presumably works only because she needs the money. Her job is portrayed as a nuisance that complicates her domestic life, not her commitment to personal expression or autonomy. *Roseanne* thus depicts an undeniable reality for American women, married or not. On the other hand, there are other facets of reality going begging. Many women work not because of the money, or because of it alone, but because they have energies and talents that they want to apply in a career. Many women take satisfaction from their careers as significant as what their family life yields or they anticipate that it could yield. In some cases—a manifest threat to the system—the significance of women's careers may be greater yet, even when they are not safely widowed like author and crime-sleuth Jessica of *Murder She Wrote* or single but thousands of miles away like the nurses of *China Beach*. Such disorder, however, must be contained.

It is possible, even simple, nonetheless to find scattered instances of programs or episodes that manage to see woman less as Other than as existing in her own right, and engrossingly so, whatever her age, shape, or affiliations. *Roseanne* and *Annie McGuire* provide immediate illustrations that looks and youth do not signify. To keep up with awarenesses spread by the women's movement, occasional narratives try hard to do what Roseanne does when she changes her foreman's favorite metaphor of football teamwork to that of a quilting bee: redirect their imagery so that it accounts for women's values and lived experiences too. When *thirtysomething* allows Melissa Stedman to decide that she can undertake single parenting without mocking her for it, it grants her her desire to nurture without compromising her taste for independence (even if it never puts her to the test by letting her conceive). Or *HeartBeat* makes the aim of its medical clinic to treat women patients with respect for their individuality and dignity, and contends with the prejudices against midwives. But the preponderant impression produced by prime time television of 1988–89 is that the more things change with respect to women, the more they remain the same.

Television mythology continues to guard against chaos and creates order by refurbishing the old images.[29] Why? Probably not because the women's movement has failed to make an impression on American culture, but rather because it has been only too effective. Speculating in 1984 on the "insistent thematic" of the nurturing good father in recent films, De Lauretis wonders if such an emphasis does not reflect "the need to reaffirm a patriarchal order that has been badly shaken by feminism and the lesbian and gay movements."[30] The traditionalism of later eighties television, in which the old fairy tales are still being told and the familiar archetypes still flourishing, doubtless reflects the same benighted attempt to safeguard the world for patriarchy, lest the Great Goddess reclaim her own.

ACKNOWLEDGEMENTS

I am grateful to Dr. Doris Earnshaw, Dr. Carolyn Hadley, and Ms. Debbie Odell for the critical acumen, feminist awareness, and television lore they contributed to this chapter.

NOTES

1. Program of 3 January 1989.
2. Sarah Ruth Kozloff, "Narrative Theory and Television," in *Channels of Discourse*, ed. Robert C. Allen (Chapel Hill: Univ. of North Carolina Press, 1987), 56–57.
3. Robert Scholes and Robert Kellogg, *The Nature of Narrative* (New York: Oxford Univ. Press, 1966), 137.
4. Kozloff, 49; Roger Silverstone, *The Message of Television: Myth and Narrative in Contemporary Culture* (London: Heinemann, 1981), 71, 196.
5. By the third millenium B.C., the supreme Great Goddess appears to have been displaced and to have lost her all-encompassing attributes. See Gerda Lerner's judicious discussion in *The Creation of Patriarchy* (New York and Oxford: Oxford Univ. Press, 1986). For a more conjectural theory about the conquest of goddess religion and its influence on myth, see Merlin Stone, *The Paradise Papers: The Suppression of Women's Rites* (London: Virago, 1979).
6. Jennifer Waelti-Walters, *Fairy Tales and the Female Imagination* (Montreal: Eden Press, 1982), 5; Marcia Lieberman, " 'Some Day My Prince Will Come': Female Acculturation Through the Fairy Tale," in *Don't Bet on the Prince: Contemporary Feminist Fairy Tales* . . . , ed. Jack Zipes (New York: Methuen, 1986), 185; Andrea Dworkin, *Woman Hating* (New York: E. P. Dutton, 1974), 47–48.
7. Simone de Beauvoir, *The Second Sex*, trans. and ed. H. M. Parshley (New York: Random House, 1974), 161, 163.
8. Northrop Frye, *Fables of Identity* (New York: Harcourt, Brace and World, 1963), 15–16; Joseph Campbell, *The Hero With a Thousand Faces*, 2d ed. (Princeton, N.J.: Princeton University Press, 1968), 36; C. G. Jung, *The Archetypes and the Collective Unconscious*, vol. 9.1 of *The Collected Works*, eds. Herbert Read, Michael Fordham, and Gerhard Adler, trans. R. F. C. Hull, 2d ed. (New York: Bollingen Foundation, 1968), 6, 154.
9. Silverstone, 70; Teresa de Lauretis, *Alice Doesn't: Feminism, Semiotics, Cinema* (Bloomington: Indiana University Press, 1984), 119, 121.
10. Martin Esslin, "Aristotle and the Advertisers: The Television Commercial Considered as a Form of Drama," in *Television: The Critical View*, ed. Horace Newcomb, 4th ed. (Oxford: Oxford University Press, 1987), 309.
11. Ovid, *Metamorphoses*, trans. Rolfe Humphries (Bloomington: Indiana University Press, 1973), 243.

12. Karen E. Rowe, "Feminism and Fairy Tales," in Zipes, *Don't Bet on the Prince*, 216.

13. E.g., 30 December 1988; 6 January 1989.

14. Specifically Jungian archetypes have elsewhere been identified in television criticism. Peter H. Wood, for example, feels that "TV is built around archetypes, many of them similar to the primordial images which Jung believed to be stored in the 'collective unconscious' of the entire species" ("Television as Dream," in *Television: The Critical View*, ed. Horace Newcomb, 3d ed. [Oxford: Oxford University Press, 1982], 517). Although Wood nonetheless does not investigate such Jungian archetypes, Stuart M. Kaminsky, with Jeffrey H. Mahan, does so in "A Jungian Approach to Science Fiction and Horror," chapter 9 of *American Television Genres* (Chicago: Nelson-Hall, 1985). While it is undoubtedly true that Jungian archetypes can be found in television narratives, the "Remember Love" episode of *Beauty and the Beast* is distinctive in being an apparently deliberate attempt to employ Jungian concepts.

15. Campbell, 30.

16. A comparable list is discussed in *Women's Realities, Women's Choices* issued by the Hunter College Women's Studies Collective (Oxford: Oxford University Press, 1983), 28–36.

17. Sarah B. Pomeroy, *Goddesses, Whores, Wives, and Slaves: Women in Classical Antiquity* (New York: Schocken, 1975), 6.

18. 27 December 1988.

19. Tania Modleski, *Loving with a Vengeance: Mass-Produced Fantasies for Women* (Hamden, CT: Archon Books, 1982), 113; Ellen Seiter, "Semiotics and Television," in *Channels of Discourse*, ed. Allen, 73; N. D. Batra, *The Hour of Television: Critical Approaches* (Metuchen, N.J.: Scarecrow Press, 1987), 94.

20. 30 December 1988.

21. Kathryn Weibel, *Mirror Mirror: Images of Women Reflected in Popular Culture* (Garden City, N.Y.: Anchor Books, 1977), 83–84, 88.

22. Weibel, 78.

23. Reported by Julie D'Acci, "The Case of Cagney and Lacey," in *Boxed In: Women and Television*, eds. Helen Baehr and Gillian Dyer (New York: Pandora, 1987), 213–15.

24. Chicago's distinctive three-dimensional art work, *The Dinner Party*, a celebration of women's heritage completed in 1979 with the help of hundreds of other women, honors women's traditional arts such as needlework and china painting.

25. Nancy Signorielli, assisted by Elizabeth Milke and Carol Katzman, ed. and comp., *Role Portrayal and Stereotyping on Television: An Annotated Bibliography of Studies* . . . (Westport, Conn.: Greenwood Press, 1985), xvi. Signorielli includes a 1982 report by the National Commission on Working Women ("What's Wrong with This Picture?") according to which women over sixty, in Signorielli's summary, "were almost totally absent" among television portrayals. Moreover, "the overall image of women changed very little between 1972 and 1981" (p. 17).

26. "Women and television: an overview," *Boxed In*, 7.

27. Lillian Robinson, *Sex, Class, and Culture* (Bloomington: Indiana University Press, 1978), 312.

28. David Marc, *Demographic Vistas: Television in American Culture* (Philadelphia: University of Pennsylvania Press, 1984), 19.

29. This propensity has been amply documented for the past. Diana M. Meehan, for

example, has done a book-length qualitative examination of thirty years of television series to conclude that during 1950–80 female portrayals were negative and unfair, limited in number and type (*Ladies of the Evening: Women Characters of Prime-Time Television* [Metuchen, N.J.: Scarecrow Press, 1983]). Signorielli's book-length bibliography of role portrayals and stereotyping, which extends to 1983 but mostly covers studies done in the seventies, reveals an "overall similarity and stability" in television's treatment of women. Compared to men, they are outnumbered and younger; they take more orders and are more limited in employment possibilities. Moreover, their home-related roles are over-emphasized yet accorded low status (p. xiv). See also my note 24.

30. de Lauretis, 116.

Part II
Television Programming as Art

5

Ariosto and Bochco: Polyphonic Plotting in *Orlando Furioso*, *Hill Street Blues*, and *L. A. Law*

James V. Mirollo

In *Channels of Discourse*, the recent anthology of contemporary criticism and television edited by Robert C. Allen (1987), an excellent essay by Sarah Ruth Kozloff on "Narrative Theory" applies some of the insights of contemporary narratology to television narration.[1] One of the latter's most common traits, she concludes, is "multiple storylines intertwined in complex patterns and frequently interconnecting." If one were to change "and frequently interconnecting" to "not necessarily or at most infrequently connecting," a literary historian would recognize in Kozloff's common narrative trait the particular kind of multiple storytelling that I refer to as polyphonic plotting, also known as *entrelacement*, or *intrecciatura*.[2] As the French and Italian terms suggest, polyphonic narrative technique involves interlacing, interweaving, or braiding of narrative episodes— what television critics, borrowing as they often do and must from the vocabulary of film criticism, call "multiple story lines" or "cutting from one story line to another."

As Kozloff admits, a historical overview of narrative form, such as can be found in Scholes and Kellogg's *The Nature of Narrative* (1966) is "an important antidote to ahistorical theorizing." The relentlessly synchronic approach of recent narrative theory would also benefit from awareness of antecedent theory and practice, especially when the phenomenon under consideration, here multiple plots, has a rich history. On the principle that what once pleased will please again, it should not surprise us that polyphonic plotting has contributed crucially to the success on television of both daytime soaps and prime time series or serials like *Hill Street Blues* and *L. A. Law*, both produced by Steven Bochco in collaboration with Michael Kozoll and Terry Louise Fisher. Nor should we be surprised that this kind of storytelling, then and now, has aroused and continues to provoke both delight in its audience and scorn from some of its critics. In order to establish the continuity of this narrative tradition, I propose to compare and contrast an undoubted masterpiece of polyphonic plotting, the *Orlando Furioso* (Roland Mad) of Ludovico Ariosto (1474–1533), published in its definitive form in 1532, with *Hill Street Blues* and, especially, *L. A. Law*. I hope thereby to illuminate these juxtaposed texts, the nature of interwoven plotting, and the traditional roots of a significant kind of television narrative.

MULTIPLE AND POLYPHONIC PLOTTING

An important distinction has to be made between other kinds of multiple storytelling and the polyphonic version. The essence of polyphonic plotting is that in the course of a long overall performance many different stories are told in episodes that *interrupt* each other, are displaced and yet return, are developed and yet do not necessarily proceed to closure. The guiding fiction of this kind of interweaving is *simultaneity*, the insistence that all of the stories begin more or less at the same time and are happening at the same time. Obviously, the authors of such stories as well as their audiences experience them successively, even though an author might compose some parts of his overall work out of its final order and the audience, especially when reading, might skip to chosen passages. Even then, however, the passages thus composed or selected would be subject to the law of temporal succession that governs the reading or viewing of narrative. Succession also created the polyphonic narrator's chief dilemma: he always knows where all his plots are going, and regularly flaunts that dazzling omniscience; but he must minimize instances of one plot getting too far ahead of the others before he is ready, requiring that he make suspense-generating but potentially irritating promises of future clarification. These may endanger verisimilitude by foregrounding the selfconscious artistry of the interlacing, as Cervantes knew all too well. Hence the fictive ideal is actually spatial, as though one were watching a large blackboard on which different story lines were shown proceeding, with the author or narrator, chalk in hand, and apparently arbitrarily, lengthening now one line, now another. If we were to look at or down on the completed work, and not at the work "in progress," we would need a different spatial analogue. Here one might imagine a verbal equivalent of Romanesque ribbon ornament, as Eugène Vinaver has pointed out in a brilliant comparison of such ornament and the interlaced narrative structure of medieval cyclic romances.[3]

A third crucial feature of polyphonic narrative, in addition to *interruption* and *simultaneity*, is *progressive digression*, as succinctly characterized by Rosemond Tuve:

One must distinguish entrelacement from the mere practice, ubiquitous in narrative, of taking one character through a series of actions, then deserting him temporarily—often with the object of introducing suspense—while another character is given primary attention, then returning to the first, and so on. . . . But events connected by entrelacement are not juxtaposed: they are interlaced, and when we get back to our first character he is not where we left him as we finished his episode, but in the place of psychological state or condition of meaningfulness to which he has been pulled by the events occurring in following episodes written about someone else. . . . we digress, or seem to, and then come back, not to precisely what we left but to something we understand differently because of what we have since seen.[4]

As Tuve has shown, polyphonic or interwoven narrative can be profitably compared and contrasted with other types of storytelling, monocentric or multiple. In antiquity, Homer's *Odyssey* offered an example of an attempt at simultaneity by the juxtaposition of the final stages of Odysseus' return home and the brief "growing up" journey made by Telemachus, but these are not interlaced; and after the appearance of Odysseus in the poem, the many stories that are told for the most part feature only him as protagonist. Similarly, in the *Iliad*, Achilles is the chief protagonist, but in his absence from the Greek camp the other Achaean lords as well as Hector and the other Trojan heroes take their turns at the center of the action, thus temporarily allowing the multiple actions of several protagonists if not multiple interwoven stories. The *Aeneid*, though blending the Odysseus and Achilles plots, maintains the principles, cherished by later neoclassicists, of unity and continuity as these had been enunciated by Aristotle in the *Poetics*:

Imitation through narrative in verse obviously must, like tragedy, have a dramatic plot structure; it must be concerned with one complete action, it must have a beginning, middle, and an end, in order that the whole narrative may attain the unity of a living organism and provide its own peculiar kind of pleasure.[5]

Aristotle in the same place also praises Homer's self-effacement as narrator, which would be remembered later by those neoclassicist opponents of medieval polyphonic technique who derided its penchant for an intrusive narrator.

Since the *Poetics* was not well known and certainly not fully recovered until the Renaissance, the preference for unity and continuity, for the single, linear, and unified discourse, was preserved by the literary-minded rhetorical tradition and its rules for the oration. Here is Quintilian:

The orator, who speaks methodically, will above all take the actual sequence of the various points as his guide, and it is for this reason that even but moderately trained speakers find it easiest to keep the natural order in the statement of facts. Secondly, the orator must know what to look for in each portion of his case: he must not beat about the bush or allow himself to be thrown off the track by thoughts which suggest themselves from irrelevant quarters, or produce a speech which is a confused mass of incongruities owing to his habit of leaping this way and that, and never sticking to any one point.[6]

Despite this prejudice against "leaping this way and that," several types of multiple narrative flourished in antiquity. For example, there is the story-within-a-story or framing device used by Apuleius and Petronius. And also, a variant that has Eastern roots, the so-called "boxed tales," which feature not one, but several frames embedded within frames. Perhaps the best known examples are *The Thousand and One Nights* and Ovid's *Metamorphoses*, the latter considered by C. S. Lewis to be the ultimate source of entrelacement in medieval Arthurian romances.[7] But entrelacement or polyphonic plotting differs from either single-framed stories or boxed tales, as can be seen if we compare the latter to the medieval and Renaissance Arthurian and Carolingian romances in which narrative interweaving predominates. First, unlike boxed tales, the romances do not have a narrative frame beyond the voice or manipulating control of an omniscient and omnipresent narrator, although there may be intercalated stories from time to time. Second, polyphonic structure is not centripetal, as in boxed tales, but centrifugal; the actions are narrated, fragmentary episode by fragmentary episode, as a succession of narrative panels that refer to antecedent pieces and future continuations of their potentially, but rarely actually, whole selves. More and more different protagonists and their actions are introduced, like threads in a tapestry, but completion and closure are perpetually postponed. Third, the protagonists of interwoven plots enact their own adventures or quests but occasionally "aggregate," or participate in a community or fellowship to which they previously belonged or newly join, from which they depart (and to which they may ultimately return) when an individual adventure beckons and is undertaken. Thus, while individual adventures are sometimes completed by the protagonist and the narrator, others begin or are in store, thereby keeping the larger narrative of multiple fragments ongoing or open-ended. The audience knows that much has happened before the narrative begins and much will continue to happen afterwards. Fourth, the physical, moral, and psychological terrain outside of the community is often a realm of nonculture, or magic, and therefore dangerous and threatening, even destructive. But as such, it also provides a test of one's worth, even if it can also precipitate a loss of self. Fifth and finally, the goals of the multiple adventures or quests are likely to be love, fame, and knowledge, which in turn require the pursuit of desirable men or women, often in conflict with duty; engagement with and conquest of worthy opponents, resulting in possession of their celebrated (because magical or legendary) swords, lances, helmets, and horses; acquisition of maturity, wisdom, spiritual enlightenment— in sum an enhanced identity with future political or historical, as well as personal consequences. Rather than gradual psychological moral or spiritual development and change, the romance protagonists experience polar conversions, from love to hate or the reverse, from infidelity to fidelity, from pagan to Christian, from lack of control to control of passion, from madness to recovered sanity.

ORLANDO FURIOSO

The generic complexity of Ariosto's romance-epic reflects his heterogenous cultural formation.[8] A product of a classically oriented Renaissance Humanist education, he was obliged to regard medieval polyphony, whether in music or narrative, as Gothic barbarism. Yet the chivalric values and narrative delights embodied in romances of chivalry still attracted the rulers and courtiers of Ferrara, and the library of the Estensi lords whom he served had an impressive collection of such texts that he knew well. Their stories of the Arthurian and Carolingian knights came to assume for Renaissance authors like Ariosto the status of a mythology, parallel to the classical one, which then could be used for its sheer narrativity, exploiting its variety and richness of plotting, while at the same time alluding to and commenting upon contemporary events and issues. Because of this ambiguous attitude to the romances of chivalry—regarding them as generically impure but taking advantage of their literariness to both entertain and inform—the leading European Renaissance authors of chivalric romance, from Pulci to Cervantes, inevitably produced parodies of their sources, and especially of their narrative techniques.

The exigencies of an entertaining performance, deliberately prolonged and interwoven to sustain audience interest, may well account for the original creation and later continuity of polyphonic plotting, from the Middle Ages to the present, where it appears most conspicuously in television series. Prior to Ariosto's time, Arthur and Charlemagne stories in prose and verse had been both written *and* performed in Franco-Venetian and Tuscan, and some of those performed by minstrels (*cantastorie*) in the piazza for popular audiences had been written down and preserved for reading. Imitating written polyphonic narrative sources, these minstrels commonly sang their *cantari* in octave stanzas to the accompaniment of a stringed instrument; they thereby spun out on successive days a series of interwoven tales about such heroes as Orlando (Roland), creating suspense by interruption, and prolonging audience attention and interest by pauses that effected division into cantos or narrative units appropriate to a single "show." The technique of these popular minstrels, and in particular their blatant narratorial manipulation of polyphonic story threads, was in turn imitated and parodied by Ariosto's two sophisticated literary predecessors, Luigi Pulci (1432–1484), in his *Morgante* (1483), and Matteo Maria Boiardo (1441–1494) in his *Orlando Innamorato* (1482–1483, left unfinished at his death).[9]

The *Orlando Furioso* is a romance-epic divided into forty-six cantos of *ottava rima* which have a total of 38,736 lines.[10] Already one of the longest narrative poems in our literary tradition, its continuation of Boiardo's poem posits a total "story" that is staggering in its hundreds of characters and incidents. In Boiardo a significant if not pioneering merger of the Carolingian epic and Arthurian romance had produced a Count Roland or Orlando overcome by Petrarchan love for Angelica, the beautiful princess of Cathay. It was Ariosto's contribution to have the nephew of the Emperor Charlemagne lose his sanity as a result of her alleged infidelity and thereby provide its title and one of the poem's major themes or threads. The others are the background war between Christian and Infidel, Charlemagne besieged at Paris by Agramante, commander of the African, Spanish, and Eastern pagans. A third interwoven motif is embodied in the dynastic pair, Ruggiero and Bradamante, whose marriage after much tribulation and his conversion to Christianity will produce the glorious progeny that is the Este family, the poet's patrons. Other major characters among the dozens who appear are Orlando's cousin Rinaldo (brother of Bradamante) who, along with several pagan knights, pursues Angelica; Astolfo, the English prince; Rodomonte, king of Sarza and Algiers and the most ferocious of the pagan warriors; Ruggiero's sister, Marfisa, who is a female warrior like her future sister-in-law, Bradamante; and several pairs of unfortunate lovers: Zerbino and Isabella, Brandimarte and Fiordiligi. As their scary names alone would suggest, the infidels are represented by such estimable warriors as Sacripante, Mandricardo, Ferraù, Gradasso.

In order to illustrate Ariosto's polyphonic narration, I will drop in on the "singing" of canto VIII and record its narrative episodes as he presents them to his audience, including his own intrusive comments on and manipulation of his plots. While it is unlikely that Ariosto actually performed his poem for the Ferrara court, and we have no certain evidence that he even read it on a succession of evenings, he does assume, and parodies, a minstrel performance:

Canto VIII (ninety-one octaves)

Proem:

the narrator praises Angelica's ring, which discloses truth, and which Ruggiero was fortunate to have as a means of escaping the wiles of the sorceress Alcina.

1. Ruggiero, escaping from Alcina, uses the magic shield made by his sorcerer-protector Atlante to defeat one of her armed minions and his threatening accompanying animals (ott. 1–11).

2. The good sorceress Melissa liberates Alcina's prisoners, including Astolfo, while Ruggiero makes his way along a sunbaked shore to the benign enchantress Logistilla (ott. 12–21).

Interruption:

> Now since it is not appropriate that I go on and on,
> Nor that I keep you occupied always with the same thing,
> I will leave Ruggiero in this heat,
> And make a tour of Scotland to find Rinaldo.

(ott. 21, 11.5–8)

3. Rinaldo pleads successfully with the King of Scotland and the Prince of Wales to send aid to Charlemagne besieged at Paris (ott. 22–28).

Interruption:

> My lord, I must do as the good musician
> Does playing his subtle instrument, who
> Frequently mutes his strings, varies his sound,

Seeks now the soft and now the shrill;
While intent on telling of Rinaldo,
I remember the gentle Angelica,
Whom I left fleeing from him,
And that she had encountered a hermit.

(ott. 29)

I'd like to continue her story for a bit.

(ott. 30, 1.1)

4. Aroused by Angelica's beauty, the lecherous old hermit tries to keep up with her as she flees, then arranges to have a demon enter her horse:

Interruption:

What his plan was, I know well:
And I'll tell you also, but later.

(ott. 34, 11.1–2)

5. The demon causes Angelica's horse to carry her off into the water, like Europa, then return to a bleak shore lined by rocks and caverns. Night falls, Angelica laments her fate. The hermit reappears, tries to violate her as she sleeps, but fails; he too falls asleep beside her (ott. 34–50).

Interruption:

But before I tell you what happened next,
I must deviate a bit from the straight path.

(ott. 51, 11.1–2)

6. The island of Ebuda, the sea monster, Orc, the legend of how an angered Proteus once demanded and still receives the tribute of a maiden to be sacrificed to the Orc each day (ott. 51–57).

Interruption:

Whether this story about Proteus is
True or not I'm not able to say, but
On its basis a wicked ancient law
Against women was in force in that land.

(ott. 58, 11.1–4)

7. The Ebudans seize Angelica and after hesitating a while because of her beauty finally expose her to the sea monster (ott. 58–66).

Interruption:

I can't go on: grief [over Angelica's fate] so moves me
That I must turn my poem elsewhere.

(ott. 56, 11.7–8)

8. Paris besieged by Agramante. God sends a rainstorm, in response to Charlemagne's prayers, that puts out threatening fires. Orlando laments his fate, has restless thoughts about Angelica, dreams that he has lost her for good. He awakens, dons his armor, and deserts the Christian camp. Charlemagne is distressed. Brandimarte, Orlando's devoted friend, departs stealthily to retrieve the Count, leaving behind his grieving wife Fiordiligi, who soon also sets off from Paris in order to find him (ott. 57–90).

Interruption and *Transition*:

> Looking for him she [Fiordiligi] travelled many lands,
> As the story will reveal in the proper place.
> But about these two I will say nothing more,
> Since I'm now more concerned about Orlando, lord of Anglante.

(ott. 90, 11.5–8)

> He took the road leading straight to the enemy camp,
> And what happened next you will learn in the next canto.

(ott. 91, 11.7–8)

Thus Ariosto ends this segment of his larger narrative with what Daniel Javitch has felicitously labeled "cantus interruptus."[11] As Javitch has also pointed out, contemporary Aristotelian critics of the *Orlando* disapproved of these interruptions as well as the intrusive and manipulative narratorial voice.[12] Opposition to such narrative discontinuity was based in part at least on aversion to its popular origin and flavor, but officially on the newly recovered and revered *Poetics* of Aristotle, in particular passages like the one cited above and the following:

Epic differs from tragedy in the length of its plot and in its meter. We have already indicated the adequate limit of length, namely that one must be able to grasp the whole, from beginning to end, as a unity. . . . tragedy cannot represent different parts of the action at the same time but only that part which is enacted upon the stage, whereas the epic, being narrative in form, can make different parts of the action come to a head simultaneously, so that these scenes, appropriate to the epic, increase the bulk of the poem.[13]

Here is one of Ariosto's cinquecento defenders, the critic Giraldi Cinthio coming to grips with the issue:

Romances are not in the manner of Vergil's and Homer's, both of whom undertook imitating only one action of one man, whereas ours have imitated many actions not of one man only but of many, since they build the whole fabric of their work upon eight or ten persons, but they give to the work the name of that person or that action which is dominant in the whole work and on which all the others depend, or at least to that which reasonably binds them together. . . . it has rather been their technique, first to speak of one person, then to interpose another by interrupting the first subject and entering upon the deeds of others, and on this design to continue the matters to the end of the work. . . . In their breaking off of one matter for another, they lead the reader by such endings that, before they break off, they leave in his mind an ardent desire to return in order to discover the matter that was broken off. Their whole poem is thus read, since the principal matters are not concluded until the completion of the work.[14]

And here is Tasso's neoclassicizing reply:

Although *Orlando Furioso*, which contains several fables, gives more delight than any other Tuscan poem or even the poems of Homer, this is not because of unity or multiplicity of fable, but for two reasons that detract nothing from our argument. One is that the *Furioso* treats of love, chivalry, adventure, enchantment, in short of inventions more charming and more adapted to our ears; the other that Ariosto excels many other poets in propriety of manners and decorum of character. Both reasons are accidental, unrelated to multiplicity or unity of fable.... We should not therefore conclude that multiplicity delights more than unity.... Since variety is thus delightful to human nature, it might be said that much greater delight can be found in a multiple than in a unified fable.... I say that variety is laudable up to the point where it turns into confusion.... if such variety is absent from a poem with a single action, it should be thought rather the artificers' lack of skill than a defect in the art.[15]

The battle lines were thus drawn between those who defended polyphonic plotting on the grounds of its modernity, variety, suspense, and sheer delight, and those who insisted that such plotting created confusion, and furthermore sacrificed concentration, unity, gravity, and verisimilitude. Of course Ariosto's readers ignored the critics and read the poem to pieces.[16] In the end, nevertheless, or at least until relatively modern times, neoclassicists won out as multiple plotting generally ceased to be widely employed in lengthy fictions in verse or prose. Beginning in the last century, however, with the revival of interest in medieval and Renaissance romance, the advent of the bulky serialized novel, and later with modernism's penchant for discontinuity, multiple plotting of both the juxtapositional and interwoven types comes to life again, as is evident in a host of novels, films, and television series from Manzoni's *I Promessi Sposi* to *Intolerance* and *Hill Street Blues*.

The elements of interwoven plotting that variously resist modern narrative retrieval are the intrusively manipulative narratorial voice claiming simultaneity, the consequent plot interruption, the avoidance of extended aggregation of many protagonists, and the lack of story closure. Many modern novels and plays prefer the "realism" of Aristotle's self-effacing and dramatizing narrator of a linear plot, mimetic showing to diegetic telling. In films and television, given the limitations of a continuing voice-over, or other kinds of intermittent internal narration, it is any one, or any one of several possible combinations of writer, director, film editor, camera-as-editor, or parallel editing, that can be claimed to "tell" the polyphonic story.[17] As for aggregation, whether frequently at one site, or for a climactic occasion, many modern novels, films, and especially television series, favor a continuous place, often urban, professional, or domestic, where a varying number of protagonists related to or associated with each other have frequent encounters. As regards closure, the television series is the glaring non-Aristotelian exception to the self-enclosed narrative norm. As John Ellis has pointed out, "the series implies the form of the dilemma rather than that of resolution and closure." Ariosto and his readers might be surprised, however, to hear Ellis's further claim that "this is perhaps the central contribution that broadcast TV has made to the long history of narrative forms and narrativised perception of the world."[18]

In Ariosto's poem, unlike the typical episode of a narrative television series, his principal protagonists rarely encounter each other. And if they do so because they are related, or lovers, or allied in combat, or because chance (i.e., the narrator) brings them together they do not stay together for long and do not stay in the same place for long. They do *not* all come together even at the siege of Paris (from which several Christians and pagans in fact depart, though all *should* return and stay), or to attend the wedding of Bradamante and Ruggiero. Paradoxically, the wedding itself, though ending the poem, does not suggest a final or culminating event precisely because it is postponed and delayed so many times. As is indicated by violent Rodomonte's last minute challenge to Ruggiero and the latter's need to destroy him before the nuptials can at last take place, the wedding actually opens a new era of ongoing bitter struggle that will continue for its progeny, the Este dynasty, down to and in Ariosto's own times, hundreds of years later. The *Furioso's* narrative style has no exact modern counterpart in its manipulation of a largely discontinuous space. However, its most faithful successors—as regards the interlaced stories of multiple protagonists, assumed simultaneity, interruption or temporal discontinuity, and avoidance of closure— are television series like the two I have chosen to discuss as continuing the tradition of narrative entrelacement.

HILL STREET BLUES AND *L. A. LAW*

In a recent discussion of the television western, and in particular the series *Have Gun, Will Travel* and its hero Paladin, Werner L. Gundersheimer has argued that "this cowboy was modelled on much earlier knights-errant like Orlando, Rinaldo, and Ruggiero, *mutatis mutandis*." He then adds that "it might be enlightening to see the resume of the creator of this remarkable character; does the intellect of a cultivated humanist lurk behind the screenwriter's suave rhetoric?"[19] I can appreciate Gundersheimer's reaction since it parallels my own during the recent past while negotiating what Wayne C. Booth has called "the many imaginative worlds we live in."[20] For me it was the experience of watching and rewatching *Hill Street Blues* and *L. A. Law* while reading and rereading Ariosto's poem for scholarly and teaching purposes, and immensely enjoying all three, even though my literary historian's instinct kept prodding me into historicising if not theorizing their intertextuality as the analogies and homologies piled up. I too wondered about Steven Bochco's cultivated reading, speculating at one point that he must have majored in Renaissance literature at Columbia!

Alas, as I have since learned, Bochco went to Carnegie Tech, where he was a Theatre Arts major, and his preparation for *Hill Street Blues* was not a course in the Renaissance epic-romance, but lots of television writing and producing, and lots of talking to cops and lawyers, not to mention involvement with several previous police shows. Clearly the analogies I was sensing would be better explained by recurring narrative needs and gratifications, *and* recurring critical response. When asked, for example, about NBC's objection to "incomplete story lines," Bochco has said that he agreed with the criticism and responded in the show's second season by putting at least one story into each episode that finished within the hour: "In that way the casual viewer, even though he was tuning into an episode in which four other story lines were ongoing, could latch onto at least one story that had a beginning, a middle, and an end."[21] This echo of the sixteenth century critical debate over the *Furioso*'s polyphonic plotting is rather startling, but as we shall see, hardly unique.

When *Hill Street* was first broadcast in January of 1981, the focus of critical reaction was on its formal and thematic innovativeness—the overall grimy and cluttered look; the density of images and sounds created by the crowded precinct house and the overlapping dialogue; the use of hand-held cameras; the large ensemble cast (fourteen) enacting multiple, frequently intercut story lines that blended professional and personal conflicts; the appeal of its urban topicality and its obvious production quality to a sophisticated if not elite audience that might be able to buy the product of the sponsor, Mercedes Benz.[22] Later, television critics like Todd Gitlin would trace its generic ancestry and note its combination of previously successful generic types, so that Jane Feuer can say that *Hill Street* might be described as "a crime show soap opera documentary that resembles the medical show *St. Elsewhere* far more than other crime shows or soap operas."[23] And John Fiske, noting the link between genre and gender and opposing "the freer segmentation of soap opera" to "the masculine laws of cause and effect," can argue that *Hill Street's* popularity with women is due to its combining "many of the elements of soap opera with the action and achievement characteristic of masculine narrative."[24] Much attention has been paid also by Thomas Schatz, Paul Kerr, and others to imitations of previous shows such as *M*A*S*H* and *Lou Grant*.[25]

Many of these same issues arise in one's reading of and response to the *Furioso*. The poem is long and divided into serial episodes or cantos. It has a large cast of characters and multiple interwoven plots. The adoption of the rhetorical stance of a performing minstrel or bard implies orality, an audience that is present and listening, just as in television generally there is a sense of "nowness" and "bardic" communication created by the rhetoric of the camera and the sounds of "living" characters. Ariosto's narrator has to deal with problems of "interruption" or "cutting," especially "textual gaps," and with what Fiske and Hartley refer to as "anamnesis," or reminding the audience of what it already knows or is about to see.[26] The narrator of the *Furioso* must create suspense but not confusion, and he must avoid closure by not only stretching out the "story lines," but also introducing new characters and their stories, often out of the past of, or presently connected with, one of the other protagonists, as when Ruggiero's sister Marfisa and Bradamante's twin brother Ricciardetto are introduced one-third of the way through the poem, or Leone, son of the Emperor of Constantinople and rival for Bradamante's hand, appears as late as Canto XLIV. As happens in television series, the departure of leading characters may occur and must be accommodated, as when Ariosto has Angelica leave his poem, proposing that perhaps in the future another will sing her remaining story (XXX, 16–17). Considering that several other Renaissance poets did in fact take up the challenge and write entire Angelica romances, one could characterize these continuations as "spinoffs" of the *Furioso*!

The *Furioso* itself, of course, "recombined" romance and epic generic features and continued Boiardo's poem, which was innovative too in that it fused Carolingian and Arthurian narrative and the amatory lyric psychology of Petrarchism. The "listener" to the *Furioso* and *Hill Street*, then, hears many textual and generic echoes. Nor are these limited to these two works, since a viewer of *Hill Street* who has a head well stuffed with previous texts is bound to notice, for example, that the "innovation" of overlapping dialogue has some rather illustrious precedents in the fifth chapter of Rabelais' *Gargantua* and the Yonville fair episode of *Madame Bovary*.

As in the *Furioso*, *Hill Street* has a central place of authority and an authority figure, the precinct house and Captain Furillo (Paris, Charlemagne) under siege from evil forces without and plagued by occasional internal dissension. The individual knights or cops (Bobby Hill, Andy Renko, Mick Belker, Johnny La Rue, Neal Washington, Howard Hunter, Henry Goldblume, Joe Coffey) individually or in pairs leave from and return to the precinct house, where they aggregate every morning for the roll call. There are women warriors who join them in fighting the criminals or enemy warriors "out there" (Lucile Bates, Robin Tartaglia, Patricia Mayo, Tina Rossi) and one who "defends" them (Joyce Davenport). Love relationships among the warriors or with outsiders (i.e., Grace Gardner) develop into several marriages (i.e., Furillo and Davenport, Belker and Tartaglia) with subsequent temporary separations. Charlemagne-Arthur-Furillo has an entourage of courtiers, precinct house advisers, and tormentors (Sergeants Esterhaus and Jablonski, Ray Calletano, Leo Schnitz, Fay Furillo, Irwin Bernstein) and is subject to the occasional punishment-harassment of a divine super-authority (Chief Daniels). The exit of some characters (i.e., Alf Chesley) is compensated for in narrative terms by the introduction of others (Norman Buntz). "Bad guys" (pagan knights) are converted occasionally (Jesus Martinez), but most are violently killed or at least imprisoned, with the "good guys" ("our" knights) often themselves wounded or discomfited (dishonored) by loss of their weapons or police cars (swords and horses), or by the failure of, or the failure to wear, bulletproof vests and other "armor."

As in the chivalric combat of the *Furioso*, violence in *Hill Street*, and indeed in other cop shows, tends to be ritualized as to opponents, modes of engagement, and outcome. But precisely because of the existence of a ritual norm, outbreaks of abnormal, violent behavior on the part of both heroes and villains are considered outrageous. Fiske and Hartley have argued that television violence in general, unlike that in real life, has its own internal rules, externalizes motives and status, and is intended to convey social values to the audience rather than have any meaning for the combatants themselves.[27] The contrast with chivalric combat would suggest, however, that there is also something at stake for the combatants themselves. Especially for the good Christian knights or cops, what is critical is the acquisition of experience, the testing of one's mettle, the display of professional pride, and the securing of a reputation for professional skill and thus advancement (promotion)—even if these turn out frequently to be as disappointing or disillusioning for *Hill Street*'s warriors as they do for Charlemagne's paladins. All of these motives require that combat be normative but not predictable. A possible exception to the analogy with chivalric violence is, however, the romance motive of fighting for the honor, attention, and protection of beloved women and men, with less emphasis on defending the weak generally. In contrast, the *Hill Street* warrior, as his job primarily requires, must rescue or try to protect all helpless victims of criminals, in order to be "a good cop."

The analogy of character is particularly intriguing when one juxtaposes the *Furioso* and *Hill Street*. Do the characters of the latter develop over the many episodes or do they, like the personages of the *Furioso*, merely swing in polar oscillation for the convenience of the narrative? My own conviction has been that interwoven narrative, whether in a poem or a television series, even a semiserialized one, is too "segmented" to allow for slow personality development, even if one were to imagine watching nightly reruns or listening to nightly readings or performances at the court of Ferrara. As we have seen, the polyphonic genre assumes "textual gaps," or performance intervals. Since interwoven plotting is an end in itself, character must serve that end in the best way it can, by oscillating change. Once the psychology of a character is established by the initial episodes (Orlando naively idealistic, Furillo quietly strong but besieged at all times, Bradamante in love and desperately faithful, Joyce Davenport cynically disillusioned but professionally committed) they can show the opposite traits during one episode, but then return to their initial personalities as multiple plotting requires. Plots or story lines are created to test or exploit their established personalities, or to show them momentarily turned around—as in Orlando's madness and sanity, Furillo's struggle with alcoholism, Rinaldo's alternate love and hatred of Angelica, the oscillating relationship of Renko and Hill—but do not involve gradual adjustment as much as weekly polar responses to specific new plots. Like the need to finish at least one story line in each episode, it may well be that the tendency to character change rather than development accepts the exigency of a series audience, which cannot be expected to retain calibrated personality growth or decay.

It is interesting in this connection that John O'Connor, in a recent *New York Times* article, accused *L. A. Law* of precisely such polar changes, in this case from wicked to lovable, and particularly in the characters of Brackman and Becker. According to O'Connor, *Hill Street* had earlier succumbed to "terminal cuteness" when the growling and biting Belker became a mamma's boy and the bigoted Renko became racially enlightened as the series continued.[28] This argument, however, ignores not only the nature of polyphonic narrative but also the facts, since these alleged "likability" transformations were temporary, as plot required, and were duly followed by regressions and future oscillations. Indeed, the total effect of such character oscillations over a long period of viewing might well be to suggest that people are not allegorical, not monolithic embodiments of one personality type but both complex and unpredictable. I am not necessarily asserting, of course, that the conscious purpose of such character presentation is mimetic realism and valuable insight into "human nature," nor am I fashionably ruling these out either. My concern here is to focus on the "internal" requirements of polyphonic plotting as they affect character.

In the case of the *Furioso*, Javitch, as noted above, has argued that the creation of frustration by interruption in its interwoven plotting serves not just to arouse in the reader an appetite for more, a motivated return for the next episode (the "suspense" argument), but structurally to replicate, and therefore to italicize, the frustrating experiences of the protagonists of the poem. What is more, "Ariosto also meant to exploit the formal necessity of interrupting his many plots . . . to condition that reader for the time when that frustration would not be merely literary."[29] In sum, how do discontinuous narratives like those of the *Furioso* and *Hill Street* relate to their worlds, given their narrativity, and even assuming that they embody "constructions" rather than "authentic" reflections of reality? Both the *Furioso* and *Hill Street* exploit past mythologies (medieval martial and amatory chivalry, "cops and robbers"), but both manage also to embody or allude to specific topics of contemporary interest (European warfare and politics in Ariosto, race relations and urban decay in Bochco). And, if Javitch is right about the effect on an audience subjected to its technique, it may well be that polyphonic narrative also has the effect of adequating us to our existential condition.

At least one contemporary critic has suggested that since *Hill Street*'s "multilinear plot structure is soap operatic, ... Some situations get involved, others continue and dissipate, which makes the show coterminous with life's happenings . . . ."[30] But whereas Ariosto's purpose was moral, and therefore assumed the possibility of acquired adequation and endurance, if not redemption or reform, some contemporary ideological critics of *Hill Street*, while acknowledging that it is after all "the best on the box," nevertheless point to its "postliberal" paralysis—bourgeois realism retreating from the issues it raises. Its imaginative world is the contemporary postmodern one, in which nothing works and everything breaks down.[31] If on this view *Hill Street* is a multidimensional world where the planes of compassion, brutality, and cruelty crisscross to create "a helterskelter sense of reality" and "mockmelodrama,"[32] with Furillo trapped as quintessential "corporate man,"[33] then the polyphonic plotting may indeed be more likely to confirm than to mitigate our painful awareness of postmodernist anomie.[34]

I turn now to *L. A. Law*, which because of its relative newness yet obvious succession to the defunct *Hill Street Blues* has not yet received intense critical scrutiny, although it has already indicated a capacity for gathering awards and "upscale" audiences.[35] I will begin by outlining a typical episode, first broadcast in December and repeated in May of 1987–88, the show's second season. I have italicized the recurring places but not indicated the times of the action—while the time is not indicated as precisely as in, for example, *St. Elsewhere*, there is no doubt that at least two days and two nights elapse as the events unfold. It is also clear that except for the partners' conferences, the events are assumed to be occurring simultaneously with others.

CONTENT SUMMARY

Reprise: "Previously on L. A. Law":

    a. Jonathan Rollins's unprofessional prolonging of a divorce settlement,

    b. The unexpected appearance of Michael Kuzak's ex-wife upsets his relationship with Grace Van Owen,

    c. Ann Kelsey and Stuart Markowitz quarrel, and

    d. Douglas Brackman's brother breaks in on him and the "buxom bailiff" Rhonda.

Prologue Scene: Brackman explains to Rhonda that he must break off their relationship, quoting Byron from a concealed slip of paper.

Recurring Preliminaries: Music and Title: License Plate and City.

    a. *Law office* of McKenzie-Brackman and *court corridors*, with characters moving about, passing, or pausing to converse with, each other; *cast* identified, and

Break

    b. View of Los Angeles: list of *guest actors* superimposed.

Episode Proper Begins:

1. Meeting of partners in conference room: discussions of current cases being handled by Kuzak, Markowitz, Abby Perkins; argument between Perkins and Brackman leads to adjournment.

2. Markowitz and Kelsey converse about her mother being in town for their impending wedding; *credits*: producers, director, writers, etc.

3. Victor Sifuentes meets Lauren, just divorced and distressed, in a stuck *office elevator*; they talk of lunch.

4. *Courtroom*: Kuzak defends a young celebrity against charges of assaulting a fan.

5. Markowitz, Kelsey, and her mother at *dinner*, have awkward talk about how Jewish men make good husbands.

Break

6. Markowitz and his client, angry movie producer Bass, talk in former's *office* about the producer's stalled suit against a movie producer.

7. Perkins's *office*: she tries to resolve old legal quarrel between two friends turned enemies.

8. Rollins and Benny Stollwitz converse in hall of firm *office*.

9. Sifuentes and Lauren converse in his *office* and plan dinner.

10. *Courtroom*: Kuzak and the district attorney argue about a plea that will get his client into a drug program instead of into jail.

11. *Court conference room*: Kuzak's client refuses the deal.

12. Kuzak drops in on Van Owen in her *office*, asks for a kiss, passionately caresses her; they leave for a hotel.

13. *Conference room at firm*: Brackman argues with Perkins again about her case; Kuzak arrives late, looking sheepish; Kelsey defends Perkins; Rhonda breaks in, accuses Brackman of having her transferred, mistreating her; Brackman leaves, embarrassed, after Rhonda departs in a huff.

Break: News Brief

14. Rollins and McKenzie chat about Markowitz's angry client in McKenzie's *office*.

15. *Men's room*: Sifuentes and Kuzak talk about Lauren; Becker, Brackman chat about Rhonda, possibility of Brackman having contracted AIDS from her.

16. *Office*: Kelsey introduces her mother to Sifuentes and Rollins, provoking her prejudiced comment on minorities.

17. *Courtroom*: In Kuzak's case testimony is given about assault and cocaine possession.

18. *Home* of movie producer Bass; Rollins feigns toughness in order to regain the case.

19. Perkins's *office*: she tries to reconcile the former partners, who quarrel again, one hurling the other through a glass partition wall.

Break

20. *Office*: glass being repaired; Kelsey and Perkins chat.

21. Bass and Rollins in McKenzie's *office*; the latter bawls out Rollins for soliciting Bass's business under false pretenses.

22. *Courtroom*: Kuzak's client is found not guilty; he and Kuzak converse about the future.

23. View of the city at night; Kuzak and Van Owen in *restaurant*: He pleads for her return; is then called away to the phone.

24. Markowitz, Kelsey, and her mother, at *house* of friends; Markowitz hears a friend ask Kelsey's mother why her daughter is marrying a Jew; in anger, Markowitz overturns a hutch filled with dishes and glasses.

25. *Jail*: Kuzak's call was about his client being arrested again for possessing drugs; Kuzak threatens to quit him unless he does something about his habit.

26. Outside the *house*: Kelsey and Markowitz talk about his angry rage, his Jewishness; she asserts she still wants to marry him, will make him some chicken soup.

Final Credit: Executive Producer, Steven Bochco.

ARIOSTO AND BOCHCO

The affinities of *L. A. Law* with both *Hill Street Blues* and the *Furioso* are obvious. As for *Hill Street*, one notes that *L. A. Law* also uses a large ensemble cast (approximately the same number); a central professional place where all of the cast aggregate daily (the firm, the conferences of the partners); interwoven plots which feature combined professional and personal tensions and crises; the goals of love, reputation, wealth and, occasionally, chivalric service to the community (*pro bono* cases) and to the cause of justice—when not a serious threat to the profits of the firm of McKenzie-Brackman, the last being an ongoing concern that definitely gives a satiric edge to the depiction of the legal profession. Like the earlier series, *L. A. Law*'s principal site (the firm's office) is crowded and noisy, with lots of coming and going and passing by others. There is inevitably much more talk than action, with brisk personal exchanges often interlaced with legal jargon. The overall appearance of *L. A. Law* is slick rather than grimy (it even features scenes in upscale *working* bathrooms); the cast of characters, like the plots, are very sexy, postyuppie, affluent. The courtrooms "out there" are certainly no match for the squalid mean streets of the decaying "out there" of *Hill Street*. Since the latter's exteriors are mostly shot in the same city of Los Angeles, *L. A. Law*'s firm is obviously located uptown, or on the other side of town.

These differences—raising the economic and social scale, but lowering the level of social and moral idealism or pessimism, putting a premium on blunt sex and clever talk while diminishing significant action—urge a question to which I will return, whether *L. A. Law*, like the *Furioso*, is a parody of its predecessors.

The coincidences of *L. A. Law* and the *Orlando Furioso* range from examples of character reincarnation—Ariosto's archetypal thieving dwarf Brunello turning up as Schuyler Kimball, the dwarfish lawyer who steals cases—to larger structural and thematic coincidences. The office of McKenzie-Brackman is the Paris from which the lawyers depart to take on (duel with) other lawyers in trials (combats). The authority figure is the senior partner, Leland McKenzie, who adjudicates quarrels among his knights and is subject only to punishment from *the client*, who might withdraw his business from the firm. There are women lawyers inside and outside of the firm who, like the female cops of *Hill Street* and the female warriors of the *Furioso*, must deal with gender prejudices and conflicts. There are love relationships and marriages within the firm and with outsiders (Kelsey and Markowitz, Kuzak and Van Owen) that are stormy, along with a good deal of frustrated seeking after the amatory ideal (Brackman, Roxanne Melman,

Sifuentes, Perkins). In matters of love, *L. A. Law* even has its *furioso*, Arnie Becker.

A closer look at the summaries I have given of Canto VIII of the *Furioso* and my chosen episode of *L. A. Law* reveals other affinities. Like Ariosto's narratorial poem, *L. A. Law*'s "previously" over-voice reprises the previous episode and is then followed by four recapitulative fragments and one prologue scene. The camera's presentation of cast and credits parallels Ariosto's virtual announcements of artifice, that he is creating and manipulating literary plots. He continues four of these (Ruggiero, Rinaldo, Angelica, the seige of Paris/Orlando) with six narrator's interruptions, and a transitional closing intervention that promises to continue the Orlando plot in the next canto. In *L. A. Law*, after the reprise and prologue scene, there are at least twenty-six narrative segments created by camera cutting and film editing, four larger interruptions for commercials, and a news break. In all, there are five story lines continued from the previous episode: 1) the relationship of Kuzak and Van Owen threatened by the appearance of his ex-wife; 2) the parallel relationship of Kelsey and Markowitz threatened by the appearance of her mother (the familiar polyphonic romance—and television series—ploy in both cases being the introduction of a "new" character from the main character's past, as happened also earlier with Brackman's half brother); 3) Brackman and the bailiff; 4) the Perkins case; and 5) the continuing aggressive behavior of Rollins. The new plot lines are Kuzak's case, and Sifuentes' meeting with Lauren. There are some apparent closures (i.e., Brackman and the bailiff, but this plot will return in the next episode) and two reliable and "just" closures (it does happen): Kelsey's mother has her hash settled, and Kuzak's client is duly punished. The next episode will continue the Sifuentes affair and the other plot lines, with greater prominence given to Becker, who is the only major protagonist not given story attention in this episode.

Just as Ariosto's sophisticated audience of courtiers was alert to and consumers of contemporary high culture, the implied viewers of *L. A. Law* are definitely addicted to "chic" in lifestyle and issues: witness the relationships, the clothing, the restaurants, the apartments and houses in which events outside of the law office occur, not to mention the frank eroticism and crisp talk. Rollins and Sifuentes assure minority presence and tensions, a concern shared by the younger members, especially with instances of exploitation. The problem of the retarded is embodied in the sympathetic figure of Benny Stollwitz, to whom, however, all of the firm's members take turns being unbearably condescending. Rape and drugs are frequent topics, while feminist issues such as sexist attitudes and equal pay for equal work get attention fairly regularly—in the next episode, in fact, Perkins's handling of her case earns her equal pay, at last! It is also shown that ambition, success, affluence, and power do not necessarily guarantee prolonged happiness. Hence it may well be that watching *L. A. Law*, like reading the *Furioso*, adequates us to an existence that is hectic, complex, materially rewarding, and intermittently satisfying, but also considerably, disappointingly, and unexpectedly, frustrating—and this, if it has any, may be its minimal ethical value.

I conclude with the question of literary or critical parody. The *Furioso*, as is well known, is masterfully ironic in its narrator's simultaneous distancing of himself from a repudiated romance genre, and his unabashed appropriation of its themes and narrative technique. Like his successor in this mode, Cervantes, Ariosto manages to have it both ways. As is usually the case with the critical literary parodist, however, there is a delicate balance to be sought, avoiding satire or burlesque and instead exploiting the kind of subtle appropriation that requires both empathy and deep understanding—and eventual recuperation—of the nature and literary value of the parodied text. When watching *L. A. Law* I have an uneasy feeling about its relationship to its predecessor—it is certainly appropriative, exploitive, and even parasitic, but also, I find, clearly repudiating rather than recuperative. It certainly does not have it both ways, and therefore does not, like the *Furioso* and *Don Quixote* for that matter (not to mention Joyce's *Ulysses*), permanently invoke and preserve the predecessor, the (only apparently) debased source.

Insofar as it is probably impossible for any television series to persist in the ironic mode, I may be asking too much, even considering the precedents of *M*A*S*H* for war story and *Moonlighting* for detective story. It may well be that the failure of *L. A. Law* to take a more imaginative stance toward its genre than merely to be an "uptown" *Hill Street* will doom it to the kind of self-satirization that has now terminally afflicted *St. Elsewhere*. Unlike the *Furioso*, in that case, which owes its greatness in large measure to a successful absorption and recycling of its generic predecessors, with the result being a fresh and enduring creation, *L. A. Law* may be destined for future recollection as only a failed generic "spinoff" of *Hill Street Blues*, Bochco parodying himself rather than renovating the genre. But this does not or would not prove that the fault lies with polyphonic plotting. In his account of the "inside" story of how *Hill Street Blues* came to be, Todd Gitlin mentions that at one point NBC, concerned that the test audience found the multiple stories and plots unsatisfactory, asked a consulting psychologist for "a scientific opinion about the number of plots an audience could hold in its mind simultaneously."[36] The conventional wisdom having been that three plots were manageable, there must have been some consternation when the reply came that an audience could handle "seven, plus or minus two" plots, and that increased familiarity would make it easier to retain them. For as it turned out, a compromise was required, as we noted above, that would have at least one plot achieve closure in each episode, a compromise between Ariostean multiplicity and Aristotelian unity. Ariosto himself might have added that not only are we able to bear much polyphony, but we may well need it in order to experience a kind of harmony between ourselves and our discordant world.

NOTES

1. Sarah Ruth Kozloff, "Narrative Theory" in *Channels of Discourse*, ed. Robert C. Allen (Chapel Hill: University of North Carolina Press, 1987), 42–73. Recent narrative

theory is conveniently surveyed in Thomas M. Leitch, *What Stories Are: Narrative Theory and Interpretation* (University Park: Pennsylvania University Press, 1986) and Wallace Martin, *Recent Theories of Narrative* (Ithaca, N.Y.: Cornell University Press, 1986). It should be noted that Gérard Genette mentions Ariosto but once in his very influential *Narrative Discourse: An Essay in Method*, trans. Jane E. Lewin and Jonathan Culler (Ithaca, N.Y.: Cornell University Press, 1980 [1972]), 231, and then in connection with embedded tales, not polyphonic plotting.

2. For background see Eugène Vinaver, "The Poetry of Interlace," in *The Rise of Romance* (New York: Oxford University Press, 1971), 68–98, and Rosemond Tuve, *Allegorical Imagery: Some Medieval Books and Their Posterity* (Princeton, N.J.: Princeton University Press, 1977 [1966]), 359–69. Also, in Italian, C. P. Brand, "L'*entrelacement* nell '*Orlando Furioso* e il romanzo cavalleresco medievale," in *Giornale storico della letteratura italiana* 154 (1977): 509–32; Giovanni B. Bronzini, *Tradizione di stile aedico dai cantari al "Furioso"* (Firenze: Leo S. Olschki Editore, 1966); Daniela Delcorno Branca, *L'"Orlando Furioso" e il romanzo medievale* (Firenze: Leo S. Olschki Editore, 1973); Giuseppe Dalla Palma, *Le Strutture narrative dell' "Orlando Furioso"* (Firenze: Leo S. Olschki Editore, 1984); Leonzio Pampaloni, "Per una analisi narrativa del *Furioso*," *Belfagor* 26 (1971): 133–50; Elissa B. Weaver, "Lettura dell 'intreccio dell' *Orlando Furioso*: il caso delle tre pazzie d'amore," *Strumenti critici* 34 (1977): 384–406.

3. Vinaver, 77ff. Note in contrast, Stephen G. Nichols' treatment of binary structure in *Romanesque Signs: Early Medieval Narrative and Iconography* (New Haven: Yale University Press, 1983), especially his interpretation of the *Song of Roland* in the light of the Italian Orlando poems (148–203).

4. Tuve, *Allegorical Imagery*, 363.

5. *On Poetry and Style*, trans. G. M. A. Grube (Indianapolis, Ind.: Bobbs-Merrill Educational Publishing, 1985), 49.

6. *Institutio Oratoria*, vol. 4, trans. H. E. Butler (Cambridge, Massachusetts: Harvard University Press, 1979 [1922]), Book 10, 135–36.

7. C. S. Lewis, *English Literature in the Sixteenth Century Excluding Drama* (Oxford: Clarendon Press, 1954), 332. Lewis points out that "Our own taste in fiction has not yet lasted as long as the taste for the interwoven sort lasted."

8. A flurry of recent books in English on Ariosto has now made the poet more widely accessible: Peter V. Marinelli, *Ariosto and Boiardo: the Origins of "Orlando Furioso"* (Columbia, Mo.: University of Missouri Press, 1987); Peter DeSa Wiggins, *Figures in Ariosto's Tapestry, Character and Design in the "Orlando Furioso"* (Baltimore and London: The Johns Hopkins University Press, 1986); Albert Russell Ascoli, *Ariosto's Bitter Harmony: Crisis and Evasion in the Italian Renaissance* (Princeton, N.J.: Princeton University Press, 1986); "Perspectives on Ariosto," the Italian Issue of *Modern Language Notes* 103 (1988), with essays on Ariosto by Italian and American scholars; see also, Marina Beer, *Romanzi di cavalleria: l'"Orlando Furioso" e il romanzo cavalleresco* (Roma: Bulzoni, 1987).

9. Bronzini, 1–65; Delcorno Branca, 57–79; Marinelli, 1–51.

10. See the detailed characterization of the poem's organization and themes by Barbara Reynolds in the introduction to her translation in verse: *Orlando Furioso (The Frenzy of Orlando): A Romantic Epic by Ludovico Ariosto*. Part One (Harmondsworth, England: Penguin Books, 1975), 11–113. I use the text of Lanfranco Caretti (Milano and Napoli: Riccardo Ricciardi Editore, 1963 [1954]), and my own translations throughout.

11. Daniel Javitch, *"Cantus Interruptus* in the *Orlando Furioso," Modern Language Notes* 95 (1980): 66–80.

12. Daniel Javitch, "Narrative Discontinuity in the *Orlando Furioso* and its Sixteenth-Century Critics," *Modern Language Notes* 103 (1988): 50–74.

13. *On Poetry and Style,* 51.

14. *Giraldi Cinthio on Romances,* trans. Henry L. Snuggs (Lexington, Ky.: University of Kentucky Press, 1968), 11–12, 37. Note also Northrop Frye's remark in *The Secular Scripture: A Study of the Structure of Romance* (Cambridge, Mass.: Harvard University Press, 1982 [1976]), 23: "Any serious discussion of romance has to take into account its curiously proletarian status as a form generally disapproved of, in most ages, by the guardians of taste and learning, except when they use it for their own purposes. The close connection of the romantic and the popular runs all through literature."

15. *Discourses on the Heroic Poem,* trans. Mariella Cavalchini and Irene Samuel (Oxford: Clarendon Press, 1973), 76–77.

16. On the quarrel over the *Furioso,* see Bernard Weinberg, *A History of Literary Criticism in the Italian Renaissance,* 2 vols. (Chicago: University of Chicago Press, 1961), I, 450–52; II, 652–53, and especially 954–1073, 1106–10.

17. Sarah Ruth Kozloff, *Channels of Discourse,* 73, refers to her forthcoming study of "invisible storytellers" (voice-over narration). See also, David Barker, "Television Production Techniques as Communication," in *Television: The Critical View,* ed. Horace Newcomb, Fourth Edition (Oxford: Oxford University Press, 1987 [1976]), 179–96; Seymour Chatman, "Covert versus Overt Narrators," *Story and Discourse: Narrative Structure in Fiction and Film* (Ithaca: Cornell University Press, 1986 [1978]), 196–262.

18. John Ellis, *Visible Fictions: Cinema: Television: Video* (London: Routledge & Kegan Paul, 1985 [1982]), 154; On closure and serialization see also, Raymond Williams, *Television Technology and Cultural Form* (New York: Schocken Books, 1975), 60–61; John Fiske, *Television Culture* (London: Methuen, 1987), 142–48; Jane Feuer, "Narrative Form in Television," in *High Theory, Low Culture,* ed. Colin MacCabe (Manchester: Manchester University Press, 1986), 101–14.

19. I am grateful to Gundersheimer for allowing me to see a copy of his as yet unpublished lecture, "Paladins and Heroines: Ariosto and the Western Epic Tradition," given at the Folger Library in February of 1988. I quote from pp. 6–7 of my copy of his talk.

20. Wayne C. Booth, "The Company We Keep: Self-Making in Imaginative Art, Old and New," Newcomb, ed., *Television: The Critical View,* 382.

21. Richard Levinson and William Link, *Off Camera: Conversations with the Makers of Prime-Time Television* (New York: New American Library, 1986), 17–35.

22. Tim Brooks and Earle Marsh, *The Complete Directory to Prime Time Network TV Shows, 1946–Present,* 3d. ed. (New York: Ballantine Books, 1985), 370–71. On the show's production techniques and audience see Kozloff, *Channels of Discourse,* 58–59; Jane Feuer, "The MTM Style," Newcomb, ed., *Television: The Critical View,* 66–69, 80–81; David Barker, "Television Production Techniques as Communication," Newcomb, ed., *Television: The Critical View,* 179–96; John Fiske, *Television Culture,* 312; Todd Gitlin, *Inside Prime Time* (New York: Pantheon, 1983), 273–324.

23. Todd Gitlin, *Inside Prime Time,* 275–78; Jane Feuer, "Genre Study and Television," *Channels of Discourse,* 131. See also, Steve Jenkins, *"Hill Street Blues,"* in *MTM 'Quality Television',* ed. Jane Feuer, Paul Kerr, and Tise Vahimagi (London: British Film Institute, 1984), 183–222.

24. John Fiske, *Television Culture*, 198–223, discusses gendered television with occasional reference to *Hill Street Blues*, that is, " . . . with its multiple plots and characters, its rapid switching from plot to plot, its sense that characters live between episodes, its "memory" from episode to episode combines many of the elements of soap opera with the action and achievement characteristic of the masculine narrative" (p. 219).

25. Thomas Schatz, "*St. Elsewhere* and the Evolution of the Ensemble Series," Newcomb, ed., *Television: The Critical View*, 85–100; Paul Kerr, "Drama at MTM: *Lou Grant* and *Hill Street Blues*," in *MTM 'Quality Television,'* 132–65; N. D. Batra, "The Case of Recombinant Progeny," in *The Hour of Television: Critical Approaches* (Metuchen, N.J.: Scarecrow Press, 1987), 74–81.

26. John Fiske and John Hartley, *Reading Television* (London: Methuen, 1985 [1978]), 84–100, 124–26. On disruption, interruption, cutting, etc., see also John Fiske, *Television Culture*, 180–84; Robert C. Allen, "Reader Oriented Criticism and Television," in *Channels of Discourse*, 85–86. See also Bernard Timberg, "The Rhetoric of the Camera in Television Soap Opera," Newcomb, ed., *Television: The Critical View*, 164–78. See also Caren J. Deming, "*Hill Street Blues* as Narrative," *Critical Studies in Mass Communications* 2 (1985): 1–22. Deming discusses *Hill Street*'s "complexity, ambiguity, and discontinuity" as creating a "modernist text cast primarily as melodrama" (p. 2).

27. John Fiske and John Hartley, *Reading Television*, 34–35. They add, "Our familiarity with the genre makes us react to violence according to its own internal rules, and not as we would to real violence" (p. 35). But see also Barry Castro, "Middle-Management Blues: Notes from Hill Street," *Soundings* 68 (1985): 435–43, and Thomas H. Zynda, "The Metaphoric Vision of *Hill Street Blues*," *Journal of Popular Film and Television* 14 (1986): 100–113.

28. *New York Times*, 17 May 1987, section C, p. 8. O'Connor argues that polar change of character "leaves *L. A. Law* teetering on the familiar television abyss of terminal cuteness."

29. Daniel Javitch, "Narrative Discontinuity," 57.

30. Batra, "The Case of Recombinant Progeny," 76–77.

31. Gitlin, *Inside Prime Time*, 309; Zynda, "The Metaphoric Vision of *Hill Street Blues*," 103, 111.

32. Batra, 75.

33. Castro, "Middle-Management Blues: Notes from Hill Street," 442–43.

34. Deming, "*Hill Street Blues* as Narrative," 18.

35. For example, see Harry F. Waters and Janet Huck's article in *Newsweek* 110 (16 November 1987), 84–88, entitled "Lust for Law" and touting "Prime Time's Hottest Series Has Sex, Style and Plenty of Smarts."

36. Gitlin, 296.

6

The Good, the Bad, and the Counterfeit: A Tolstoyan Theory of Narrative

Mary Sirridge

> If a man is infected by the author's condition of soul, if he feels this emotion and this union with others, then the object which has effected this is art. . . . And not only is infection a sure sign of art, but the degree of infectiousness is also the sole measure of excellence in art.
>
> Tolstoy, *What Is Art?*

In 1898, Leo Tolstoy, the famous novelist, critic, and social reformer, published his extraordinary popularist manifesto concerning art and criticism. Tolstoy surely felt he was proposing a comprehensive, revolutionary model showing that "high" or "exclusive" art was either not art at all or bad art; this polemical conclusion was one of his main objectives. In fact, I think he produced criteria of evaluation largely inappropriate for "exclusive" art; but in proposing his theory, he made a significant contribution to art theory. He produced a theory of art particularly illuminating with respect to such popular art forms[1] as folk art and the art of our mass media,[2] art forms not dealt with very satisfactorily by the standard post-Renaissance aesthetic theories.

ART AS THE EXPRESSION OF FEELING

Art for Tolstoy is essentially an expression or externalization of feeling causing others to have that feeling also: "Art is a human activity consisting in this, that one man consciously, by means of certain external signs, hands on to others feelings he has lived through, and that other people are infected by these feelings and also experience them."[3]

An object or activity qualifies as art to the extent that it succeeds in promoting this sharing of feeling, to the extent that it is "infectious," to use Tolstoy's term.[4] Purported art that is not genuinely infectious is just not art, though it may be a counterfeit of art (i.e., something arousing feelings by some other mechanism and therefore easily mistaken for art).

"Feeling" has a very wide range for Tolstoy: emotions like anger or fear, a sense of the humor of a funny story or the tranquility of a landscape, perceptions of good and evil or the meaning of life.[5] All the objects and activities of a culture that externalize and transmit feelings are art in a very broad sense: "We are accustomed to understand art to be only what we hear and see in theaters, concerts, and exhibitions, together with buildings, statues, poems, novels. . . . But all this is but the smallest part of the art by which we communicate with each other in life. All human life is filled with works of art of every kind—from cradlesong, jest, mimicry, the ornamentation of houses, dress, and utensils, up to church services, buildings, monuments, and triumphal processions. It is all artistic activity."[6]

Tolstoy does not spend much time on art in this wide sense. His principal interest is art in the more usual and less inclusive sense—the buildings, statues, poems, and novels. Such art has, he says, the special property of expressing those feelings he calls "religious perceptions," perceptions of the meaning of life, of the good and the evil in life.[7] In defining art in this sense in terms of its expression of religious perceptions, Tolstoy is, of course, presupposing his view that art generally is defined in terms of the expression of feeling. He is also looking to the larger societal function or purpose he assigns to art:[8]

As, thanks to man's capacity to express thoughts by words, every man may know all that has been done for him in the realms of thought by all humanity before his day, and can, in the present, thanks to this capacity to understand the thoughts of others, become a sharer in their activity and can himself hand on to his contemporaries and descendants the thoughts he has assimilated from others, as well as those which have arisen within himself; so, thanks to man's capacity to be infected with the feelings of others by means of art, all that is being lived through by his contemporaries is accessible to him, as well as the feelings experienced by men thousands of years ago, and he has also the possibility of transmitting his own feelings to others.[9]

Thus feelings, like thoughts, have to be externalized in order to exist in a form in which they can be perceived by others, and remain accessible after the subject who feels them has gone or gone on to other things, just as one researcher's scientific insights have to be announced for others to build on those insights and in order to survive their biographical instant. It is Tolstoy's view that art as it is usually thought of—the plays, stories, and music—represents an attempt to concretize and express the essentials of human existence. As the principal means of externalizing feeling, art is the main means through which humankind advances from a lower and more obscure perception of life's meaning to one more lucid and more universal.[10] The evolution of feeling thus achieved is the ultimate purpose art serves, and the justification for its existence, despite its terrible costs in individual lives and happiness and the competition it offers for scarce resources.[11]

Tolstoy judges art to be good or bad on the basis of whether it furthers this evolution of level of feeling. Good art represents the best or highest level of religious perception of its own age.[12] As Tolstoy sees it, the highest level of religious perception of the modern age is the sense of brotherhood under God. Good modern art is therefore of two kinds: universal art, which expresses feelings common to all;[13] and art which, though less universally accessible, expresses directly the ideal of brotherhood or horror at man's inhumanity to man. In Tolstoy's thinking, the first criterion shades into the second; he seems to think that as a result of feeling the simple feelings everyone shares, people also sense their unity with those others, thus coming to have, in a dim and general way, the best feeling of the modern age, the very feelings they would come to have more explicitly and clearly by reading works specifically engendering them. But there is an obvious tension between the two criteria, and a work has to uplift feeling very clearly and to an extraordinary extent—Tolstoy's favorite examples are Dickens's *A Christmas Carol* and the works of Dostoevski—to escape condemnation for lacking universal appeal. The reason for this is clear enough. The audience of a work which lacks universality—Tolstoy calls such works "provincial"—revels in a sense of separateness and superiority, a perception contrary to the religious perception of the modern age. The only obvious exceptions to this phenomenon are works that by their very "message" discourage such feelings.

Tolstoy's theory has an obvious bias against "high" or "exclusive" art; he ends up condemning Beethoven, Baudelaire, the Impressionists generally, and his own early novels, to cite but a few examples. The problem with Tolstoy's proscriptions is not so much the specific judgments, any one of which some critics might accept, as it is the intrinsic discrimination against what is original, subtle, complex or esoteric. Whatever Tolstoy may have thought, this theory is not a very good tool for evaluating "exclusive" art, where originality of vision and unity in complexity are genuine desiderata and canons, and where limited *versus* wide appeal is a hit-or-miss matter. (Van Gogh's *Starry Night* is a great painting, and it is very popular; but why not El Greco's *The Burial of Count Orgaz* as well? And why, of all of Andrew Wyeth's paintings, is *Christina's World* as popular as Gainsborough's *Blue Boy*?)

Nevertheless, Tolstoy's theory has crucial strengths regarding art forms that depend on mass appeal, art forms for which many post-Renaissance aesthetic theories are not very helpful. Tolstoy's theory addresses the intuition that a dimension of the aesthetic problem is disregarded when *War and Peace* is judged immeasurably better art than *M.A.S.H.* because *War and Peace* is much more subtle, complex, powerful, deep, and timeless (though all of that, of course, is true).

First, Tolstoy's theory explains the relation between popular acceptance and artistic value. Popularity is an effective condition for widely consolidating the level of feeling and fostering the feeling of belonging. Such goals can be achieved only by works expressing feelings that many people identify as their own in artistic frameworks that they identify as familiar. Similarly, the further agenda of the advancement of feeling depends upon art's ability so to interweave the higher and more lucid levels of feeling with the lower feelings many people actually have that the higher feelings are not perceived as "other" and are therefore easily appropriated by each as "my own." An important corollary of this first characteristic of Tolstoy's theory is that it has no critical bias against repetition of form or subject matter, the two touchstones of familiarity. Indeed, art fitting Tolstoy's theory normally introduces innovation, if at all, only within repeated patterns.

Second, like many nineteenth century theories which are "evolutionary" in a broad sense, Tolstoy's theory of art does not require that individuals consciously strive to attain the larger objective that art serves. In Tolstoy's theory, individuals are motivated characteristically by the desire to communicate their feelings, and those motives are likely in the case of universal art to be mixed liberally with the other motives of daily life. It is consistent with Tolstoy's theory that some individuals have a larger "design" perspective and produce works fostering a higher level of feeling—one would expect such motivation fairly often in the case of creators of explicitly "religious" art—but it is also consistent with the achievement of the larger objective that individuals be selfishly devoted to self-expression *per se*, or that this desire in turn serve a drive for power or monetary gain or whatever. Like the assignment of a theoretical role to popularity, the positing of a shared achievement indifferent to individual motivations is a requirement for a good theory of folk art, and probably even for a theory which fits collective art works like the buildings of the Acropolis and the cathedrals of the Middle Ages.

Finally, the art Tolstoy describes has its significance against a broader background of objects and activities expressing the felt life of the community, for example, jokes and utensils. With his characteristic theoretical impatience, Tolstoy gives no account of the function of such items in the popular life of feeling, or how their function is a background for art in the less inclusive and more usual sense, though a more searching analysis, however, establishes clearly the connection between the art that interests Tolstoy most and the popular life of feeling.

Humor, for example, is crucial background for many popular narratives—tall tales, fables, and such. Since it involves incongruities and reversals, humor depends heavily on entrenched attitudes and expectations. Sharing the humor of the "Aggie" joke in which the Aggie who has suffered stock market reversals puts a gun to his head and shouts at his broker, "Be quiet! You're next!" requires a fairly complex common stock of expectations, attitudes, and values. There is a ghastly misalignment here—and misalignments and reversals are expected subjects for humor—between the Aggie's perception of reality and the way things are: any fool knows that there is no "next," once one shoots oneself. "Any fool" is an important tag; this is a *so-stupid-that* joke, a genre joke. (It is also a *too terrible-to-say* black humor joke, for suicide is, of course, too terrible to joke about.) In its university context, this joke about the market crash of October, 1987, served to focus and defuse shared anxiety about the economy and shared disdain of a provincial university, and thereby confirmed a common ground of feeling and a shared understanding of what things are ghastly, what things are frightening, and what things and what people are just deplorably stupid. In its local newspaper context, the joke had a considerably more complex function related to the relationship between university and town and to a kind of customary regional inversion of *so-stupid-that* jokes, in which the object of the joke is in fact being praised and singled out for a rough demonstration of admiration and affection. I have belabored this example to make a point. Very simple jokes involve very complicated patterns of affect and apperception, and people who "get" other people's jokes share those patterns of feeling. It is against such a background of shared values, stereotypes, expectations, and attitudes that the comedy of popular narrative functions.

Utensils and building patterns, too, establish a certain "floor" of familiarity. The ordinary things people use to perform ordinary, daily actions establish a uniform background of action patterns and expectations. Not being able to figure out what the things in the bathroom are for or how to use the potato peeler, unfamiliar glassware and flatware patterns, curved construction instead of rectilinear, monuments to unfamiliar people or to people famous for things hard to appreciate, not being able to find greeting cards that say the usual things—these are all telltale signs of being "other," of being among people from whom one is divided by a difference in low-level action patterns and spheres of familiarity. And these low-level patterns of expectation are value laden. Our expectations about how space, lived and auditory, is to be filled; our understanding of desirability, reassurance, respectability, "class," and elegance; our perceptions of heroism and the usual dimensions of contentment, normalcy and fulfillment— these all find their most basic expressions in our sense of the objects surrounding us daily. These objects therefore embody a basic level of felt communion within a culture. Against this background the narratives of popular art take shape—the parable, the *Red Book* story, the folk ballad, and the tall tale. By virtue of such a background the audience understands the significance of objects and actions in a narrative. "Exclusive" art, too, invariably depends on context to complete its meaning; yet, unlike popular art, esoteric art characteristically aims to defy this dependence and to create an object self-sufficient in meaning and therefore free of its context of creation to the greatest possible extent.

THE TELEVISION NARRATIVE: A TOLSTOYAN ART FORM?

Perhaps the most visible and most criticized feature of the television narrative as an art form is its *de facto* susceptibility to the demand for popular appeal and accessibility. Television series and other television narratives are continued if enough people prefer them over concurrent offerings and removed if they receive inadequate popular support; prospective shows are chosen on the basis of their probable audience appeal. This is part of the conventional wisdom about television programming, and it is pretty well documented as well.[14] The result, it is claimed, is a systematic bias against programs with original content, subtle and innovative form, or any characteristic rendering them esoteric in their appeal (i.e., insufficiently popular). Despite the validity of occasional critical claims that some series are formally innovative[15] or revolutionary in content,[16] these charges are, I think, largely true. If television narratives had to be measured against the criteria for good or great "exclusive" art, very few of them would fare well. But if the television narrative should prove in important respects to fit the conception of art that Tolstoy offers us, it would gain both a more sympathetic set of evaluative criteria and a moral and anthropological *raison d'etre*.

Obviously, the dependence of the television narrative on popular appeal and the predominance of repetitious form and content is not enough to guarantee its conformity to Tolstoy's model, though these characteristics serve to alert us to a possible theoretical fit. But there are further parallels. The most important of these is a general orientation to the stuff of life that is heavy handedly evaluative. Situation comedies, situation dramas, day and nighttime "soaps," made-for-TV movies, and the minidramas in television advertising all work out of current problems and preoccupations, and, as a rule, they deliver evaluations. The daytime soaps show (repeatedly) that new social developments[17] can fit a known pattern of significance: that events have a communal meaning;[18] that life has meaningful patterns, despite its lack of closure; and perhaps most importantly, that personal identity survives traumatic change. The Good Characters share this outlook. Bad Characters either act without regard for the communal consequences of their actions or constitute a continuing (and ultimately unsuccessful) assault on meaning, community, and the identities of others. The "minidramas" of television advertising are similarly oriented to current life realities. Since these advertisements depend on presenting ways of being—"cool" in Levis, competent in a multi-purpose vehicle, or a beautiful and happy little girl—the ways of being presented have to be imaginable, present, real-life alternatives. And the proposal of values in advertising is obvious: these are valuable ways to be, and so one has to have the Levis, the multi-purpose vehicle, or the white plastic pony with a pastel mane in order to be that way. Thus television narratives are markedly oriented toward the meaning of life and the good and evil in life by which Tolstoy's theory defines art in the less inclusive sense.

Moreover, the television narrative resembles the popular narrative structurally in depending upon a broader context for significance. The broader context is network programming, which includes commercials, news shows, game shows, sports, children's programs, talk shows, science specials, and variety shows. This list is incomplete, and cable television increases the alternatives geometrically. This broader context may well secure a continuity with daily activities and basic community values; very probably it establishes some *felt* continuity of this sort. But far more central to its operation than any real connection to the world of attitudes and objects from which popular narratives usually arise is the fact that it *constitutes* a context of activity and valuation relatively complete in itself. Television creates a background on which its narratives rely in much the same way as the *Red Book* story relies on the objects embodying the common experiences and attitudes of its culture. Television gives advice (how much insurance to buy, how to get floors to shine, what toys are fun this year) and passes communal values along in the process (fun is important, responsible people have adequate insurance, and people whose floors shine are fulfilled). Television news and its accompaniments offer a rhythm of reality—tuning in to reality at daybreak, getting things summed up as the work day ends, getting reality "talked down" at 10:00 P.M., or thereabouts, and getting things pulled together on the weekend. Whatever the facts about its real objectivity or lack of it, television news conveys in the process the sense that Ideal People first collect the facts objectively, then judiciously react and act. Some of this value material and information is appropriated, some is rejected, and some is accepted in name only. How it is processed does not matter, as long as a large segment of the population becomes familiar with the values and information, a kind of cultural common property.

This larger context and the cultural reality it purveys is the necessary environment for television narratives. Narratives depend on the lowest level on an audience's ability to fill in gaps. Television narratives depend on the viewer's sense of what the reality in the narrative is like, from the unseen next room to the world at large. The interiors and neighborhoods of television advertising and the maps and clips of network news are crucial for the construction of this reality. Situation comedy humor depends heavily on the character types behaving according to or contrary to expectations in situations whose parameters do not have to be explained: the father who suddenly has to manage house and children, young women trying to be independent in the face of well-meaning overprotection, and the ups and downs of the family five with one child of each age. Situation dramas suppose that the audience is familiar with their problem *foci*. Whether or not the types, situations, and problems of television narratives are really those of daily life, they are surely those of television reality, which gives them completeness, significance, and relevance.

Generally television narratives present us with an art context resembling, in many respects, the kind of art of which Tolstoy meant to give an account, and not just because popularity is the operative criterion of evaluation. There are dissimilarities too, of course. The degree to which television constitutes an *ersatz* reality has no parallel in Tolstoy's theory, and there are many features of twentieth century sensibility that Tolstoy could not have anticipated. Still, if essential features of Tolstoy's model apply, television narrative has a general role to play in consolidating and raising the level of feeling in the culture; if he was at all correct about the direction of this upward development, then the television narrative should move the culture towards an increased perception of brotherhood among humankind. Obviously, Tolstoy could have been right about the general evolutionary claim and wrong about the specific direction the evolution of sensibility would actually take. He was, I think, generally right about both, though some of his specific "hobby-horse" prejudices are as wrong for the twentieth century as they were for his own century.

It is fairly obvious that there are and have been successful series that embody Tolstoy's ideals generally and specifically. *M.A.S.H.* fairly consistently stressed the brotherhood of humankind, deplored racial prejudice and warmongering, and reinforced these perceptions with the message of God's fatherhood and the blessedness of children in the persons of Father Mulcahy and Radar O'Reilly— all to eventual warm, popular approbation. *Hill Street Blues* regularly attacked racial prejudice, class prejudice, sexual prejudice, and mistreatment of the old, the young, and the uniformed; ultimately the message that beneath the skin, the age, the income, and the uniform all good people have a lot in common, was warmly accepted. Similar claims can be made about *L. A. Law*, *St. Elsewhere*, and *SOAP*. It seems obvious that such series are popular precisely because the feelings expressed are generally ahead of their time; these series are popular because they express feelings that a large number of people want to feel and feel they ought to feel, not because they express that unquestioned consensus of sentiment on which the majority daily act.

Certainly some popular series are intended to be ahead of their time. In one of the late episodes of *St. Elsewhere*, for example, a homosexual dying of AIDS asks a resident, who has become a "born again Christian," how it can be that God will not accept him unless he surrenders the very self that he has begun to find through his homosexual relationship. The religious perspective is not being mocked; though the viewer knows about the resident's fear that he has the AIDS virus, the resident is not presented as a hypocrite or as a Pascal-type believer. In this fair debate, the dying AIDS patient emerges the moral victor. This scene is not entirely an anomaly for *St. Elsewhere*; it is an extension, though a problematic and controversial one, of the usual message that the true perspective is one of the brotherhood of man under God without regard for sexual preferences, race (Luther, the one-time orderly, latterly medic), weight (Eliott, the obese resident), or personality quirks (Craig, the overbearing surgeon, and Ehrlich). Moreover, *St. Elsewhere* itself is not an anomaly. Something like this general ideology underlies a large number of situation comedies and dramas.

Of course, *St. Elsewhere*, like most situation dramas, regularly offers emotional truisms, sex, and violence. A Tolstoyan theory does not discriminate against truisms, however hackneyed. On the contrary, they have an important role to play. Truisms provide occasions for a broad range of feelings the average viewer can easily identify as his own best feelings and those of other good people who are united by a sense of rightness and humanity in a world increasingly complex and threatening: pity for children in pain and forsaken, the joy of Christmas, laughter at the foibles of the self-important, and anger at evildoers.

The less conservative message of brotherhood is all the more likely to be appropriated by the viewer, since it is embedded in a context which is to an appreciable extent unproblematically conventional in the emotional responses it elicits. If Tolstoy is right, it is reasonable to expect that these feelings are likely to surface in real life as well, partly by virtue of their having been appropriated by viewers as their own while watching these narratives.

Tolstoy would, of course, have deplored the sex, violence, and sensationalism of *St. Elsewhere* and its kind; but it is exactly this kind of "hobbyhorse" that renders his theory fanatical. For there are probably few feelings so universal as the love of high melodrama, curiosity about the lives of the young and the beautiful, sexual voyeurism, and amusement at banana peels, pies, and open trapdoors. The popularity of art which expresses such feelings is no problem for a Tolstoyan theory generally, however much it might have offended Tolstoy's personal sensibilities.

It is important to remember that the Tolstoyan model does not require that anybody intend the evolution of feeling principally, or even at all; "giving the viewers what they want" will, if Tolstoy is right, produce art works that effectively promote the best common denominator and gradually raise the level of perception in the culture. Equally important, it cannot be expected that in a diverse art context, *all* art will be forward moving. Much of art will simply serve the *status quo*. Finally, as long as earlier modes of feeling and sectarian differences are significantly represented, there will continue to be art that answers to these lower levels of feeling and to special, "provincial" interests.

Tolstoyan optimism seems to be seriously challenged, however, by very popular series which are arguably below the general level of feeling of the culture. In the face of great popularity, it is difficult to argue that some faction with reactionary sensibilities or some "provincials" are getting their way. Art that the general population seems deliberately to select for its lower levels of feeling is a problem for a Tolstoyan theory because it poses a counterinstance to the kind of benevolent "anthropology" of mass behavior that gives rise to the whole Tolstoyan perspective.

Certain kinds of problems can be singled out as particularly vexing for the Tolstoyan perspective. *Miami Vice*, for example, is a very popular police (good guy-bad guy) drama, conspicuous for its existential callousness and moral superficiality. *Smurfs*, a perennial Saturday morning cartoon favorite, is simplemindedly moralistic. *The Cosby Show*, a sitcom of record breaking popularity, seems to belong to a much earlier level of development of the TV sitcom; it has been criticized as dangerously bromidic and quietistic.

Miami Vice: **Dream Violence and Disaffection**

Miami Vice is an unusual good guy-bad guy drama because it has no moral center. *Vice* is low-slung, vacuous and highly polished. There is no sense that evil touches those outside the world of vice, and thus no contrast with innocence or right. Moreover, the main characters participate in the moral decentration in an unmotivated way. Detectives Crockett and Tubbs are regularly touched by evil because, as we are reminded by the ambiguity of *Miami Vice*, they are themselves vaguely within its circle. There is, however, no good reason for their being there. They are not pulled into a position of compromise by compassion or by the complexity of human situations or by their own mixed natures (a frequent theme of *Hill Street Blues*). They are not drawn by forces around them into an area where the moral order blurs beyond recovering (the theme of *Wise Guy, The Equalizer*). *Miami Vice* is morally unfocussed. It is hard to see what this sort of narrative could contribute to the consolidation and advancement of the evolution of feeling.

Miami Vice also has very little narrative or psychological order. The plots are either insubstantial or inchoate—sometimes both. In one 1987–88 episode, a well-to-do middleman (whom we meet alive only to see him snatched into a motel room and dropped over the balcony) is murdered because he is skimming the profits of a Japanese crime organization. The black prostitute who was with him at the time is eventually murdered too, though for no clear reason. On a psychological level, the episode is even more inchoate. Is Christine, the Madam for whom the prostitute works, and with whom Crockett has become involved romantically, just selfishly careless in sending the girl back to her own apartment . . . or does she more or less knowingly send her to her death? (Is *that* supposed to be the point of the silent, dreamlike, gold-and-green-tone sequence in which Christine's lovemaking with Crockett fades back and forth with the strangling of the prostitute? Does this interweaving of sex and violent death have a more sinister meaning? Or are we just being told that the strangling seen through a fishbowl greenly is occurring at the same time as sex between Christine and Crockett?) The lack of focus in plot, characterization, and imagery leaves questions about motivation and guilt forever hanging. The episode ends with a final exchange of disaffected remarks between Crockett and Christine:

Christine: You know the newspaper that's been crucifying me. . . . The publisher was one of my biggest clients. So was that little worm that does the editorials on Channel 8. They're bastards, all of them.

Crockett: That go for me too?

Christine: You might be the biggest one of all.

Now what is that supposed to mean? That Crockett is as hypocritical as the Johns *qua* reformers? Why should she think that? Again, this sort of question has no answer. Everyone on *Miami Vice* is just his or her superficial presence to the other. The characters have no emotional stake in each other, and the viewer thus has no avenue for emotional involvement with the characters. The lines talk of trust and betrayal, but there is no emotional reality underneath them, either for characters or for viewer.

The "culmination" to this episode is visual; it comes in the form of a climactic shootout with the Japanese Crime Lord in a white dreamscape interior with a wall of aquaria; the aquaria collapse in the gunfire, sending waterfalls cascading through the dreamscape, while a number of people are shot in slow motion. But the culmination answers no questions, moral or narrative. In "We Build Excitement," Gitlin says of *Miami Vice*: "Everything happens for the sake of display; *Vice* only makes sense if the viewer is willing to regard images as self-sufficient . . . that hurdle crossed, the viewer has to agree to suspend narrative disbelief and surrender to the trashy pleasure of sheer look and sound."[19] The "suspension of narrative disbelief" Gitlin refers to is no return to the ordinary, but the viewer's ceasing to expect a coherent fictional universe peopled with real characters.

Disordered narratives and a repeated thematic formula: moral miasma, dream violence, and disaffection. The popularity of *Miami Vice* offers a challenge to a Tolstoyan theory of television narrative, for it suggests that Tolstoy was wrong in thinking popular taste will effectively select works expressing the best values of the time. Todd Gitlin offers a critical account of *Miami Vice* which suggests a solution of sorts to the problem. Gitlin tends to see *Miami Vice* as an artistic expression of something unattractive, but perhaps unavoidable, in the spirit of our age (i.e., a deliberate lack of depth and definition—"blankness"). Like the "Lone Rider" of the car commercials with his sunglasses, who is all surface, all machine, *Miami Vice* reflects a modern perception that reality and relationships are all surface, all environment, that the ideal existence is a lone existence apart from the existing order:[20] "At one point the Renault driver, wearing mirror sunglasses, actually metamorphoses into his marvelous vehicle, his sunglasses turning into headlights. . . . Gazing into his sunglasses, his ensemble of admirers see only themselves; there is no one home, nothing but the reflection of his beholders. This might stand as a chilling image of his nothingness—but in a world composed of surfaces, it is only to be expected that a man is nothing but pure surface either."[21] Thus in Gitlin's account, *Miami Vice* is a genuine expression of a response to the modern predicament; its lack of meaning and depth are means to this expressive end. He is inclined to see the same message in much of modern art. This frightened and defiant retreat to the life of surfaces is perhaps not a very good response; Gitlin is inclined to believe that it is not. Yet a defiant and disordered recognition of a problem of insurmountable dimensions may yet be genuinely and widely felt. Indeed, though we have to go beyond Tolstoy to do so, it seems sensible to suggest that such a work may constitute a moment of some more lasting and lucid resolution.

Gitlin's critical estimate, in effect, asks us to construe superficiality as an obsession with surfaces and to equate lack of meaning with the denial of meaning; *Miami Vice*'s flaws are thus turned into artistic "virtues." *Miami Vice* becomes a piece of popular art which begins to approach, in its effect, the aggressively stark and alienating character of much of "exclusive" art.

Gitlin is undoubtedly right about the frequency *Miami Vice* operates on, and about the meaninglessness and the surface quality of *Vice* existence. *Miami Vice* is, however, very badly made; and this casts suspicion on the attempt to explain it as an artistic success, even an unappealing and disturbing one.

The *Miami Vice* narrative is incoherent because it is technically incompetent. It is often impossible to understand the lines. To some extent the problem is drawled and growled diction; to a greater extent, it is a mismatch of lines and body and eye movement. Lines that are ostensibly directed to another character are delivered instead to the camera or to the floor (to the lower left, as it happens); they fail to convey the sense that something is happening between these people. Thus no true dialogue occurs. Moreover, *Miami Vice* has serious problems with movement, which affect its credibility as fiction. The television drama relies very heavily on intention and direction in body movement to create a sense of narrative spatiotemporal continuity. When, for example, detective Hunter of *Hunter* charges out of an office, body tense with the press of anxiety, we have no doubt that the apartment we next see him charge into is where he was headed— and that he has "in the meantime" run the whole unseen "distance between." Intention physically manifest creates a coherent narrative space-time. *Miami Vice* tends, in contrast, to leave characters standing or slouching and pick them up standing somewhere else—or to show two characters leaving one scene and another character entering the next—with the result that it establishes no coherent narrative space and no sense of time elapsed during effort. Under these circumstances the plots have to be banal to be comprehensible; since the plot cannot be read narratively, the viewer has to rely on formulae and stereotypes known beforehand. The story of Crockett, Christine, and the Japanese Crime Lord falls apart precisely because it presents an unfamiliar formula to a viewer without supplying the information necessary for constructing a narrative. The result is an inchoate fictional universe, and the problem is further reinforced by nebulous characterization and ideological diffusion. Far from being a clear expression of blankness and formlessness, then, *Miami Vice* is distinguished by lack of coherent meaning on any level.

We have to search elsewhere, it seems, to explain *Miami Vice*'s popularity— or admit that it represents a puzzling counterinstance to a generally well-supported theory. Gitlin is drawn to his position because he assumes without question that *Miami Vice* is genuinely artistic. Why not start instead by questioning this assumption? In Tolstoy's theory, a "work" not arising from the need to express some genuine feeling, is not art at all.[22] Tolstoy calls such art "insincere." The absence of genuine feeling is notoriously difficult to verify, and Tolstoy adds that works not springing from genuine feeling can almost always be recognized by their lack of individuality and clarity. According to Tolstoy, works self-consciously put forward as art are, paradoxically, always in danger of ceasing to be genuine artistic expression. The artist surrenders to the pressure to produce successful art and loses touch with the real life of feeling: "Becoming ever poorer and poorer in subject matter, and more and more unintelligible in form, that art of the upper classes in its latest productions has even lost all the characteristics of art, and has been replaced by imitations of art . . . it has in the course of time ceased even to be art at all, and has been replaced by counterfeits."[23]

Counterfeit art arises, according to Tolstoy, when the idle demand for amusement is brought to bear on an artist already demoralized by the search for rarefaction and refinements. The "artist" is then driven to counterfeiting as a way of affecting the audience, an audience easily confused with the characteristic effect of art. Tolstoy's example of the "stupid, but highly cultured" lady author makes it clear that counterfeiting need not involve calculating cynicism, any more than creating genuine art requires being motivated by a sense of art's real mission. Counterfeiting is born of the spoiling atmosphere of an art culture eager for novelty, the self-delusion of the artist, and the pressure to produce.

One mark of the counterfeit is the presence of

action, often purely physical, on the outer senses. Work of this kind is said to be "striking," "effectual." In all arts these effects consist chiefly in contrasts—in bringing together the terrible and the tender, the beautiful and the hideous, the loud and the soft, darkness and light, the most ordinary and the most extraordinary . . . in painting, besides all kinds of other contrasts, one is coming into vogue which consists in giving careful finish to one object and being careless about the rest. . . . In drama, the most common effects besides contrasts are tempests, thunder, moonlight, scenes at sea or by the seashore, changes of costume, exposure of the female body, madness, murders and death generally: the dying person exhibiting in detail all the phases of agony.[24]

Another technique is "borrowing," which consists "in borrowing whole subjects, or merely separate features, from former works recognized by everyone as being poetical, and in so reshaping them with sundry additions that they should have an appearance of novelty. Such works, evoking in people of a certain class memories of artistic feelings formerly experienced, produce an impression similar to art."[25]

In employing the "striking effect," the artist seeks out an element that has a natural "charge," then exploits that undigested charge; the audience, having been powerfully affected, assumes that it has experienced a powerful work of art. Tolstoy clearly thinks that contrasts have a natural "charge" themselves, probably because sharp juxtapositions jar the senses and the imagination. He is thus led to construe contrasts of "rhetoric" or "finish" as instances of "striking effect." In "borrowing," on the other hand, the remembered effect of the individual "poetic" item affects the audience; because the remembered effect of the item is artistic, the audience mistakenly assumes that it has been affected by an art work. In each case, the strategy is in a sense the same: elements in the work affect the audience, but not by contributing to an organic, expressive whole (i.e., not artistically).

Clearly, *Miami Vice* lends itself to analysis as counterfeit art. A fair number of the striking effects on Tolstoy's list are, in fact, commonly found on *Miami Vice*. More importantly, *Vice* is a sustained study in contrast and "striking effects" strung together for visceral, serial effect. In the episode under discussion, for example, the final shootout occurs in a white dreamscape, a wall of water cascading through the fray, bodies flying backwards slowly with the impact of being shot; the viewer is offered the striking combination of slow motion, violent death, and flowing water. The dreamlike juxtaposition of sex and strangling is undeniably "effectful" in the same way—love and death in a slow motion dance.

Moreover, these scenes have an effect because novel camera techniques, interposed images, and jarring juxtapositions help to convince the viewer that he is in the presence of something Artistic. The clear indication that this is borrowing, and not genuine art, is that *Miami Vice* strings such elements together undigested, creating the ambiance of art, but no meaning. The water cascade has visual importance, but no meaning; there is really no point to anybody dying in slow motion here—there is nobody whose final moment it is significant to draw out. Similarly, there is no plot context for the sex-violence image to reinforce—these people are not doing violence to each other . . . they are not even interacting. Even the disaffection of *Miami Vice* is borrowed from classic tales of love, corruption, and betrayal in films and television series in which the characters have developed reasons for presenting only emotional surfaces to others. *Miami Vice* uses the ruse of existential lack of commitment to cover for acting without conviction.

Miami Vice gets a lot of mileage, too, out of not asking the viewer to take its narrative seriously. Like much "esoteric" art of the twentieth century, it calls attention to itself as art object. The white dreamscape interiors are not spaces for real existence, but objects of attention in themselves. *Vice* violence and *Vice* sex are usually in slow motion, often in monochrome, and frequently supplied with rock video sound; again the viewer is invited to watch the technique, appreciate the artistry, see how smoothly sex and violence can be filmed. The result is distance and viewer disaffection from the narrative. The car and boat chases for which *Miami Vice* is famous are narratively fractured by obviously unusual camera angles. Again the same message: think about the camera angle, the space . . . but don't take the story seriously . . . it's all done with surfaces.

Miami Vice is in fact seriously trying to establish the semblance of art that expresses the genuine sentiment credited to it by Gitlin. *Vice* pretends to be art which deals through innovative form with distance and disaffection as a response to the predicament of modern man: moral ambiguity, alienation, the threat of meaninglessness. It even pretends to that reflexive self-presencing quite common in twentieth century "esoteric" art. The result is the calculated illusion of moral and artistic sophistication. The illusion of sophistication sells. The *Miami Vice* viewer is rewarded with a warm sense of self-congratulation at having seen something morally and artistically worthwhile, the sort of program which appeals to people who can see through the moral blacks and whites of *Barnaby Jones* and *Dragnet*.

There is some question, I think, about whether *Miami Vice* would be popular on prime time TV if it were what it pretends to be, if it really forced viewers to face disaffection and the disintegration of meaning, or if it really had the aggressive self-presence and hostility of much "esoteric" art in this century. *Miami Vice is* popular because it is a slick counterfeit which makes none of the emotional and intellectual demands of genuine art, though it gives its audience the sense of having understood and responded to the real thing. Its popularity leaves open the question of whether there could be a real challenge to the Tolstoyan perspective in the form of a prime time popular series that really did express negativity, callousness, "blankness," and disaffection.

Smurfs: **Categories and Communal Values**

Saturday morning cartoon fare has been deplored for a generation. The time spot is a market place for anything that bleeps and squeaks at some inordinate price or rots teeth and upsets the healthy diet. With the exception of the moralizing cameo series, *One to Grow On,* the main Saturday morning fare is notable for the absence of an educational agenda (as compared to *Sesame Street*) or a serious moral program (as compared to, say, *Fraggle Rock*). It is fairly often assumed that Saturday morning cartoon series are of uniformly poor entertainment quality as well.[26]

Smurfs is a very popular, perennial Saturday morning cartoon series. The Smurfs are little blue creatures: Jokey Smurf (given to practical jokes), Farmer Smurf, Painter Smurf, Brainy Smurf (an intolerable pedant with glasses), the three young smurflings, Smurfette (the girl), Baby Smurf, and so on. There are occasional cameo appearances by Wild, who has grown up outside the village and squeaks and babbles in animal language, and Grandpapa Smurf, who is magical and constantly threatened with not being taken seriously by the younger Smurfs. The village is presided over by Papa Smurf, who perceives—more rarely pronounces—the moral of each episode. The Smurfs are menaced by the evil wizard Gargamel with his cat Azriel and apprentice Scruple and occasionally by other forces, like Morpheo, the Demon of Bad Dreams, Petulia, the narcissistic plant, and the various evils the Smurfs bring on themselves by the mindless search for novelty, carelessness, selfishness, shortsighted pedantry, scapegoating, and worse. Other series come and go, but the Smurfs stay on and on. If this series is really as bad artistically and as vapid morally as is commonly supposed, then either it has to be shown to be counterfeit art like *Miami Vice* or it presents a problem of sorts for a Tolstoyan theory—for its popularity would force us to suppose that children are insensitive either to art or to the claims of good feelings.

Certain charges which have been levelled at *Smurfs* (e.g., involvement in pernicious commercialism) fail to gain a purchase within the framework of a Tolstoyan theory. It may well be true that *Smurfs* is part of a deplorable strategy of scheduling cartoon series so as to profit from a terrible discovery: it is possible to sell anything to children from dolls to lunchboxes, when they are dazed by familiar cartoon images reflecting off every object that catches their eyes.[27] This alone, however, is not enough to condemn the series according to Tolstoyan theory. First, a distinction must be made between the execution or making of a work of art and the process of implementation, which has to do with the way the work is made present in the culture.[28] The artistic integrity of a work is not automatically impugned by even grossly nonartistic motivations in its implementation. Moreover, a Tolstoyan theory does not require pure motives from the artist; the desire to express feelings may easily come mixed with the ordinary diversity of motives found in everyday life—including self-importance and the desire for gain. To be condemned on Tolstoyan grounds, *Smurfs* has to be either counterfeit like *Miami Vice* or retrograde in the sentiments it expresses.

Unlike *Miami Vice*, *Smurfs* does have a clear positional orientation with respect to what it expresses and an integral relationship between narrative and what the narrative expresses. The variety of Smurfs serves to address the puzzling (to the child) fact that people are not all alike by offering a system of psychological types. The unresolvable differences between kinds of people is a pervasive and important theme; at the ends of most episodes, Papa Smurf turns to his audience with an all-expressive wink, as if to say, "The peculiar excesses of Brainy's or Handy's or Jokey's type can be curbed, and ought to be, but you can't change the way people are . . . and we wouldn't want to, would we?''

Equally important thematically is the reduction of situations to situation types. Gargamel's newest smurf-catching contraption is just another overcomplicated snare that can be eluded by cooperation and by using every smurf's absosmurfly special talents.[29] Indeed, *Smurfs* generally brings a wide variety of problems down to their common denominator. For example, Lazy eventually realizes he can rescue his companions from the land of Morpheo only if he can realize that he is not helpless before the nightmares that are *his particular* Nemesis—*Smurfs* never has the theme that a personal Nemesis is not real—just as all the Smurfs learn that they have to face and take control of the situation to rejoin the Good Papa Smurf and the Bad Papa Smurf into their familiar and beloved father figure. All of the really knowing characters on *Smurfs* are distinguished by being able to predict behavior and outcomes using their knowledge of character types and situation types.

The other consistent focus of *Smurfs* is the problem of individual versus community. Again and again the Smurfs learn the consequences of one individual's pursuit of his/her own interests without thinking of the consequences for the community. The smurflings want to bring their new playmate to the village festival, despite the safety rule that strangers are never to be brought to the village; their playmate turns out to be Gargamel in disguise. Handy builds a smurfominium (!), indulging his passion for the new and technological at the expense of others' comfort and well-being and ignoring the claims of the tried and the true; the thing burns, nearly burning all of them with it. Brainy gets carried away with the intellectual sport of winning his court case and nearly gets someone convicted of letting Baby stray into danger when he is himself guilty of the offense; they are all so absorbed in their courtroom drama that Baby gets away again. And so on. *Smurfs* is obviously dealing here with the problems of a very young audience that is beginning to realize that actions have social reality and consequences. As in dealing with the problem of differences among people, *Smurfs* has a very consistent ideological focus. This focus is embodied in the narratives, that actually turn on the issues they raise, though they have their liberal share of banana peel humor, crazy chase scenes, and Road Runner gags. Papa Smurf normally does not pronounce the moral of the story at the end of the episode. He winks. He shrugs. As if to say, "Well, you see how it is." And the young viewership certainly does see how it is. (In such series as *She-ra* and *He-man*, by contrast, some character has to announce the moral as an afterthought, since it is more or less extrinsic to the action of the episode; more often than not, the moral is some sort of mishmash about being true to oneself.)

Smurfs clearly does not have the marks of counterfeit art. Is it, then, an estimable artistic series? That depends on whether what it expresses is true and "forward moving." The moral psychology of *Smurfs* is not very sophisticated. At the risk of belaboring the obvious, it has to be remembered that *Smurfs* is aimed at a very young audience. Tolstoy does not consider the problem of children's literature, and would very likely not have conceded that the special needs of the child audience place special demands on the artist. Common sense would seem to dictate a modification of theory here, however. Surely a sensible Tolstoyan theory can require at most that children's art express feelings that are not retrograde *relative to the child's position.*

Smurf episodes are, of course, repetitive and unsurprising in their themes. But Tolstoyan theory does not condemn an art work because it is repetitive in form and content or because it expresses predominantly truisms. If the truisms are genuine truths of the heart, however simple, and not empty platitudes or dangerous oversimplifications and bromides, and if these truths find genuine artistic expression, then the work stands vindicated on a Tolstoyan theory, however little competition it may offer to the outstanding works of "exclusive" art favored by most post-Renaissance theories of art. Moreover, here the repetition and the truisms serve a purpose that is genre specific. Young viewers are learning, much as they would from beast fables, to accept human character types as fact, and even to think of differences of this sort as good and interesting. Moreover, they are learning to type, generalize, project and solve human equations. They are learning, too, as they would from "Dance of Death" literature, that each kind of person confronts the ultimate problems of existence in the form that speaks to his or her character. *Smurfs* is properly classed with these other kinds of parable narratives, and thus genre considerations alone suffice to defeat the charge that the series is predictable and moralistic. It belongs to a predictable and moralistic genre family that has traditionally had a pedagogical focus and purpose.

Smurfs does not, however, stand wholly vindicated. Despite the general value of learning to classify by psychological type and character traits, there are problems with the particular scheme *Smurfs* adopts. Smurfette, for example, is an unfortunate type. Handy builds things. Painter paints pictures. Smurfette is A Girl. Jokey and Brainy are personifications of morally relevant character traits. Smurfette has some morally relevant character traits—she loves beauty, is vain and superficial, but warmhearted; but she has these traits *by virtue of being a girl*. Smurfette has also got an unfortunate history. She is a kind of gift to smurfkind, since she was, it turns out, invented by Gargamel, and sent to spy on and betray the Village. Papa Smurf's magic turned her into the good Smurfette, now blond; but there lurks ever in Smurfette the possibility of turning once more to evil, as well as Pandora's talent for opening things and inviting things home that would be much better left alone. Smurfette is an instance of an undesirable icon for a children's program, since it reinforces the following view: girls are fundamentally weaker morally, sexual differences are morally relevant, and girls do not do the sorts of things that can be taken seriously in the real world.

The typing of Smurfette is not part of the message of the series; it is instead a fact of the narrative universe. But it is not thereby rendered innocuous. On the contrary, as a "fact" it is all the more likely to be assimilated without question and stored in a general memory of "the way things generally are" until a later point in the child's development; then it can emerge to do some real motivational damage. Tolstoy was himself not very sensitive to artistic effects that are not part of the intended, expressed message, but certainly this is a deficiency in any theory which makes essential use of the role of art in the cultural development of feelings and perceptions.

The communalism of *Smurfs* is problematic as well. Handy learns from the fate of his smurfominium to give up his dreams of innovation and go back to fixing mushroom-shaped houses for his little friends. Harmony Smurf learns it is better to play with the group so everyone can have fun than to play beautifully but in a way that makes others feel bad. Such episodes are mindlessly positive about the value to be found in community, and viscerally negative about independence, innovation, and resistance to authority.

The mindless communalism of *Smurfs*, which is not just a narrative fact, but something explicitly expressed, is a problem because it is a half-truth, an oversimplification. As such it is not very likely to be perceived as false by a viewership having as yet very little articulate experience against which to measure it. Again, it is not clear that the communalism of *Smurfs* would have been perceived by Tolstoy as a problem. This is partly because communalism would have had to be very mindless indeed in order to have been perceived negatively by Tolstoy, and partly because he was epistemologically insensitive to problems of oversimplification and half-truths.

There are, then, good reasons for objecting to *Smurfs*, though they are not the ones usually given, and not ones obvious to the intended viewers, who respond favorably to the persistent sense of moral order in the universe and to a well-integrated and good natured mix of laughs, magic, adventure, and folk wisdom. The popularity of *Smurfs* is not a mystery or a problem in principle for a Tolstoyan theory, but it motivates a demand for a more sophisticated and highly differentiated epistemology and a more complex theory of modes of artistic meaning.

The Cosby Show: **Home Truths or Bromides?**

After watching Rudy's daddy spend the better part of an afternoon staging a fashion show so the little darling can regain her equilibrium by modeling her crisp weather designer threads before her admiring mother and siblings, the folks at home presumably rise from their chintz sofa vowing to spend more afternoons restoring one another's self-esteem.

But does it really work that way? Do all those scenes of TV families venting their feelings really facilitate communication between aloof, hostile, or withdrawn family members in the real world? . . . Better to trust our own reactions—including the depression evoked by the show's idealized images. In real life, if not on TV, we are painfully aware of the powerful forces working to make us strangers to those who ought to be our loved ones.[30]

The members of the Cosby TV family certainly *are* unrelentingly constructive. They certainly do succeed in solving all their problems by talking and thinking and acting them through. In the end, father's or mother's perspicacity and love always win the day. The real world, Bayles says, is not very much like the Huxtables' world; the forces at work are too powerful, she thinks, to be dealt with as the Huxtables deal with their problems. Indeed, viewers who take the Huxtables as their models are likely to end up disillusioned and depressed by the distance between ideal and reality. Bayles' review ends by recommending, reasonably enough, several television narratives which deal more realistically with the psychological and social evils surrounding us.

A Tolstoyan theory does not discriminate against truisms which are true, but well-worn. Platitudes and bromides, by contrast, are false. Sometimes they are dangerously false, since they can create a false sense of reality. The sense of reality expressed by platitudes like, "Like father, like son," is impoverished by the false economy of a hasty, usually one-sided summation. Bromides like "Love conquers all," license quietism where energy and vigilance are called for. The immense popularity of *The Cosby Show* poses a problem for a Tolstoyan theory if what it expresses is misleading in either of these senses, no matter how pleasant and loving its overall message is.

This sort of criticism is typical of one source of resistance to *The Cosby Show*. The series is also, in many respects, a throwback to the *Father Knows Best* period. The problems are defined within the family circle, realized in a shallow way, and invariably resolved; all of this seems to ignore the advances of MTM and Norman Lear sitcoms. In *The Cosby Show*, the characters and their ranges of reactions are strongly stereotyped by age and sex. Most of the dialogue is half-addressed to the audience, so that the viewer becomes a shadow participant in the narrative. Partly as a result of this, narrative integrity and plausibility are generally very low; it is not possible to believe the events are happening and not just being acted. Unlike *Happy Days*, which always played with an ironic distance from its 1950s model, *The Cosby Show* follows its paradigm with simple fidelity. A Tolstoyan theory does not, of course, discriminate against a return to simpler, purer forms. But atmospheric archaizing is, as Tolstoy points out, a conspicuous and cheap form of counterfeiting;[31] and the unimaginative adoption of older forms is borrowing, pure and simple.

In order to assess the force of these criticisms, we need to make explicit a distinction we have had occasion to invoke before, the difference between *what properties a narrative has* and *what the narrative expresses*. *Miami Vice is* meaningless, but it does not express meaninglessness, since it does not express anything. *Smurfs has* a girl-type who does girl things; but it is not part of the message of the series that this is what girls are like. This second example shows that a feature of a narrative need not be part of the work's explicit message or theme to have a problematic moral-psychological effect on viewers. Traditional Tolstoyan theories are concerned mainly with problems having to do with expression. But once it is recognized that properties can possess moral and artistic importance, even if they are not expressed, a theory relating art to moral evolution is obliged to take cognizance of such properties.

The Cosby Show is a genre comedy, a 1950s father-knows-best comedy. It has the usual characteristics of its type: contrived spaces, blurred viewer distance, family orientation, and overresolution. It also *expresses* the typical themes that life with kids is cute and that love and understanding conquer all.

If *The Cosby Show* conveyed to viewers, even by virtue of its constitution as a fictional universe, literal models for talking and acting out problems, then Bayles' half-serious vision of viewers rising from their sofas and acting like Huxtables and becoming disillusioned and depressed as a result would have negative force. But the talk and actions of works in this genre are not simple facts of the narrative like Smurfette and her ways; they are rather a conventional externalization of thought and feeling, like Hamlet's soliloquies. The verbalizations are partly addressed to the audience, the intended perceiver of the cuteness, transparency, or natural wisdom of what has been said. The other characters' reactions serve to include the audience. (Cliff Huxtable's indulgent smile is not directed at his daughter Rudy; that kind of reaction would stop her cuteness dead. It is intended to say to the audience, "See how cute and how universal this child's reaction is . . . smile with me at her and all the children among us." His smile does not occur in the narrative; it is commentary.) *The Cosby Show* does not teach a literal behavioral lesson because it is precluded from doing so by its dramatic form. Instead, it uses a transparently conventionalized situation in order to express a comment, in this instance the comment that children's balkiness (and maybe balkiness in general . . . who knows? . . . who knows indeed?) may well be due to their not understanding situations. *The Cosby Show* is thus importantly different in dramatic form from such shows as *The Waltons*, where people observe unrevealing silences, react dramatically to each other, and fail to come to a resolved understanding of their situations. The kind of work it *is* protects *The Cosby Show* from a part of Bayles' objection.

The Cosby Show would have the literal consequences Bayles worries about, then, only if its conventions were taken literally (i.e., if it were misread). Whatever potential for misreading the genre may have had in its period of first currency, its conventions are now so thoroughly entrenched that we can safely banish the half-serious vision of audiences rising from their sofas for family fashion shows.

On the other hand, this sort of defense focusses much more on the second objection that what works of this kind *do* express is wrong. For example, there are, as Bayles thinks, problems within the family circle for which the love-and-understanding formula is drastically inadequate. More seriously, perhaps, there are problems in the family circle whose manifestations cannot find adequate resolution there because they are due to imbalances outside the family. There is here a certain confluence of the criticisms of substance made by Bayles, and others' criticisms of *The Cosby Show* for being a throwback artistically, for it is partly due to this lack of honesty regarding its problem focus and the deficient scope and depth of its solutions that the series is alleged to compare unfavorably with such series as *All in the Family*.

In fact, why would anyone want to create a show like this in the 1980s, when even the popular viewer is accustomed to much more sophisticated and complex material and modes of presentation? The answer, I think, is fairly clear: The known properties of 1950s family comedies, *and* the themes such works typically express, are being exploited to some further end. In addition to the properties which father-knows-best series had in their period of currency, they have *now* the properties of understandability, transparency, and familiarity. It is principally these latter properties, which have to do with presenting an earlier form to a later audience, that are being exploited by mounting *now* a show of this kind. The black family is being assimilated to the familiar, the ordinary, the next-door. More ambitiously, the black male professional is being presented as ir-refragable fact, as the usual, the familiar, in his exercise of authority. With respect to the facts of its universe, with respect to what it presupposes, *The Cosby Show* thus has a considerably more advanced agenda than *Good Times* or *The Jeffersons*, which intended to express the perception that black people are people too. *The Cosby Show* never expresses this theme because it is determined to establish a universe where race is not an issue.

In its expression, *The Cosby Show* conveys truisms at best and bromides as a rule. In contrast, by *using* this sort of narrative with its traditional expressive qualities in combination with the kind of properties such narratives have now acquired, the series presents a radical revision of feelings and perceptions about racial differences. This is an ambitious strategy, and one whose effectiveness has yet to be proved, whereas the more conservative approach of giving a realistic exposition of the problem and coming to a well articulated sense of its sources and a mature nonsolution has been well established, notably by Norman Lear.

The strategy of *The Cosby Show* has heavy costs artistically. Restriction to the familiar, the nonthreatening, the unchallenging, is bound to produce a lack of dramatic tension at best; at worst, the result is a desperate reaching for the viewer's sympathy and laughter through cloying and belabored stereotypes. Moreover, in order radically to exclude serious issues, *The Cosby Show* must operate within a very circumscribed physical universe, leaving a lot of questions unanswered. (What are the schools actually like that these children attend? How do the neighbors feel about having the Huxtables on the street?) More seriously, episodes involving the older children are inevitably shallow because the universe of discourse, too, is narrowly circumscribed; the family is made to serve as the whole universe for problems which are obviously broader in scope (e.g., Theo's underachieving and Denise's choice of a college). This is perhaps just another way of observing that *The Cosby Show* cannot be seriously problem-oriented if it is to deal with the main problem it has set itself.

The Cosby Show is popular partly because its truisms of feeling and perception are in fact true and are identified by the audience as good. The falsity of the bromides and platitudes is to some extent discounted because they are dispensed with charm, humor, and conviction, and are known to be genre specific; to some extent, no doubt, they are embraced because the audience so wishes they were true. It may be, too, that the deeper agenda of the series exerts an attraction, if only as a perceived easing of a tension felt culturewide.

CONCLUSION

Unlike the two previous cases, *The Cosby Show* raises unavoidably a problem in the cultural psychology of art which requires resources technically beyond Tolstoy's theory, and indeed beyond the resources of any theory that makes expression the sole significant dimension of aesthetic meaning. This problem was raised in passing by *Smurfs*, as it became obvious that some of the effects of the series having to do with moral psychology are not really part of its expressive ideology, but are due to the constitution of the fictional universe. *Miami Vice* ends up not causing a problem because it is not art, even on the popular level; but it raises in theory the problem of how to deal with a popular work that expresses meaninglessness, alienation, and the threat of inhumanity as a condition of existence. A Tolstoyan theory can, of course, condemn such works as genuine, but bad art. But this vastly underestimates the complicated course of moral development, in which the desperate and disordered response, the moment of defiant acceptance, and the deliberate embracing of evil, all have their role to play in creating a pattern which is positive in the larger scheme of things.

Each case, at least in its broader applications, indicates a need for modification and for further articulation of a Tolstoyan theory. For example, there is a need to better understand how fictional universes function cognitively and to develop a more sophisticated moral epistemology. None of these cases or their broader applications, however, pose a serious challenge to the validity of Tolstoy's general picture concerning art's cultural function or to using his theory about the evolution of sentiment as the basis of an aesthetic theory for the television narrative. This, I think, is because Tolstoy's account is essentially correct for this sort of art form.

Attempts to deal with the television narrative as myth or ritual go in somewhat the same direction as Tolstoy's theory. A Tolstoyan account has the advantage, however, of being more inclusive; in addition to being a theory connecting art to its roots in everyday life and cultural fact, it is an aesthetic theory, and one explicitly designed to include art conscious of itself as art. As a result it can ground, as theories of myth and ritual cannot, a responsible and insightful critical practice.

It is certainly not ruled out that some television narratives may also fare well under the critical theories customarily used to evaluate esoteric art. In fact, it is probably to be hoped that an increasing number of television narratives will be of this kind. But it seems clear that television narratives belong fundamentally to an art which demands a different kind of aesthetic theory, one connecting the TV narratives to the important popular art of ages past. It is this essential desideratum for a theory of television narrative that the Tolstoyan theory satisfies.

NOTES

1. "Popular art" has no special technical force here. It applies to art having wide acceptance and for which this acceptance plays a decisive role in determining the survival of works and developmental trends. It follows from this specification that a work may be popular art at one time and not at another; many nineteenth-century novels may have undergone a change of status of this sort.

2. A theory does not count as useful or sympathetic with respect to an art context simply by ruling works acceptable or good which other theories condemn. Rather, a useful or sympathetic theory is one that (a) can accept and explain the canons of the area (e.g., that simple repetition is the canonical form of recapitulation in folk music); and (b) can validate intuitively obvious quality distinctions within the area.

3. Leo Tolstoy, *What Is Art?*, trans. Aylmer Maude (New York: Liberal Arts Press, 1960), 51.

4. Ibid., 139.

5. Ibid., 51. For an examination of the meaning of "feeling" as Tolstoy uses the term, refer to Gary Jahn, "The Aesthetic Theory of Leo Tolstoy's *What is Art?*," *Journal of Aesthetics and Art Criticism* 34(1)(Fall 1975), 60–62.

6. Ibid., 52–53.

7. Ibid., 53–54. For an examination of Tolstoy's notion of religious perception, including important material from the later essay, "What is Religion and Wherein Lies Its Essence?" see Jahn, "The Aesthetic Theory," 63–64.

8. Tolstoy never actually addresses the question of the individual's purpose in sharing his feeling artistically, indeed in sharing them at all. The boy in Tolstoy's example, ibid., 50–51, who has been frightened by a wolf, just does set out to try to make everyone else feel the fear he has felt. For Tolstoy, this personal impulse to bring others to share one's emotions seems to have the status of a basic human fact not subject to further explanation or analysis.

9. Ibid., 52. The claim of Gary Jahn, in "The Aesthetic Theory of Leo Tolstoy's

What Is Art?,'' p. 60, that "the perceiver of a work of art is infected when he understands what is expressed in the work,'' is not correct, since it implies that there can be infection in Tolstoy's sense without participation in the feeling.

10. Tolstoy, *What Is Art?*, 54.

11. Tolstoy spends the first chapter of *What Is Art?* on a description of an opera rehearsal and its human costs which anticipates the wicked humor of the film *Network*.

12. Tolstoy is surely tempted to reserve the designation "religious perception" for the best level of feeling of an age. (Cf. ibid., 54, where he says, "Religions are the exponents of the highest comprehension of life accessible to the best and foremost men at a given time in a given society—a comprehension toward which, inevitably and irresistibly, all the rest of that society must advance.") But he cannot afford to yield to this temptation, theoretically speaking; and his overall position is that "religion" designates an area of content—the meaning of life, etc.,—and that the lower, more obscure and retrograde feelings of a culture are religious, and therefore capable of being expressed artistically, but badly.

13. Ibid., 151–52. Tolstoy sometimes seems to require only that universal art cause all people to have the same feelings. He says on page 151, "draw them to greater and ever greater union and make them ready for and capable of such union." On this account it is the role of art with an explicitly Christian content to bring mankind to a consciousness of this united feeling which universal art causes to exist. More often he seems to require, in addition (or more probably, to assume), that in feeling such universal feelings people *also* sense the feeling as universal and uniting. This is clearly the thrust of his example of the performance that "unites them all as by an electric flash, and in place of their former isolation or even enmity they are conscious of union and mutual. Each . . . feels the mysterious gladness of a communion which, reaching far beyond the grave, unites us with all men of the past who have been moved by just the same feelings, and with all men of the future who will yet be touched by them," 150–51.

14. Todd Gitlin, *Inside Prime Time* (New York: Pantheon Books, 1983), 47–55.

15. Thomas Schatz, "*St. Elsewhere* and the Evolution of the Ensemble Series," in *Television: The Critical View*, 4th ed., ed. Horace Newcomb (Oxford: Oxford University Press, 1987), 85–100. Cf. also Gitlin, *Inside Prime Time*, 273–324.

16. Jane Feuer, "The MTM Style," in *Television: The Critical View*, 4th ed., ed. Horace Newcomb (Oxford: Oxford University Press, 1987), 52–84.

17. A spot check of the plot synopses of daytime "soaps" revealed, in addition to the usual stock of births, deaths, marriages, infidelities, mental illness and market intrigues, the following: two cases of AIDS (*All my Children, Another World*); sending aid to South American Freedom Fighters (*Another World*); breast cancer (*The Bold and the Beautiful*); sexual molestation as a child (*Loving*); alleged wife abuse (*One Life to Live*); a lawsuit against a surrogate mother (*Santa Barbara*); computer theft (*Days of Our Lives*); and drug selling and alleged drug selling (*Guiding Light*).

18. Robert C. Allen, "*The Guiding Light*: Soap Opera as Economic Product and Cultural Document," in *Television: The Critical View*, 4th ed., ed. Horace Newcomb (Oxford: Oxford University Press, 1987), 149–162.

19. Todd Gitlin, "We Build Excitement," in *Watching Television*, ed. Todd Gitlin. (New York: Pantheon Books, 1986).

20. Ibid., 156–161.

21. Ibid., 139.

22. Note that although Tolstoy does not require that the artist intend to achieve the

consolidation and advance of better feelings, he does strongly require that the artist intend to infect others with his own feelings—for whatever reason.

23. Tolstoy, *What Is Art?*, 99. cf. n. 3.

24. Ibid., 102.

25. Ibid., 100.

26. *Berenstain Bears* and the cartoon series *Fraggle Rock* are obvious exceptions to such generalizations, but neither is a true member of the Saturday tradition. *Berenstain Bears* is a development of a best-selling series of books about children's problems, and *Fraggle Rock* is derived from the puppet show of the same name, again an exercise in child-level moral psychology.

27. Tom Engelhardt, "The Shortcake Strategy," in *Watching Television*, ed. Todd Gitlin (New York: Pantheon Books, 1986), 73–74.

28. Nelson Goodman, "Implementation of the Arts," *The Journal of Aesthetics and Art Criticism* 40.3 (Spring 1982): 281–83.

29. No one who values the English language is going to have much appreciation for "absosmurfly," "everysmurf," "unsmurfy," "smurf over here," and the like. In general, however, it is likely that young viewers learn something about word structure and creative word use from this butchery. Such gaffs as "absosmurfly," show that the principles are sometimes misapplied, since syllabic interchange is not a live option in English.

30. Martha Bayles, "Christmas With the Huxtables," *The Wall Street Journal*, 24 December 1987, 20.

31. Tolstoy, *What Is Art?*, 103.

7

Richard Chamberlain's *Hamlet*

Theoharis C. Theoharis

Like Shakespeare's theater, American television presents its narratives virtually indiscriminately. Anyone can afford admission, and almost anyone can find something to like. Such accessibility has earned television much of the suspicious censure it earned Shakespeare's Globe, which was located outside city limits because London's government deemed the copious world mirrored on that stage not properly governed or governable morally. That Shakespeare's art now appears on television as sanctified programming that validates the medium, as experience twice deemed fit for inclusion in the elite grandeur of *The Hallmark Hall of Fame* series, is one of life's more delicious ironies. It was not ever thus. Throughout the nineteenth century, Shakespeare's plays were immensely popular on stages all over America, in authentic and bowdlerized versions whose inventive transformations far exceeded the extravagances of a Tate, for instance, in their free appeal to contemporary morals and taste. Lawrence Levine's *Highbrow/Lowbrow: The Emergence of Cultural Hierarchy in America* offers an account of how our present intimidated, dutiful, and secretly bored official approbation of Shakespeare came about.[1]

The first *Hallmark Hall of Fame Hamlet*, which was broadcast in 1950, and starred Maurice Evans, is as fustian an example of reverent TV homage to "the Bard" as can be found. The second, which appeared twenty years later and starred Richard Chamberlain, has none of the first production's fraudulent artiness, but relies for its force instead on the genial romantic appeal which Chamberlain had established as the fabulously popular intern in *Dr. Kildare*, which went off the air in 1966, four years before his *Hamlet* was broadcast. Directed by Peter Wood, adapted for television by the eminent English Shakespearean John Barton, distinguished by Michael Redgrave's dapper and comically accomplished performance as Polonius, this production set Chamberlain in very elegant company. Having performed the role in Birmingham two years earlier, Chamberlain gave the television version as much elegance and technical mastery as it demanded. He is not an actor memorable for projecting an inexplicable variety of thought and emotion through short or extended sequences, but despite the fact that this was a production of *Hamlet*, such a performance was not required of him. Powerful and very suave, the second *Hallmark Hall of Fame Hamlet* presents Shakespeare's most extravagantly copious and problematic work as a revenge melodrama with a romantic lead who suffers no ambiguity or ambivalence. This Hamlet is a charming, put upon subordinate, moving in a world where life and death decisions for which he is held responsible are controlled by older and not better men. For all the publicity to the contrary preceding the broadcast, there is more than a whiff of the revolted intern in Chamberlain's and Wood's conception of this handsomely troubled Prince. Whether deliberately or not, the popular reputation of the star lead set the aesthetic direction of this performance.

The necessary conditions for that outcome were quite deliberately chosen, as Richard Chamberlain made clear in a short essay that appeared in the Sunday Leisure Section of *The New York Times* two days before the broadcast.

My Hamlet is, I confess, against the prevailing fashion. Contemporary Hamlets, from Sir Alec Guinness twenty years ago to Nicol Williamson the other day, have been determined antiheroes, rough figures slouching to their fate. Our version is, avowedly and unashamedly romantic, a revival of that earlier and longer-lived tradition that includes such Hamlets as those of Irving, Barrymore, Gielgud, and Redgrave, the prince as a Byronic hero. Peter Wood has set *Hamlet* in the Regency period. In its shortened (two-hour) television version, the play becomes more of a revenge melodrama, the popular entertainment of the early nineteenth century. That era was close to our own in its fashions and attitudes, so that the play's contemporary qualities are emphasized.[2]

The logic of such a paragraph might well cause the most generous academic's knotted and combined locks to part. Here we have revenge melodrama cited as an early nineteenth century popular form resurrected and dressed out in Regency period as a means of making *Hamlet* current for a late twentieth century audience. Quixotically and regretfully one thinks of Thomas Kyd, or more ruefully, of the notion that the permanently contemporary qualities of inherited dramatic masterpieces are evident enough in their intellectual and mimetic structures not to require representation in antiquarian costuming.

Succumbing however to the little learning displayed in these remarks, fretful academics can discover that this performance operates on clear aesthetic principles of heroes and villains, driving action, and thrilling entertainment guaranteed by the sexual appeal of a maligned righter of wrongs. The Byronic paradox of criminal virtue and Satanic salvation is a cogent dramatic conception of the Prince, and apparent in Shakespeare's text, but absent from Chamberlain's performance, which is Byronic only because it is sexy and often self-consciously overwrought. But that combination made Chamberlain popular on television long before he appeared as Hamlet, and popular appeal in and of itself is not damaging to any performance of Shakespeare's plays, in fact belongs to them intrinsically. That *Hamlet* should be popular on television is all to the good, politically and imaginatively. In fact, one good reason to reconsider Chamberlain's performance twenty years after it was last broadcast rests in the special way his fashionable appeal clarifies Shakespeare's more problematic presentation of conventionally approved heroism. As should be the case, what this Hamlet cannot do is as important as what he can.

That television can narrate with aesthetic self-consciousness, complex plotting, and ideational tension and scope is rarely apparent in this performance. All dramatized narratives reach us through the eye and ear more or less simultaneously. Television's primary narrative distinction from the theater lies in that ability, which it shares with cinema, to control what we see with complete authority. Working with synchronized electronic sounds and images instead of living bodies moving in three dimensional space, televised drama can articulate the action of a play, its pace and structural values, with much more precision than virtually any theatrical performance. In its composition and camera movement in individual shots, and its continuity from shot to shot, this *Hamlet* is technically accomplished and often beautiful. Resourcefully grafted onto Chamberlain's doe-eyed television fame, this production makes good use of the medium's special capacity for intimate development of characters and their relations. The following analysis of two scenes indicates what dramatic substance that beauty draws the mind's eye to watch through the camera's.

In act I scene iv Hamlet, Horatio, and Marcellus have come to the battlements (where the opening scene is shot) to wait for the midnight reappearance of the ghost. A trumpet flourish announces the revel promised by the king to celebrate Hamlet's decision to remain in Denmark. Hamlet describes the king's drinking games to Horatio and complains that the reputation for drunkenness those games have gained the Danes abroad has preempted recognition of their courageous deeds. He then moralizes on the lethal damage which even trivial faults wreck on the honor of otherwise blameless men. The ghost appears and beckons Hamlet away. After threatening to murder his comrades when they, fearful of his safety, restrain him, Hamlet leaves. In the play's text they follow him on the famous line "Something is rotten in the state of Denmark." In the broadcast their departure and the line are omitted.

Hamlet's moralizing on virtue and reputation in this scene can be played in many ways, but two basic readings of the lines cover most interpretive possibilities. Investigating the fortunes of honor, contemplating the life of active virtue, Hamlet begins to establish his heroic identity in this scene. Till this point in Shakespeare's text, Horatio has taken on the exemplary Renaissance role of scholar/soldier, the man adept at active and contemplative life; now Hamlet, by association, and substitution, assumes the role. Where Horatio's sighting and interpretation of the ghost make up the dramatic action of the first battlement scene, Hamlet's sighting and response to the same ghost in the same place, an event arranged by Horatio, forms the action of this scene. Horatio expatiates on history and queries the meaning of portents after seeing the ghost, correctly surmising that Hamlet could summon more meaning from the apparition. In all this there is no change of fortune for Horatio. Hamlet observes how frail the possibilities of honorable action are before seeing the specter, and after the visitation is left with a command to revenge which he carries out only after three dishonorable murders. These changes in fortune certainly violate the stipulation that Hamlet should not taint his mind in acting virtuously for the sake of his father's and Denmark's honor, and in retrospect, make Hamlet's exposition of honor's weakness ironically confessional. But when he talks so poignantly of honor, Hamlet could only hypothetically be observing his own case at this point in the drama. If Hamlet directs the analysis of vainly soiled honor to Horatio or Marcellus, or to both, the emphasis shifts from establishing his identity to dramatizing some attitude he has about either or both of theirs. Of course, both intentions could be dramatized simultaneously in the scene, since they are not mutually exclusive. Hamlet could be defensively musing about his own future actions as well as warning his friends about theirs. Wood shoots the conversation as an intimate recognition scene for Hamlet and Horatio, with Marcellus moving into Hamlet's loving instruction of an adoring, much younger Horatio, to announce the fearful interruption of the momentarily forgotten ghost. Hamlet's dismay over the exaggerated censure heroic men suffer for incidental deviation from a sanctioned norm has little conscious self-absorption in it, as shot in this production. It is all done for Horatio.

The scene opens with a medium shot of the misty battlements, cuts to a profile of Hamlet rocking his head on the line "The air bites shrewdly," and muffling his neck on "it is very cold," loosens to include Horatio in a close-up two-shot which includes a cross to the rear for Marcellus on Horatio's line "It is a nipping and an eager air", cuts to Hamlet in profile again for "What hour now?", and cuts to a three shot for an announcement of the time. On the flourish of the trumpets, the camera cuts to a close-up of Horatio for the line "What mean's this, my lord?" which is followed by the longest shot so far, four lines for Hamlet, done in close-up during which he describes the king's drinking games, turning his face partly toward and away from Horatio. In this sequence, Chamberlain archly derides Claudius and all his works, and lets Hamlet enjoy charging the vowels in "Rhenish," "bray," and "triumph," with a contempt that proclaims his own immunity from Denmark's vice.

The cut to a close-up for Horatio's line "Is it a custom," followed by a long two-shot during which Hamlet starts his moralizing on reputation, changes the mood. As Horatio laughs at Hamlet's irony about custom's breach and observance, Hamlet turns the conversation immediately serious for three lines, forgetting his hatred of Claudius to impress upon an abashed Horatio the significance of the moral loss carousing costs in the world at large. On the line "So, oft it chances in particular men," the camera cuts to Hamlet in close-up, who with a softened face, and lowered, slowed voice delivers his regretful analysis of un-merited scorn. On the word "guilty" the camera cuts to Horatio, who opens his chastened eyes in surprise and alarm till the camera returns to Hamlet, whose voice has become even softer and more conciliatory. His words measured with more and more gravity, the Prince spins a startling sardonic note over the word "grace," in the line "Their virtues else, be they as pure as grace," lowers his face and raises his brows on the word "corruption" in the next line, and gives a muffled staccato to the word "particular," which precedes his final word "fault." The camera then cuts to a medium three-shot, where silence reigns for a few seconds, while Hamlet, with an arm across his chest to hold his cloak, watches the effect of his speech on Horatio, who with downcast eyes nervously shuffles his fingers, while only Marcellus, seen between and behind them, watches for the ghost.

At Marcellus' call that the ghost has come, all three stare forward, and Hamlet gasps, clutching his hands to his face. The camera cuts to a close-up of Hamlet, delivering the line "Angels and ministers of grace, defend us" with his face still covered, lifting his head so that only the eyes are revealed after he finishes the prayer. After a medium shot of the ghost walking, the camera cuts back to Hamlet, who is in the same posture for two more lines, until he has resolved to speak to the apparition. On "I'll call thee Hamlet," the camera cuts back to a three-shot of Horatio and Hamlet in the foreground, Marcellus behind them, moving forward as the camera tracks in for one line. After a cut to the ghost beckoning with an upraised sword during a voice-over in which Hamlet and Horatio describe the event, the camera cuts to a three-shot during which Horatio repeatedy obscures Marcellus while embracing Hamlet. The Prince, gazing al-ways on the ghost, in breathless half-voice, reasons frantically with Horatio. There is another cut to the ghost beckoning, again with a voice-over from Hamlet saying he'll follow, this time followed by a three-shot in which Marcellus and Horatio hold the Prince, who gives an operatic push to the line "My fate cries out" before the camera cuts to a two-shot, this time for the ghost in the back-ground and Hamlet in the foreground on the line "By heaven I'll make a ghost of him that lets me." Father and son with uplifted swords fill the screen for a few seconds, the camera cuts to a two shot for Marcellus and Horatio, in medium close-up in which Marcellus watches Hamlet's off-screen departure to the right while Horatio, blinking tears, turns away from Hamlet on the line "He waxes desperate with imagination." The scene finishes as the camera cuts to a final medium two-shot in which the ghost exits through a portal on the battlements, Hamlet glares briefly at his off-screen comrades, and follows through the portal. Fade to black.

This scene, one of the best in the broadcast, lasts for three minutes, during which there are twenty-two cuts, and six close-up shots of Hamlet alone, four extended through three to five lines of verse. Horatio is seen alone in close up twice, both in conversations with Hamlet, in one two-shot with Hamlet, and one with Marcellus. The ghost and Hamlet appear in two two-shots together, the ghost appears alone twice, leaving eight three-shots in which Horatio, Hamlet, and Marcellus appear together. Three purposes govern the shooting: description of the situation (Hamlet jerking his head into his cloak in a close-up indicating that the air bites shrewdly); thematic visualization of shifting alliances (Hamlet at the end pictured twice waving a sword with his father, newly absorbed into a world of violence inaccessible to his friends); and finally, revelation of characters' changing relations and fortunes (intimacies Hamlet shares with Horatio, and significantly not with Marcellus, being violently sundered by the guard's announcing the father's nightly march).

Shakespeare does not specify any particular peccadillo as specially lethal to reputation in Hamlet's speech to Horatio, and this production does not either. Isolating the Prince and his friend during the conversation, and directing it as a lesson anxiously received by Horatio from a wise, rueful, and forgiving authority, Wood makes the scene a moral rite of passage. Hamlet, who will be tested immediately after this by his father, and found apt, seems more than anything to want Horatio to understand the difficulty of being morally adequate to life's adult demands. His denunciation of Claudius' hedonism shifts quickly into a preemptive exoneration of some unnamed innocent and natural inclination which very likely will ruin any chance the two friends have to be regarded as virtuous men of action.

The relationship between Hamlet and Horatio governs much of the play's action, and displays as many enigmatic ambiguities as that between Hamlet and Ophelia. Incapable of delivering Hamlet, though faithful, Horatio's love balances Ophelia's equally failed, and under compulsion less faithful, devotion. Horatio's steadfastness costs him survival at Hamlet's insistence, Ophelia's lapse costs her death, accidentally through Hamlet's dishonorable action. Wedded spiritually to Horatio, by his own proclamation in act III, scene ii, lines 60–71, Hamlet substitutes sexless male intimacy for the ruined marriage to Ophelia, whom he has renounced with unreasonable but intelligible violence, as irretrievably promiscuous in the immediately preceding scene. Hamlet's loving discourse on honor with Horatio in the second ghost scene of this production anticipates that substitution. When at the end of her mad-scene, act IV, scene v, Ophelia kisses Horatio as she exits on the line "Sweet ladies, good night, good night," Ophelia unwittingly completes the transfer herself.

Horatio's adolescent slightness, Hamlet's manly bearing, the camera's focus on eyes, brows, and lips, added to such reasoning, all give the instructing moment a palpable erotic charge. Despite Chamberlain's suggestion, in *The New York Times* article already cited, that " . . . our more liberal directors might score by transforming Hamlet into one of the boys in the band," the production never makes the possibility that these men are lovers, or want to be, a coherent structure in plot or characterization.[3] Unwilling to make homosexual desire the heart of Hamlet's mystery, this television show will nonetheless make use of Chamberlain's sexual appeal when Hamlet needs to appear sympathetic, wise, and virtuous, as he does in this scene. Making erotic charm rhetorical this way is, of course, a long-lived though sometimes scorned strategy of dramatic performance, and should come as no surprise in a television performance starring a man who received over 12,000 letters a week at the height of *Dr. Kildare's* popularity. The willingness to endorse an argument even momentarily with same-sex appeal is a surprise for television in 1970, but given the imprecision of the fault which Hamlet says will stain good men's reputations, and the high-toned moralism which begins the instruction to Horatio, the audience has been provided with easy ways to ignore the object of Chamberlain's seductiveness, or, what is probably more the case, experience the appeal as a general one directed toward them.

Horatio performs his only necessary action in the plot when he brings Hamlet and the ghost together. After this, although he hears Hamlet's plans, he has no part in them. His primary function is to sustain Hamlet through reception of the Prince's secrets. Made a knower of the secret plans and deeds of Hamlet, not an agent of them, Horatio becomes a trusted analyst, at times a friendly critic of Hamlet's hopes, a way for Shakespeare to comment from inside the play on the shifting connection of character to plot, of meaning to event. In this production, Horatio's loyalty consists in a willingness to be instructed by the Prince, to be ruled by Hamlet's interpretation of events. The play presents Horatio as Hamlet's companion in knowledge, an intellectual fit to think with his friend, to advise, disagree, or concur. This performance replaces Horatio's virtuous knowledge of Hamlet's obscurely honorable purpose with adolescent admiration for a misunderstood hero, and transfigures the soldier/scholar's devotion into a moral and intellectual crush, appreciated, if not in fact engendered, by a wise and certain Prince. Little of Hamlet's doubt, speculation, and intellectual discovery are preserved in Chamberlain's interpretation of the Prince, and whatever is left has nothing to do with Horatio. The battlements scene establishes the mutually pleasing subordination uniting them, and nothing else in the production ever disrupts or transforms that union.

Affectionately grieved for Horatio's sake, perhaps for his own, that men's virtuous deeds cannot escape calumny, this Hamlet has very different feelings about the unjust reputation women acquire in their lives. Whatever good is said about women is false, since they are incapable of constancy, and even if they are constant, they shall not escape calumny, which they deserve because they are sexually faithless even if they are chaste. This horrid logic governs Hamlet's emotions, cruelly blighting his dealings with the two women in his familial world, his mother and forbidden, hoped-for wife Ophelia. Here, the relation of honor and faulted deeds is precisely reversed from the lesson given to Horatio. Where men's virtue was unfairly submerged by undue attention to their natural infirmities, women's natural vice, even when not in evidence, disqualifies them from any estimation as virtuous.[4] Adultery is so endemic to women that Hamlet concludes all future marriages must be banned, although he allows that those presently espoused, save one, may stay alive. This last conclusion comes in act III, scene i, immediately following Hamlet's "To be or not to be" speech, in his first scene with Ophelia. The reversal of an argument that previously allowed Hamlet to command affection, and the different circumstances and consequences of Horatio's loyalty and Ophelia's to the Prince, make this scene and act I, scene iv reciprocal. In both, Hamlet concludes that virtuous action can not prevail. Tragedy is made of such conclusions, whether they are just or not.

Act III, scene i begins with Claudius, in the presence of Gertrude, Ophelia, and Polonius, trying to find out from Rosencrantz and Guildenstern whether they have been able to discover the cause of Hamlet's lunacy. When they report their failure, Claudius asks if they have tried distracting Hamlet with pastimes. Eager to please by reporting success in that strategy, the spies happily tell Claudius how they elated Hamlet by announcing to him the arrival of travelling actors at the court. Polonius relays Hamlet's request that the King and Queen attend a performance that night, to which the King assents. Rosencrantz and Guildenstern leave, and Claudius ushers Gertrude out, explaining that Polonius and he have arranged a surprise meeting between Ophelia and Hamlet that hour which they plan to observe in hiding to discover whether disappointed love torments the prince. Gertrude leaves, expressing to Ophelia her wish that such an explanation may prevail, and that love may become a solution, not remain a problem. Polonius gives Ophelia a book to disguise the meaning of her encounter with Hamlet, and withdraws with the King to watch the couple prove to Claudius that unhappy love has undone the Prince. Hamlet enters, contemplates the incentives and prohibitions governing suicide, and discovers Ophelia. She enjoins him to discuss their sundering, he repudiates her, and excoriates sexual attraction and affection so wildly and violently before he leaves, that Ophelia believes they are both past hope. Polonius and Claudius emerge, disagree about whether love has distracted Hamlet (the King does not believe so, nor does he believe Hamlet is mad), and plan to send the clearly dangerous Prince into exile in England.

At the end of "To be or not to be" Hamlet is kneeling at the globe in Claudius's office. On the line "Soft you now" he turns, sees Ophelia kneeling at the statue of the Madonna and Christ child, and rises in a crane shot to address her. After a close-up of Hamlet, the camera cuts to a close-up of Ophelia with a candle at her side. She asks how the Prince is, and a medium two-shot follows in which he moves to the door as she moves toward him to stop his exit. There is a short track in for the line in which she offers to return a love-token. In the next medium shot Hamlet turns from her, denying that he gave her aught. A close-up of Ophelia follows as she describes the tender circumstances in which he gave the amulet. On the line "Take these again" the camera cuts to a two-shot, in which she gives him the amulet, he takes her hand, and begins feigning madness with a loud laugh on "Ha, are you honest." A two-shot follows, focused on Ophelia, in which Hamlet, seen from behind, questions her fairness. A reversed two-shot follows in which Hamlet, seen full face, takes Ophelia's face in his hand, holding the amulet, tenderly and sanely remonstrates with her about honesty and fairness, tells her he loved her, tells her she should not have believed he did, and commands her, with mad vehemence again, "Get thee to a nunnery." On that line he starts moving forward, forcing her backward toward the bookcase. In the next two-shot the camera pans right as Hamlet forces Ophelia across the room, never letting go of her chin, accusing himself of dishonesty with his words, but blaming her for these faults with his tone and physical dominance. At the second directive to go to a nunnery, the camera cuts to Hamlet, then in tight close-up to two eyes watching the scene through an aperture in the bookcase, cuts to Hamlet in close-up for the line "Where's your father," and cuts to a medium close-up of Ophelia who turns down her face and eyes on the line "At home, my lord." A two-shot follows, in which Hamlet shouts "Let the doors be shut on him," as he grabs Ophelia, who is standing to his right, spins her back to the camera, spins her to his left, then turns her face forward as he flings her to the globe, where she falls. At the midpoint of their encounter they are in positions that reverse the opening staging, he in the background, she kneeling at the globe. He advances, pointing at her on the line "If thou dost marry," grabs her with both hands as he scorns her chastity's defense against slander, embraces her uplifted hands on the third "nunnery" dismissal, drops them and turns his back to her. A close-up of Ophelia follows, in which she prays for his recovery. A two-shot follows, in which Hamlet turns back to her, grabs her face and twirls her round as he moves back to the bookcase, berating women for wearing makeup. At the case, he lifts his arm to point at her again, haranguing her with gruesome facial and vocal moronism on the line "I say we will have no more marriage," dragging the last word through coarse derisive mockery as an adolescent thug might. On the line "all but one" there is a cut to a close-up of the eyes in the bookcase revealed after Hamlet pulls books away. The camera then cuts back to the same two-shot, Ophelia foregrounded in profile with her hand to her face, Hamlet in the background raising the hand he pointed at her, throwing the locket back to her on "to a nunnery go," and lunging out of the scene to the left. A medium close-up of Ophelia from the waist up, with her hand over her eyes, face front follows. She turns to watch his unseen exit, hears the door close, turns left and kneels to pick up the locket, which comes into view as the camera pans down and left, following her gesture, which is made against the background of Claudius's desk, behind which a fire burns. A cut to the locket follows, in a medium close-up, into which her hand comes. As she raises the locket the camera pans up to her face, where she brings her hands together beneath her chin to begin her soliloquy. The close-up holds through her speech, as she moves the locket from hand to hand, in and out of the shot, and moves her hand or hands about her face and brow. After the last line "Ah woe is me! To have seen what I have seen, see what I see!" her hands move down out of the shot, leaving her for an instant silently in tears.

Throughout the middle acts of the play, until he is exiled to England, the question of Hamlet's sanity and the strategies of his delay make the story a series of conundrums and reflexive deceptions. Claudius, the unwitting subject of Hamlet's postponed deed, investigates his stepson's mental state through indirect means, and acknowledges Hamlet's mad behavior while constantly doubting its authenticity. Apparently he holds as low an opinion of women as his nephew, since he criticizes Hamlet's denunciation of Ophelia only because it is slightly incoherent: "Nor what he spake, though it lacked form a little,/Was not like madness." This odd, and little noticed concurrence between Hamlet and Claudius on the inevitability of feminine inconstancy conflates villainy and heroism in ways that could have powerful consequences for characterization, and thematically for the play at large. The lines are cut in this production. While he is not convinced that love has unhinged the Prince, Claudius is convinced of his dangerous lunacy here. Polonius has argued from the first that love is the problem, and maintains that conviction in the lines, also cut here, "But yet do I believe/ The origin and commencement of his grief/Sprung from neglected love." Eliminating the disputation over Hamlet's amatory life, and the King's odd assent to his nephew's misogyny, this production plays the scene as Hamlet's discovery that Ophelia has betrayed him, that she is in league with the eyes of Polonius, as Hamlet presumes them to be in the line "Where is thy father?", that glare out behind the displaced books. Throughout the scene, Chamberlain feigns lunacy, first to try Ophelia's virtuous femininity, implicit in her praying to the Madonna, and to keep the woman he loves away from him and the dangerous, impossible revenge she can not help him accomplish. After he sees the spying eyes, he uses the cover of madness to excoriate her for endangering him. There is no question of Hamlet's madness here: he and the audience know that he has justly and cleverly deceived the fathers, and that she has put herself in the way of a hero's righteous indignation, not madness, by obeying them.

The camera movement in this sequence, bringing the two together and sundering them with increasing violence, usually in close-up shots, dramatizes their clashing intentions and horrible entanglement with visual precision and intimacy that could not be accomplished on a stage. Cutting to the paternal eyes, silly as it looks, especially the second time, is not strictly required by the text. Hamlet constantly conjoins Ophelia and her father in his speech to Polonius in the mad scene preceding this one, and his line "Where's your father" could easily be played as a continuation of the same idée fixe. Hamlet's accidental discovery of Polonius gives a cruelly ironic turn to Ophelia's sad commendation of the Prince as the "observed of all observers." Here again television can make a thematic and symbolic gesture which the stage cannot, although the same interpretation is readily available if Polonius discloses himself somehow accidentally on the stage. The discovery of the meddlesome father in this blasted love scene also helps justify the sarcasm with which Hamlet dismisses murdering Polonius in the second misogynistic rampage in which the Prince condemns his mother's sexual perfidy. Up until the discovery, Hamlet threatens Ophelia only by holding her face and forcing her to retreat as he pursues her. After the close up to the eyes, he thrusts her about repeatedly, acting out the violence the eyes have initiated, playing the madness they expected, to deceive them and punish her. The violent constraining and separation of bodies here contrasts sharply with the solicitude of Horatio and Marcellus's embraces in act IV, scene i, expressing frenzied sexual antagonism and disappointment. Hamlet's earlier physical struggle was shot as a liberating effort to discover truth and a virtuous cause in the face of religious terror and awe. Here, his cruel embraces are shown as provoked chastisement of a weak, dangerous, and failed love. Gesture and movement could convey these intentions on stage, but not as accurately and inevitably as they do when there is nothing else to watch, as is true while the camera moves with moving bodies on a small screen.

Heroes in revenge melodramas are not insane, they do not abuse women, especially their mother and beloved, they do not kill the wrong people. They may, as in *The Mark of Zorro* or *The Scarlet Pimpernel* or the Superman and Batman stories, or the *Odyssey* which initiates this trope, disguise their strength and purpose by feigning various forms of innocuous incapacity, even to the point of creating alter egos. Hamlet presents his madness as such a disguise: he never mentions it when he speaks alone, and explicitly asserts his sanity when he fears the disguise will thwart him in the closet scene with Gertrude. For the last two centuries, starting for convenience with Goethe's thinking about the play, Hamlet's madness has been regarded as more than feigning. The standard accounts have it that a too delicate mind has been blasted by the horror of vice and enforced policing of it, and the vice is often presented as a sexual problem, either a maladjustment in Hamlet's own nature or an endemic murderous lust corrupting all worldly affairs. Chamberlain opts for the second account of vice, and without driving Hamlet to distraction over lust's villainy, does show him powerfully disgusted and discouraged by it. The denunciation of Ophelia could easily wreck any presentation of the Prince as a sane, Odyssean savior of Denmark, since its distorted logic and vehemence have all the marks of lunacy. The sympathetic moralizing of sexual appeal which always accompanies the romantic hero's deeds could also easily be forfeited in act III, scene i, since the scene breaks the code of courtesy to women by casting Ophelia simultaneously in the role of angelic ally and sexual sorceress. The melodramatic hero often has to remonstrate with a loyal woman who cannot understand the higher calling which takes precedence over love, and be crueller than he would like to a temptress using romance to destroy him, but he never has to do both at the same time, except in Shakespeare's plays, which routinely elaborate generic conventions by collapsing them this way. This production preserves the virtue of the lovers by showing Polonius and Claudius as the instigators of sexual cruelty and mistrust when the camera cuts to the spying eyes. Once the feigned madness is converted to defense against parental villains, Hamlet's wrath becomes compelled cruelty, an erotic anguish which continues the rhetorical moralizing of Chamberlain's sexiness. This flattens out Shakespeare's text drastically, but in a way consistent with the aesthetic of driving action and heroic vindication which governs everything in this production.

Shakespeare's Prince is not obviously in control of his moral intentions at any point in the play, but neither is he unaware that a simply virtuous role as minister of divine judgment, maybe even divine grace, is available to him. His story moves him through desperate rehearsals of those two heroic roles, and through just-avoided villainous lapses into demonic possession as Nero or the savage pagan warlord of an Icelandic saga. These roles of manly political action are interleaved with various possible enactments of the lover in marriage comedy. Some interpretations present this welter of possible actions as a maddening incoherence which shatters the Prince's reason. Chamberlain's Hamlet is spared any madness on that account. His Prince is not Goethe's too-sensitive soul, Ernest Jones' Oedipal son, or a close reader's victim of structural ambiguity. More than anything, this *Hallmark Hamlet* is interfered with by powers which accidentally cancel themselves out while he steadily advances his secret and altogether sane vengeance. That is as it should be in a popular form like the revenge melodrama, where the hero always wins by bringing his antagonists under the sway of his skillfully deployed and impeccably virtuous moral project, often with some help from providence, and the tendency of villains to defeat themselves.

While Hamlet's madness, delay, and subordination can all be absorbed into the successful strategy of a melodramatic hero, his death cannot. The Hallmark production eliminates all the complexities that make Hamlet an innocent criminal, a guilty victim, a tragic hero in short. His death, consequently, is sad but never feels frighteningly necessary or horribly right. Chamberlain's Hamlet dies of the public's veneration for tragic emotionality, a callow, sincere awe of the moral grandeur which leads heroes to fight villainy *usque ad mortem*. This lionizing of self-sacrifice coexists in popular taste alongside boostering enthusiasm for the triumph, against all odds, of an innocently powerful righter of wrongs. Popular forms can be as mixed as traditional ones; witness the necessity of so many American movies to have simple happy endings, no matter how complex and difficult the story may be. In the *Hallmark Hamlet* the handsome avenger should get his girl as happily as he gets the bad guy, but Shakespeare thought otherwise, and so the Prince dies instead. Unwilling to sacrifice the *gran finale*, but unprepared to make Hamlet's death a tragic test of justice, this production evades interpretive incoherence by simply switching at the end from one popular construction of heroic achievement to another instead of trying to blend the two.

Shakespeare proceeded otherwise. His language always provides more meanings in puns and figures than are strictly necessary to advance his plots, and his plots are normally anthologies of conflicting genres, but he manages to preserve coherence in this superabundance, usually by making the multiple structures complementary and interdependent. Television has aired complex, popular narratives ordered by such overlapping, *Hill Street Blues* most recently. Nothing in the medium automatically requires that Shakespearean complexity be handled by serial and selective presentation of conventions, ideas, feelings, and actions which the playwright has intermingled. Any interpretation transparent or flexible enough to contain or suggest the alternative readings it has superseded will successfully render Shakespeare's drama on film, or stage, or on television.

Romantic melodrama does not please by thematically copious display of inter-dependent moral and ethical structures, and cannot render, therefore, Shake-speare's *Hamlet*, no matter how winning a performance any popular male star might give. The dashing avenger Chamberlain discovers in *Hamlet* exists in Shakespeare's play, but not so freely as the *Hallmark* broadcast suggests. One topic in *Hamlet* which the television version simply ignores is theatrical aes-thetics. Specifically and repeatedly, Hamlet thinks of his life as an actor's prob-lem, as an incapacity or unwillingness to perform the inner man. The romantic avenger is the first false role Hamlet adopts, and as the play proceeds, and he fails repeatedly to succeed in the part, he relies less and less on it. Insofar as *Hamlet* is a poetics for Shakespeare's theater, and a commentary on character types, it presents the sexy righter of wrongs as a frail fantasy most suitable to excitable male ingénues. Chamberlain's popular success came as such an in-génue, a fact which might have made his Hamlet extraordinarily potent, had he followed Shakespeare's lead and grown out of the part. As it stands, he seems superannuated in the *Hallmark Hall of Fame*, almost an aesthetic criticism of himself, almost a melancholy man.

NOTES

1. Lawrence W. Levine, *Highbrow/Lowbrow: The Emergence of Cultural Hierarchy in America* (Cambridge: Harvard University Press, 1988).

2. Richard Chamberlain, "Why Does an Actor Agree to Do Hamlet," *New York Times*, Sunday, 15 Nov. 1970, Sec. 2, 21.

3. Chamberlain, 21.

4. Recent writers trace misogynistic elements in this scene to the feminist controversy of the Elizabethan period. See Katherine Usher Henderson and Barbara F. McManus, *Half Humankind: Contexts and Texts of the Controversy about Women in England, 1540–1640* (Urbana and Chicago: University of Illinois Press, 1985), especially pp. 116–118.

Part III
Television and Its Critics

8

Taking Television Too Seriously—and Not Seriously Enough

Barbara Lee

> A great agent for good, a means of education unrivaled, a source of much innocent and inexpensive pleasure, the moving picture show has come to mean, as a rule, a pandering to the lowest tastes, a misrepresentation of life as it really is, as harmful and more accessible than the dime novel, and the telling of a lie, constantly and universally.[1]

Though these words were written in 1908 about the then-developing medium of motion pictures, it would not be difficult to find parallel statements in current critical writing about television. First movies, then radio, and finally television initially were hailed as a prospective means of bringing culture and education to the masses and then condemned not only for failing to fulfill this designated potential, but also for contributing to the deterioration of moral and aesthetic values.

In this essay I will trace some of the recurrent themes that have accompanied the arrival of each new mass medium, the great expectations and great disappointments expressed in the popular press by defenders and critics. The current arguments about "trash TV" can serve as an example of how these same types of concerns easily surface and continue to be discussed on a level that provides more rhetoric than insight. And finally, I will suggest some areas that have gone relatively unexplored in the preoccupation with these sorts of debates.

A recurrent theme among both promoters and detractors of each new medium has been the "democratization of resources" that it could provide. With the advent of each mass medium, there has been a vision of the entire country receiving culture at low cost; even those in small towns or with limited income could now have access to great performers and speakers, hear music and drama previously unavailable to them.

Thus Thomas Edison promoted his moving pictures as a boon to the working classes, extolling the medium as "the greatest contribution in history to the brightening of the lives of the masses" and predicting that "the working man will be able, by laying down his dime at the modern theater of cinematography, to enjoy grand opera and dramatic productions, with sound, dialogue, color, and action."[2] Other observers shared his enthusiasm, extolling the advent of the motion picture because it "filled a long-felt need admirably and completely; because it brought to the rank and file of the American people the dramatic entertainment which had been beyond their reach; because it bridged one more point of cleavage between the large cities and the small towns and rural sections."[3] The "people in Podunk" would enjoy the blessing of "the very best in music and drama on the same day that the New York's public does, and at the same low price."[4]

Advocates of radio followed the same argument of equality of entertainment with its implied contribution to the democratic tradition. Through radio, said Owen D. Young, Chairman of the Board of R.C.A., "We can share thought and culture and knowledge, rich as well as poor, farmers as well as the city dwellers."[5] According to a *Good Housekeeping* article, radio would offer unique benefits of diversion to women at home: "Isolation, whether mental or geographical, has been the cause of much of women's restlessness and has done more to retard her progress than any other one factor. And now the radio comes as a sort of panacea to cure all the ills which isolation brings forth."[6] When David Sarnoff surveyed the future of television, the concept of popular home entertainment was a given, but he proposed that television would advance beyond radio in providing not only music, but "the best in drama, the dance, painting and sculpture" to a mass audience.[7]

The capability to reach larger groups than had ever before been gathered as one audience impressed both promoters and detractors of each new media. A writer in 1908 was enthralled by the ability of a film of the "Passion Play" to be witnessed by greater crowds than could ever be physically assembled.[8] For both movies and radio, the ability of the media to supply grand opera and great drama to a large public was presented as a prime virtue. Writing in *Scribner's* in 1929, one advocate praised radio as "offering new kingdoms of musical riches for the multitudes," awakening an enormous public to music they didn't know existed.[9] Though by the time television arrived, the fascination with startlingly large audience figures had somewhat waned, a writer for the *Nation* was still impressed by the ability of the media to bring "Pulitzer Prize plays" to the millions.[10]

The implicit assumption was that the expansion of horizons through exposure to the charismatic power of the grand and great would lead to a progressive improvement of the public's artistic tastes. Critics' bitter disappointment at motion pictures, then radio, and later television, lay in the media's failure to live up to this potential. "Mass audience" became a term of derision—"mass appeal" automatically meant appeal to the lowest common denominator, a guarantee of poor quality and low taste. Not only were the producers and practitioners guilty of this betrayal; the audience itself was derided for dictating standards of mediocrity. Movies, according to William Allen White, writing in 1926, provided "little that is much better than a glittering toy for an imbecile giant."[11] Radio was castigated for its "surrender to the current standards of mass public taste,"[12] and television was labeled "the chewing gum of the masses."[13] The media themselves were devalued on the basis of the audiences to which they appealed.

Perhaps for television, since its capabilities seemed even higher than for the other media, there was the greatest fall from grace, exemplified by Norman Cousin's attack on this new medium in 1949. After describing television as (in concept at least) "the most magnificent of all communications," he went on to detail what it had become in the face of assembly-line standards:

Out of the wizardry of the television tube has come such an assault against the human mind, such a mobilized attack on the imagination, such an invasion against good taste as no other communications medium has known, not excepting the motion picture or radio itself. In the one year since television has been on an assembly-line basis, there has been mass-produced a series of plodding stereotypes and low-quality programs. Behind it all, apparently, is a grinding lack of imagination and originality which has resulted in the standardized formula for an evening's entertainment: one poisoning, a variety show, a wrestling match.[14]

Television, to its detractors, had fallen into the vicious circle of mass entertainment: the producers appealing to "the thirteen-year-old mind" to capture mass audiences, the public responding in numbers to the lowest forms of entertainment.

So much for culture. But what about education, another great good that would be brought about by the new media? In Thomas Edison's vision, movies were to become a replacement for the usual forms of entertainment: "Books will soon be obsolete in the public schools. . . . Scholars will be instructed through the eye. It is possible to teach every branch of human knowledge with the motion picture. Our school system will be completely changed inside of ten years."[15]

While what Edison derided as "dull" conventional methods of education were never overthrown, at least one of his vivid predictions of how the moving picture could add excitement to teaching the alphabet was eventually realized:

Take the alphabet. . . . You remember how hard it was to learn the letters? Why? Because it was dry and uninteresting. Lord, how dry! But now see what we'll do: Suppose, instead of the dull solemn letters on a board or card, you have a little play going on that the littlest youngster can understand—oh, as small as that, "and the wizard's hand shot down to his knee." The play begins with a couple of lively little fellows who carry in a big letter T. They put it down, and it stands there. They carry in an H. Then a little cuss comes in, hopping and skipping and turning somersaults, and "both hands were whirling in the air now'' as he takes his place next to the H you see he is the letter I. Next to him they put down an S. There you have the word "This." In the same way they bring in the letters, or the letters run in and dodge into place, until the sentence stands there. "This is a man." Then a hand appears pointing, and up marches a man for it to point at. Of course, the teacher gives the children the name of each letter and pronounces each word as they go along. You can see how eagerly the youngsters will watch every movement on the picture-screen, for there will be something going on there every moment. Nothing like action—drama—a play that fascinates the eye—to keep the action keyed up. I don't think it'll take them long to learn the alphabet that's lively and full of character.[16]

Though few envisioned the complete overturn of the traditional classroom that Edison had predicted with the advent of broadcasting, predictions were made for a revision and enlargement of the traditional forms of education—supplementing the teacher, creating new forms of pedagogy, and making the greatest teachers available to all. H. V. Kaltenborn in 1926 stressed radio's educational value for its ability, because of the size of the class, "to have the best teachers in every subject."[17] When television arrived at the scene, readers of *Nation's Business* were told that it would be "the biggest classroom the world has ever seen."[18] David Sarnoff echoed this prediction: " . . . with [television] it will become possible for the best teachers in the land to give carefully prepared and illustrated lectures simultaneously to millions of children."[19] Whatever positive value television provided for classroom teaching, however, was soon overwhelmed by concerns about the deterioration of children's reading and writing skills in the face of the seductive visual medium.

Beyond the specifics of classroom instruction was the broader claim that the media would provide a liberal education, a means for reaching places and people unknown before and creating a presence at events that people could not otherwise witness. Early motion pictures were heralded as allowing an "eastside youngster [to] see a bear hunt in Russia, scenes from an Indian reservation, or pictures of the dredging machines at work on the Panama Canal."[20] Considering radio, one observer compared studious young Abe Lincoln lying on his stomach in front of the fire with the image of the farm boy listening to his radio, for "with a little radio set in one corner of the farmhouse . . . the plowboy of 1929 has the world at his feet."[21] And television, when it appeared, was described as the complete "window on the universe."[22]

There was a clear downside to this exposure to people, events, and concepts outside of one's day-to-day experience, especially for the young. For each innovation, objections quickly arose to lapses in moral content and particularly to what first movies, then radio, and finally television were teaching the young. As early as 1910, an article in *Good Housekeeping* objected to motion pictures because the viewer would find

depicted again and again, in living form, all sorts of acts of a criminal and depraving nature. And around it all is thrown a sentiment such as to give the minds of plastic youth a tendency to regard the coarser forms of conduct as a common thing in our daily walks of life. There he learns precisely how robberies, holdups, and murders are committed; how officers of the law, such as policemen, are false to their oath of office and to the demands of plain, everyday duty; how divorces are originated and how the various members of the family violate the most sacred laws that bind together the home circle and give it its charm and perpetuity.[23]

The theme of the media's detrimental effects on morals and behavior has been so regular and persistent that it hardly needs documentation. While children were usually presented as the most vulnerable to such influences, there was often an implication that even adult viewers were susceptible. Thus, the author of an article in *Christian Century*, speaking of movies and television together, argued that

these mass entertainment giants go far toward determining the moral climate of the nation. The record of their attainments is being daily written in the life of the nation. Part of it is inscribed on the rolls of divorce courts, on police blotters, on the admission cards of homes for juvenile delinquents and hospitals for alcoholics.[24]

A critic in 1908 was even more explicit regarding the need to protect the unsophisticated audience from the power of media influence. He detailed the damage that violent scenes in movies had on viewers:

The constant picturing of crime in any form, even if the punishment is shown at the end, is a harmful and degrading thing, especially when a large percentage of the patrons of such theatres is made up of minors or *adults without the education and point of view which will enable them to see things as they are.*[25] (emphasis mine)

Along with the concern about the media's influence on morality was anxiety about the distortion of values. The ideal against which each new mass media was measured was the provision of entertainment which was "real," which reflected a proper and correct version of life. Measured against this standard, the mass media fell woefully short. Movies were labeled by one observer in 1921, "the world's worst failure" because of their "absolute failure to present truthfully the fabric of the cosmic drama which we call life."[26] Radio soap operas were criticized for encouraging misguided views of life among their listeners, while juvenile serials were characterized as "distortions, negative and disturbing when they should be positive and beneficial," ignoring real life for the sake of excitement and suspense.[27] Television offered an even greater threat to the ability of its audience to maintain a realistic view of the world. A writer in *U.S. News* wrote of the "narcotic dysfunction" of television, as "more and more men come home in the evening, drop into a chair in front of the TV set after supper and slip into a dreamworld of unreality."[28]

The political process was another area in which the potential influence of the broadcast media (movies, much less so) was a source of debate. The announcement of the development of television in 1912 prompted one writer to ask,

"What will happen to our political forms when a candidate must appeal directly to all the electorate, revealing his personality by his close range appearance and normal voice? Will representative government survive this nationwide extension of the neighborhood in which a man can be known?"[29] More than seventy years later, much the same question is still being asked.

Some welcomed the broadcasting of radio speeches as a change that would free the audience from the influence of the crowd. The listener, alone in his home, was portrayed as no longer susceptible to the contagion of crowd psychology and "only the logic of the issue which the orator presents can move him."[30]

Other proponents of broadcasting spoke of the media as providing an opportunity to return to Athenian democracy, a shift to firsthand politics. *Saturday Review* argued in 1952 that television and radio "turned candidates into men, not names," so that

[The] vast public which is too untutored or too indifferent to apply itself with assiduity to evolving a clear conception of a candidate from his speeches as reported in the press is now able to follow his course through political events with the least possible effort over television and radio. The America of 150,000,000 souls is nearer today to the era when politicians and people met face to face than in many a long decade.[31]

A recurrent theme was that the close-up look that television provided would enable the viewer to sift out the false from the honest, exposing the candidates to judgments of their total personality. Thus John Cosby argued in 1951 that "In the long run, though, television is likely to be an unparalleled blessing to the voter. The phonies, the stuffed shirts, the liars, the crooks will have to look the camera straight in the eye and talk fast. We'll see the politicos as they are, warts and all. If, after so stringent a test, the political hacks survive, we have only ourselves to blame."[32]

Opponents of broadcasting also thought that the new media would change the criteria for judging candidates, but with the opposite results, substituting personality and appearance for the substantial qualities formerly demanded of those seeking office. As one commentator warned in 1955, describing how politicians may deceptively use television:

Here is a man who may sit in the White House, the President's cabinet, or in the United States Senate. Before the TV camera he seems to be chatting away off the cuff about the gravest of topics—taxes, the armed forces, diplomacy, civil liberties. Yet he has been tutored in this relaxed and easy manner by Hollywood stars. He is reading from the teleprompter the speech written for him by political counselors or an advertising agency. Artfully used creams and powder pare a dozen years off his normal appearance.[33]

As with the other issues I have discussed, the observer's image of the public underlies his assumptions about television's effect on the viewer. In the optimistic view, the cleareyed viewer is able to discern the true characteristics of politicians, seeks out information and education rather than mere entertainment, and is inspired by exposure to the best. In the pessimistic view, the public is easily deceived by style over substance, is readily subverted by the media's appeal to the low and common, and uncritically accepts the view of the world the media presents. In both cases, there is an underlying equation of content with perceived effect.

Why focus on technology for the playing out of these images? In part, it may be because technology is seen as having a power of its own—what technology *can* do, *will* come to be. Glowing predictions are made that ignore the reality and endurance of existing social institutions; thus once again, when computers arrived on the scene, revolutions in education were forecast that echoed Edison's prophecies for motion pictures.[34] Or it may be that new technologies simply provide a ready point of departure to express wistful desires for panaceas for intractable social problems or human frailties. A common approach is to diagnose a problem as one that television has created or, at least, exacerbated, and provide formulas for ways, with a little tinkering, television could fix it.

The intensity of public debate over what television can or should be has diminished from the early days of its introduction, as its presence in American households has become as commonplace as running water. Certainly, some of the expectations of television as a revolutionary instrument for altering tastes and institutions have been sharply curtailed. Yet debates about the potential influence of television, based on its dominance as a mass medium, can still readily surface in response to a controversial program or other shift in the medium.

Take, for example, the current furor over what has been labeled "trash TV." As a genre, it encompasses confrontational television, exemplified by Morton Downey's exchanges of insults with his talk show guests and Geraldo Rivera's bringing together representatives of opposing causes so passionate that their differences break out in brawls. Other programming that falls under the heading of "trash" seems to vary with the observer and includes *America's Most Wanted* for the violence in its recreation of actual crimes, *On Trial* for its coverage of sensationalistic court trials, real-life medical programs, and *The Oprah Winfrey Show* and *Donahue* for their excursions into tabloid topics. Producers of each of these programs deny this inclusion, claiming they serve the public interest by informing viewers, dramatizing real conflicts, and helping to catch criminals.

There seem to be only two aspects of commonality in this grouping: first, that "trash TV" programs are beyond the usual boundaries of what television presents and second, that some of them, at least, get good ratings. On both scores, the easy interpretation of these programs is that they represent a further decline in public taste. Thus a professor of broadcasting, commenting on this new phenomena suggests that "we have somehow got to get them (the audience) to have better taste, and I'm not sure how."[35]

But, as even the alternative label of "tabloid TV" that some apply to these programs suggests, the appeal of this type of material is not new. Violent crimes and aberrant sexual activities have long been a staple of the *National Enquirer* and other print tabloids. On radio, the genre of talk show that is characterized by the host's abusive interchanges with guests and listeners is heard across the country.

That this type of material is now more prominent on TV raises interesting questions. Is there a common public for these programs or does each have its own individual niche? Does the appeal lie in style or topic or treatment? Is this a temporary phenomena, overblown by the "copy-cat" tendency of television producers, or does it represent a real shift in public taste toward a gritty realism? These are valid questions, but lumping a range of programs together as a common indicator of lowbrow taste is a sure way of deflecting any serious effort at understanding.

It is also an example of the global approach that could be called "taking television too seriously," where media content is mainly treated as an opportunity for hand-wringing on the state of our culture. What may be just another blip on the long chart of TV's changing modes is not so much analyzed as cited, isolated from the complicated matrix that creates surges of popularity.

At the same time, this approach is a way of not taking television seriously enough, since it precludes the type of analysis undertaken in several of the articles in this book, which systematically examine the interaction between viewer and text. As David Marc observes, there is a new "critical dialogue" developing, but it is still easy to find commentaries on television that pay little attention to distinctions between genres and programs and even less to what they may mean to the audience.

In general, social commentators have been less concerned with what the media provides to its audiences and how the audience adopts media to its own uses. While some social scientists have pursued the question of audience gratifications from viewing, it is the research about effects of the medium that is most likely to be cited in popular debate. The interesting ways in which television interlaces with people's lives generally gets much less attention. Let me give a few examples of some commonplace aspects of the medium, easily acknowledged but rarely investigated.

One is the role of television in providing the "gossip" of society. Two recent *New York Times* articles provided vivid first-person accounts of television playing this role. In one, a man told of his discomfort in being excluded, by his lack of interest in sports, from the easy fellowship created through conversations about last night's game.[36] Another was a mother's description of the long-distance connection she maintained with her daughter by sharing the surreal experiences of the characters on their favorite soap opera, *Days of Our Lives*.[37] In both cases, the conversations described became more than simply trading notes; rather, part of the pleasure was the recreating of the viewing experience and the sharing of sophisticated commentary on what was seen.

Since television is so ubiquitous, it can play the traditional role of gossip, providing television surrogates for a common equivalent of friends and neighbors to observe, laugh at, condemn or admire. In this role, television provides a currency of discourse, a way of relating to others, and sometimes a vehicle for reaffirming values.[38] In a novel study of households involuntarily deprived of television, Winick described the decline in family communication that occurred in the absence of television.[39] We tend to think of television viewing as an isolating act, but the reality of family life is that most viewing is done with others and becomes part of the "social cement" that maintains family relationships.

On a more significant scale, television can provide the glue that holds a community together in extreme situations. Dr. Frank Stanton (then head of CBS) tells of a call he received on the eve of President Kennedy's funeral from the president of the American Banking Association, who asked if the networks intended to devote the entire day to the event. The banker had been afraid of a run on the banks, if there were not some relief of people's anxieties and emotions through the unifying experience of vicarious participation.

The integrative function of what Katz and Dayan have dubbed "The High Holidays of Mass Communication"[40] can extend to times of celebration as well as disaster. On these historic occasions—the astronauts landing on the moon, the Olympics, the Watergate hearings, Sadat's coming to Jerusalem, the Royal Wedding—the media take on importance that demands participation. In a sense, viewing is almost mandated by the need to be present at what will become history.

Such events take on a special character that goes beyond ordinary viewing, because of the symbolic overlay that invests the occasion. Eric Rothenbuler in his study of the 1984 Summer Olympics[41] described the differences from the usual viewing situation that distinguished this event as a celebratory occasion: "People looked forward to the games, they viewed large amounts of the broadcast, they rearranged their personal schedules to see more of the games, they got together with friends to watch, they ate and drank and talked, both about the Olympics and other things, they planned their viewing and they payed close attention while viewing."[42]

These events are occasions that cut across the conventional divisions of society and serve as community-wide rituals. What is interesting are the possible parallels with the individualistic rituals that families and individuals may consciously create around television—setting up a sequence of viewing that is planned, orderly, and somewhat sacrosanct. In a study I conducted at CBS, people in focus group discussions described television rituals for certain programs or certain nights of the week—times they set aside for viewing, trying not to plan outside activities that would interfere with watching, letting the children stay up late, making popcorn for the occasion, avoiding interruptions, becoming so involved that they would not answer the telephone.

There is a connective thread here that runs through these different ways of using television—whether it be as grist for commonplace gossip, as a society-level celebration or for personal or family integration. In the social sciences, a new approach is emerging that considers such everyday interactions with media, and how they relate to social roles and the maintenance of family systems and subcultures.[43] Perhaps the long-standing conception of the audience as a passive aggregate, shifted in one direction or another by the media, is beginning to erode, though it may continue as the tone of popular debate.

NOTES

1. C. H. Claudy, *American Review of Reviews*, December 1908, 161. I am indebted to Robert Edward Davis's Phd. dissertation, *Response to Innovation: A Study of Popular Argument About New Mass Media* (Salem, New Hampshire: Ayer, 1976) for this and many of the following quotations from magazines and journals. The author reviewed seventy popular periodicals chosen from Theodore Peterson's *Magazines in the Twentieth Century* for articles relating to the mass media, selecting one thousand articles for analysis. Because of the large number of sources cited, the author used abbreviated footnotes, limited to the publication date and page number, occasionally citing the specific author in the text.

2. *Independent*, 17 July 1913, 142.
3. C. B. Neblette, *PhotoEra*, Oct. 1926, 175–76.
4. Robert Grau, *Lippencott's*, Aug. 1913, 191–92.
5. *Collier's*, 8 April 1921, 4.
6. Pauline Frederick, *Good Housekeeping*, Aug. 1922, 202.
7. David Sarnoff, *Annals of American Academy*, Jan. 1941, 151.
8. *Independent*, 6 Feb. 1908, 308.
9. *Scribner's*, 23 April 1929, 410.
10. *Nation*, 13 Oct. 1951, 297.
11. *Colliers*, 16 Jan. 1926, 6.
12. *Harpers*, Nov. 1931, 720.
13. *Nation*, 9 Feb. 1946, 171.
14. *Saturday Review*, 24 Dec. 1949, 20.
15. *American Review of Reviews*, Dec. 1914, 725.
16. *Harper's Weekly*, 4 Nov. 1911, 8.
17. *Century*, Oct. 1926, 670.
18. *Nation's Business*, July 1947, 74.
19. *Annals of the American Academy*, Jan. 1941, 152.
20. *Colliers*, 25 Oct. 1913, 23.
21. *American Magazine*, Jan. 1929, 15.
22. *Senior Scholastic*, 8 March 1946, 3.
23. *Good Housekeeping*, Aug. 1910, 184.
24. *Christian Century*, 13 Jan. 1954, 37.
25. *American Review of Reviews*, Dec. 1908, 744.
26. *Outlook*, 19 Jan. 1921, 104.
27. *Rotarian*, Nov. 1930, 59.
28. *U.S. News & World Report*, 2 Sept. 1955, 38.
29. *Independent*, 17 Oct. 1912, 89.
30. *Forum*, Apr. 1929, 215.
31. *Saturday Review*, 9 Aug. 1952, 20.

32. *American Magazine*, Apr. 1951, 111.

33. *New Republic*, 9 May 1955, 12.

34. For example, in 1967, Herman Kahn and his associates at the Hudson Institute envisioned computers "giving simultaneous individual instruction to hundreds of students, each at his own console and topic, at any level from elementary to graduate school." Herman Kahn and Anthony J. Wiener, *The Year 2000* (New York: The Macmillan Company, 1967), 90.

35. Quote from Murray Yaeger, professor of broadcasting, Boston University, *Electronic Media*, 2 Jan. 1989, 85.

36. Leonard Riskin, "About Men: Un-sportsmanlike Conduct," *New York Times*, Sunday, 22 Jan. 1989, 14.

37. Mary Cantwell, "Close to Home," *New York Times*, 26 Jan. 1989, C2.

38. See Elihu Katz, and Tamar Liebes, "Decoding Dallas: Notes from a Cross-Cultural Study," in H. Newcomb, ed., *Television, the Critical View* (New York: Oxford University Press, 1987), 419–432. The authors conducted fifty focus groups with people from different subcultures in Israel to explore the varying interpretations and judgments the respondents made of this program, from one social group to another.

39. Charles Winick, "The Functions of Television: Life Without the Big Box," in *Television as a Social Issue*, ed. S. Oskamp (Newbury Park, Calif.: Sage Publications, 1988), 217–37.

40. E. Katz, and D. Dayan, "Media events: On the experience of not being there," *Religion* 15 (1985): 305–24.

41. E. Rothenbuler, "The Olympics in the American Living Room: Celebration of a Media Event." Paper presented to the International Congress on the Olympic Movement and the Mass Media: Past, Present, and Future Issues, University of Calgary, Canada (1987).

42. Ibid., 10.

43. See, for example, the range of studies, several of which used in-home observational techniques, reported in T. R. Lindlof, ed., *Natural Audiences* (Norwood, N.J.: Ablex Publishing Corporation, 1987).

9

Mass Culture, Class Culture, Democracy, and Prime-Time: Television Criticism and the Question of Quality

David Marc

Europe called for Dada by antithesis: America for analogous reasons called for the antithesis of Dada. For America is Dada. The richest mess of these bean-spillers of Italy, Germany and France is a flat accord beside the American chaos. Dada spans Brooklyn Bridge; it spins round Columbus Circle; it struts with the Ku Klux Klan; it mixes with all brands of bootleg whisky; it prances in our shows; it preaches in our churches; it tremolos at our political conventions.

Waldo Frank, 1924[1]

Getting away from the grim words "mass media," finding a new name for them, connecting their social effects with the pleasures they give—was for me an act of simple justice.

Gilbert Seldes, 1957[2]

The uniformity of intellectual response to the introduction of national television service in America following the Second World War is striking. Any enthusiasm for the democratizing possibilities of the medium or for its homegrown proces-sional Whitmanian aesthetic was quickly dispelled by the content of the actual programming presented by the three midtown Manhattan corporate giants who held the keys to the hardware store: the spectacle of Berle behind falsies vamping in drag; the ominous monosyllabic police-state diatribes of Jack Webb; the screaming winners of washing machines and trips to Florida; the brainless oh-goshisms of suburban domestic representational comedies; the hollow seductive smiles of the comedy-variety choruslines.

Given the overpoweringly masscult ambience of the new medium, even high-toned series such as Edward R. Murrow's *See It Now* and Alistair Cooke's

Omnibus—programs that during the formative years of the system served a function that has since fallen to the entire PBS network—suffered a kind of guilt by association for being TV shows in the first place. Early television at its selfconscious "best"—the live, commercially-interrupted, psychobabbling antitragic dramas of Paddy Chayefsky, Rod Serling, and Reginald Rose—was deemed a mere flirtation with midcultery. It was not until long after the death of the "playhouse" genre that kinescopes of "Marty," "Requiem for a Heavyweight," "Bus to Nowhere," and other such teleplays were canonized for middle class adoration as PBS reruns.[3] Television at its unself-conscious "worst"—the whirling checkered coat of Pinky Lee, the resurrection of the Three Stooges from the graveyard of Depression-era Saturday afternoons, gameshows hosted by Jan Murray—was apparently several rings deeper than Man Thinking cared to venture. Marxists, liberals, and beatniks stood shoulder to shoulder with genteel elitists, fundamentalist ministers, and neighborhood librarians in turning a blind eye toward a cultural delivery system that promised to make "the masses" and "the audience" synonymous terms.[4] The best minds of Allen Ginsberg's generation were still "accusing the radio of hypnotism" in 1955; television is mentioned not even once among the stunning catalogue of mass culture terrors to be found in "Howl." That very same year, Rodney-Young Productions was proclaiming "Ars pro multis" at the end of each new *Father Knows Best* episode. For the masses? Certainly. But where was the art?

Dwight Macdonald and Herbert Marcuse were leading critical figures on the Left. For progressives, television was a hopelessly vertical system of cultural distribution, more than willing and only too able to program the responses of the millions to whatever political and/or consumerist suggestions served the short-term interests of capital. The consciousness of the many—the very force that might reform and improve society—was shamelessly squandered on self-destructive romantic fantasies at the expense of the participatory urge. Marcuse warns the reader against dangerous "new forms of control." The apparatus of mass communications, in Marcuse's view, creates a "closed language [that] does not demonstrate and explain—it communicates decision, dictum, command."[5]

In his 1956 essay, "The Phantom World of TV," Gunther Anders modeled socialist response to television when he wrote, "Modern mass consumption is a sum of solo performances; each consumer, an unpaid homeworker employed in the production of mass man."[6] The viewer is seen as a pathetic stooge performing a cultural tragedy whose terrifying implications are far more aesthetically compelling than the low slapstick of a Ball, a Gleason, or a Skelton. In his 1957 film *A Face in the Crowd*, Elia Kazan speaks to the concerns of mainstream liberalism when he warns the American public that television could destroy the integrity of the electoral system by thrusting political power into the hands of opportunistic actors and spokespersons.

Questions of authorship, genre, and discourse were almost completely ignored in postwar mass media studies. Indeed, specific television programs are not even mentioned in such seminal television-era works as Macdonald's "A Theory of

Mass Culture'' or Marcuse's *One-Dimensional Man*. Described only in terms of its systemic effects, TV is seen as a kind of relentlessly ringing bell in a vast Pavlovian laboratory of culture. If the tongues salivate whether or not a stimulus is offered, why discuss the flavor or quality of the dogfood? *I Love Lucy*? Fascism with a laughtrack.

On the Right, conservatives such as T. S. Eliot, R. P. Blackmur, and Ernest van den Haag feared the intrusion of commercialization on the personal spheres of family, religion, and *volk*. As was the case with Marcuse and Macdonald, these commentators rarely mention the word "television," much less any program titles. Perhaps it was capitalism's apparently increasing dependence upon TV that provoked this caution on the part of conservatives. In his "Notes Toward the Definition of Culture" (1949), Eliot already fears the Americanization of Britain as the first television licenses are being issued in his adopted homeland. The Missouri-born poet identifies religion as the basic human impulse that makes the development of all culture possible.[7] Without tribal or national consensus on the etiology of the universe, standards of good and evil inevitably deteriorate into relativity. Lacking a clear moral foundation, art becomes pornography: gratuitous titillation at best; at worst, chaotic disruption of order and community.

America's pluralism had been its aesthetic albatross since long before the excesses of the twentieth century had sent T. S. Eliot fleeing across the Atlantic. Even before the Civil War, European cultural conservatives from Count de Tocqueville to José Ortega y Gasset had been similarly repelled by what Whitman was calling a "teeming nation of nations."[8] Television, a medium structurally compromised to serve a maximum number of segments of an already mongrelized society, was the nightmarish precipitate of the American experiment. The self-appointed keepers of the castle, charged with the eternal care of the best that has been thought and said, fretted beneath the intimidation of a cultural bomb whose fallout threatened the survival of the entire aesthetic ecos. *I Love Lucy*? Stalinism with a laughtrack.

The current of books and essays that greeted the introduction of television into American culture has since been labelled by intellectual historians as "The Mass Culture Debate." It was not, however, much of a debate. Socialist as well as conservative participants found too much common ground in their shared vocational identities. For example, in 1953 Dwight Macdonald complained of the blandness and emptiness of mass culture. He accused the great leisure-industry corporations of homogenizing the best of both high culture and folk culture in their never-ending quest for broadly marketable products. Mass culture, wrote Macdonald, "threatens to engulf everything in its spreading ooze."[9] The similarity of conservative thinking on this issue is obvious in the following passage from *The Fabric of Society*, a collaborative work by Michael Ross and Ernest van den Haag:

The mass media inexorably exclude art and anything of significance when it cannot be reduced to mass entertainment, but (instead) they divert us from the passage of the time they keep us from filling. They tend to draw into the mass market talents and works that might otherwise produce new visions, and they abstract much of the capacity to experience art or life directly and deeply.[10]

As intellectuals, all feared the threat of a total corporate takeover of culture; as professional writers, all dreaded the consequences of the outmoding of their craft. "Us" was *Kultur* (from the Bible to Picasso); "them" was television (from Madison Avenue to Hollywood). Several liberals, such as David Manning White and Melvin Tumin, could even go so far as to allow that tolerating television was an aesthetic price that would have to be paid by artists and intellectuals for the privilege of living in nontotalitarian states in the twentieth century.[11] But if there were disagreements at all motivating the "Mass Culture Debate," they were not about whether television was good or bad, worthwhile or worthless, or even structurally capable or incapable of ever improving. In each case, the latter was generally assumed as a ground rule for the serious critic.

If sales figures and Neilsen ratings meant anything, the public was frankly crazy about this household appliance that attracted the messianic hostility of so many intellectuals. Perhaps television was receiving no worse treatment than had the American cinema fifty years previously. Robert Sklar argues that during the early development of the film industry many of the traditional gatekeepers of American culture—professors and clergymen prominently—resented the way in which they were being circumvented by a bunch of upstart entrepreneurs, many of whom were neither educated nor churched, many of whom were not even native-born.[12] Television, to an even greater degree than the nickelodeon, was loud, vulgar, insufficiently deferent to traditional sensibility, and hopelessly tied up with trade (this last trait as distasteful to Tories as it was insidious to revolutionaries).

Anyone who doubted the dangers of such an instrument to a free society was referred to T. W. Adorno, Walter Benjamin, Erich Fromm, Max Horkheimer, Leo Lowenthal, and the other Frankfurt School theorists who had located the success of Nazi totalitarianism in the Party's innovative uses of mass communications technology. With the ink on the Nuremburg verdicts hardly dry, the American TV networks were suddenly using an even more advanced form of high-tech mass communications to sell toothpaste and Chevrolets. Might they not just as efficiently sell military expansionism or racial genocide, should the political trade winds shift? It is perhaps not surprising that many German-Jewish refugee college professors seemed to think so. A Luddite urge to wipe away the machine lay just beneath the surface of this fatalistic analysis. Brain workers showed themselves no less fearful of the latter stages of industrialism than brawn workers had shown themselves to be of previous stages. As a result, the question of contention that dominated media criticism as the TV networks were coming to form was this: Is it possible for intellectuals (i.e., the partisans of print) to save culture from television? The optimists said yes; the pessimists said no.

It is of course doubtful that the close reading of television texts by members of the mostly academic critical elite during the fifties would have had much of an effect on the upbringing of the enfant terrible. But the upturned noses on the Right and the wringing hands on the Left amounted to an effective disengagement of critical thought from what rapidly became the nation's most important source of drama, news, style, and language. This collective act of rejection by the intellectual community certainly did not hamper the rapid expansion of the medium or of the industries that grew out of its technological advantages. All nightmares came true: television became both the vital engine of consumerist capitalism and the intrusive disrupter of traditional gemeinschaft values.

Against this general background, three names stand out as dissenting progenitors of what would survive to the present as a usable critical past: Erik Barnouw, the only historian at work during the fifties who seemed to grasp the significance of the entertainment-industrial complex as it was being put into place; Marshall McLuhan, the cultural philosopher who attempted to make sense of the new epistemological order of the television age by searching for its contexts in the archives of Western civilization; and Gilbert Seldes, the only critic of note (as opposed to reviewer; no mass circulation newspaper lacked one of those) who dared to offer thick readings of television programs at a time when such material was generally considered beneath the contempt of educated people.

The heirs of these three pioneers became apparent during the seventies and eighties. Owing much to Barnouw's efforts, the history of American broadcasting has recently become a flourishing academic subdiscipline. Barnouw's masterwork—his three volume *History of Broadcasting in the United States*—no longer constitutes the entire bibliography on the historical formation of the industry. Its encyclopedic scope, however, has made it a primary reference text for a new generation of American historians whose efforts have gone, as one might expect, to particulars: in *Inventing American Broadcasting 1899–1922*, Susan J. Douglas focuses on the precommercial radio period; in *Media and the American Mind: From Morse to McLuhan*, Daniel J. Czitrom uncovers the response of American intellectuals such as William James, John Dewey and Robert Park to the various stages of media development that took place during their lifetimes; J. Fred Macdonald has written issue-oriented historical concordances to entire television programming eras and genres;[13] George Lipsitz has studied the presentation of class and ethnic stereotypes during the fifties;[14] Thomas Cripps has examined the context of the television adaptation of *Amos 'n' Andy* in the civil rights struggle;[15] and so on. As broadcast history moves toward a second century, the selection of definable periods and topics increases geometrically.

As for McLuhan, he has been a more difficult act to follow. With historically-based critical studies of literature and culture in precipitous decline in recent years—with the epistemological value of the humanities itself placed in doubt by orthodox number crunchers and their unwitting deconstructionist allies—few commentators have been willing or able to follow the path of inquiry suggested by *Understanding Media* and *The Gutenberg Galaxy*. A Canadian Anglo-Catholic who had written a dissertation at Cambridge on the Elizabethan writer Thomas Nashe, McLuhan insisted that the continuities bridging the pre- and postbroadcasting eras were the keys to understanding the disjunctions separating them.

Most English departments have frankly begged to differ, preferring to treat television as if it were not a momentous occasion in the development of the language. The general failure of McLuhan's lit crit brahmin colleagues to embrace his subject matter has been a disappointment to those who imagine the study of books as a service to the broader studies of language and culture. Moreover, this failure has been a strategic blow to the already shell shocked humanities, helping to marginalize the aesthetic apprehension of consciousness even further from the centers of public rhetoric.

If literature critics for the most part rejected McLuhan's mandate for the study of the mass media, the social scientists who came to thoroughly embrace McLuhan's subject matter were largely indifferent to his methodology. Having created a profitable industry for themselves by quantitatively proving and disproving the "effects" of television on "the masses," these sociologists and mass psychologists have found little of use in McLuhan's dense, allusion-laden metaphysical dovining. In an era in which the protestation of empiricism shields the analyst from the stigma of having offered a personal opinion, a freshly laundered lab coat is more comfortable working attire than a dark medieval cowl.

Most specialists with degrees from American universities in subjects such as "communication theory" and "public opinion methodology" seem to know or care little about the processes of premechanical bookmaking or the poetry of Alexander Pope (to name just two of McLuhan's "eccentric" entrances into modern media studies). Several literary artists, however, have produced works that have upheld McLuhan's humanistic approach. These include *The Consciousness Industry* (1974) by Hans Magnus Enzensberger, Umberto Eco's *Travels in Hyper Reality* (1983); any of the critical studies of Jacques Ellul, especially *La Technique*; and *White Noise*, the 1984 novel by Don DeLillo. The only American on the list, DeLillo offers a particularly dramatic narrative exploration of "industrial folklore" as suggested by McLuhan's *The Mechanical Bride*.

By contrast, the few direct efforts by American humanities scholars at McLuhanesque broadstroke techno-cultural critical writing have been pretty dismal. Typically more interested in iterating their own gentility than in examining the subject at hand, these efforts amount to endless recapitulations of the "plug-in drug" arguments. Recent books by Neil Postman and Gary Gumpert, for example, have embraced McLuhanite koans such as "the medium is the message," and "the post-Gutenberg era." But unwilling or unable to effect McLuhan's cool, clinical Empire tone, these writers take the easy way out of mass media studies, cautioning the good reader to "just say no."

Postman's clumsily written *Amusing Ourselves to Death* (1986) epitomizes this romantic regression from the media world. Citing such authorities as "the great Socrates" and "the wise Solomon" (this is actual language used by Postman), the book is a comprehensive summary of the vast range of schoolmarm objections to television. Its single departure from the "Mass Culture Debate" model of scholarly gentility is Postman's insistence on conjuring nineteenth century America (rather than eighteenth century Europe) as the preelectronic golden age that proves the evil of our current condition.

All of which brings us to Gilbert Seldes. Not nearly as well known as McLuhan or as widely read as Barnouw, Seldes does not even rate an entry in *The New York Times Encyclopedia of Television*. Nor does his name appear in the indexes of such comprehensive textbook histories of American broadcasting as Sterling and Kitross's *Stay Tuned* (1978) or Barnouw's *Tube of Plenty* (1975). Despite this neglect Seldes must be counted as the founder of the critical vocation practiced today by a host of academic and freelance television critics, including Horace Newcomb, Robert C. Allen, David Thorburn, Patricia Mellencamp, Michael Arlen, Ella Taylor, Thomas Schatz, Caren Deming, Thomas Zynda, Mimi White, Robert Thompson, Jimmie L. Reeves, and Jane Feuer. Working without VCR, TV reference books, or even entré to the stars' dressing rooms, Seldes watched television—and took seriously the task of writing about what he saw— for over twenty years. His remarkable volume of practical criticism, *The Public Arts* (1956), contains specific chapters concerning the performance art of such television stars as Milton Berle, Jack Benny, and Sid Caesar, as well as meditations on a variety of complex issues, including the relationships between cinema and video, and the prevalence of comedy on prime time schedules.

The younger brother of the eminent muckraking journalist George Henry Seldes, Gilbert Vivian Seldes was born in Alliance, New Jersey in 1893. Completing a degree at Harvard in 1914, he served as a war correspondent for the *Philadelphia Evening Ledger* before returning to America as Washington correspondent for *L'Echo de Paris*. Both of the Seldes brothers were deeply interested in politics and, like their Christian socialist utopian father, they counted themselves as advocates—as well as progressive reformers—of American democracy. George would pursue this political passion as a kind of metajournalist, becoming a print-media watchdog whose work would serve as an example for I. F. Stone and others. Gilbert pursued similar aims in his exploration of the role of popular culture in democracy, adhering to the Whitmanian principle that the measure of democracy's success as a political system would lay in the quality of the culture produced under its rule.[16] This belief took him first to the theater, then to the movies, to radio, and finally to television. His willingness to shift critical focus from one medium to the next in response to the evolution of mass communications technology demonstrates a concern in his values for the social and political consequence of art that prevails over the inevitable critical temptation to fetishize the aesthetic medium or object.

After the end of the First World War, the character of Gilbert Seldes' career quickly took shape. In 1920, he began a four-year stint as managing editor at *The Dial*. The magazine, which had been founded as a cultural monthly in 1880, had only recently abandoned the traditionalist Victorian editorial policies that could be traced to its origins. A new editor, Scofield Thayer, moved *The Dial*'s offices from Chicago to New York, attempting to put it at the crossroads of the radical literary and artistic movements that were reviving following the Armistice. The monthly became a fortnightly and it was rapidly transformed from a nineteenth century parlor review to a self-consciously freethinking champion of previously taboo culture in America. Randolph Bourne, Van Wyck Brooks, and H. E. Stearns were among Seldes' colleagues on the editorial staff. All of these critics were advocates of what Sherman Paul has described as the "green tradition" in American letters. Identifying strongly with Emerson in theory and Whitman in practice, they were bound by a common conviction that the homegrown in American literature, art, and culture was not to be measured by, or sacrificed to, the preservation of traditional European forms and standards.[17]

At *The Dial*, Seldes handled avant-garde manuscripts by such writers as Thorstein Veblen, John Dewey, and Mary Ritter Beard. He left his editorial position in 1923, but remained *The Dial*'s drama critic until the end of the decade. In his 1924 book, *The Seven Lively Arts*, Seldes proclaimed the reasons for his critical dedication to such "low" popular forms as comic strips, motion pictures, vaudeville, and pop music:

Because, in the first place, the lively arts have never had criticism. The box-office is gross; it detects no errors, nor does it sufficiently encourage improvement. . . . The lively arts can bear the same continuous criticism we give to the major, and if the criticism itself isn't bogus there is no reason why these arts should become self-conscious in any pejorative sense. In the second place, the lively arts which require little intellectual effort will more rapidly destroy the bogus than the major arts ever can. The close intimacy between high seriousness and high levity, the thing that brings together the extremes touching at the points of honesty and simplicity and intensity—will act like the convergence of armies to squeeze out the bogus. And the moment we recognize in the lively arts our actual form of expression, we will derive from them the same satisfaction which people have always derived from art which was relevant to their existence.[18]

Seldes' personal eclecticism never flagged. The author of several murder mysteries (under the pseudonym Foster Johns), an editor of the works of Ring Lardner, a daily columnist for *The New York Journal*, and an Ivy League professsor, he continued to scale the peaks and valleys of American letters for half a century. During the Depression year of 1930, for example, he completed a contemporary stage adaptation of Aristophanes' *Lysistrata* and also wrote a book on the evolving etiquette of social drinking during the Prohibition era. During the 1950s he was at the same time Dean of the Annenberg School of Communications at the University of Pennsylvania *and* a weekly series reviewer for *TV Guide*.

Just as George Seldes' belief in the crucial function played by journalism in American democracy made him a press critic, Gilbert Seldes' similar belief about the role of drama in a democratic culture put him in front of a television set. It surely took a certain amount of confidence, in the years immediately following World War II, for an intellectual to devote his career to the aesthetic examination of a medium that had established a reputation, almost from birth, as the crudest public exercise of the imaginative capacity in the history of artistic expression. Seldes' impeccable credentials—his family, education, apprenticeship, and early career—must have provided him with some of this confidence; the contingency that he could move freely from academic appointment to commercial writing must also have been a factor.

Seldes' critical embrace of what so many of his colleagues were willing to dismiss as just so much evidence of the sociopathic dysfunction of late capitalism was neither self-serving nor a patronization. In 1956, for example, the critic found himself thoughtfully perplexed by the rise of Jackie Gleason: "throwing his weight around . . . is . . . Gleason's most characteristic movement before the camera. He is a heavy man with the traditional belief of heavy men in their own lightness and grace."[19] Seldes admired Gleason's technical acumen as a comedian, but on the whole, found The Great One "distasteful." The very ambiguity of such comment concerning a leading television performer went against the tide of bland, daily "like it/don't like it" newspaper reviewing. But what is far more remarkable about the Seldes critique of Gleason is that a critic with Seldes' training found fault with the "fatman" TV clown not by way of some comparison with Falstaff or even with Fatty Arbuckle, but rather rated Gleason against the standard of Jimmy Durante, who was hosting a comedy-variety show during the mid–1950s that was much like Gleason's.[20] Seldes found Durante's grotesque mugging and posturing and his stylized Brooklyn speech supported by a humane warmth that he felt was lacking in the blustery tirades of Ralph Kramden or in the egocentric pomposity of Reginald Van Gleason III. Seldes was perhaps the first critic who could discuss matters of taste in television viewing without questioning a taste for television viewing itself.

Seldes refused to isolate television narrative from the traditional paradigms of American culture. A good example of this is his positive review of Paul Henning's *The Beverly Hillbillies*, which was published in *TV Guide* during the sitcom's premiere season of Fall 1962. Unwilling to issue a blanket dismissal of situation comedy in general or rural situation comedy in particular (as had so many reviewers in response to what would become the most popular show on American TV for the next decade), Seldes affords the text the respect of careful viewing and searches for its context:

The thumping success of *The Beverly Hillbillies* has already sent some serious thinkers to the wailing wall, and when you tune the program in, you are supposed to ask yourself, "What is America coming to?" As I am still laughing, I think back to the days when custard pies and Keystone Cops were flying through the air and a lot of people were convinced America was a cultural "desert"—the 1920 word for "wasteland." A question I asked then has never been answered: What can you do with a custard pie except throw it?[21]

Thus Seldes stands alone as a learned and sympathetic television critic during the first two decades of network broadcast. Unfortunately, that very loneliness led to obscurity rather than distinction. His writing simply did not fit into the highcult/masscult belletristic apartheid that was the substance and legacy of "The Mass Culture Debate." Simultaneously more complex than the bubble gum reviewing of the tabloid TV sections and too simplistic (as much for its lack of disciplinary jargon as for its subject matter) to be taken seriously as academic criticism, the body of Seldes' work simply fell through the cracks in American letters.

Seldes seemed very much aware of this. In his last book, *The New Mass Media: Challenge to a Free Society* (1968), he attempts a metacritical overview of American television, focusing on the philosophical implications of the mass media for American democratic traditions. Abandoning practical criticism completely, the short, pamphlet-like book takes on the character of a Mass Culture Debate tome; it does not mention the name of even a single performer or program. While this attempt at a "respectable" treatise is evidence of Seldes' frustration, the critic ends on a hopeful note in the final chapter, reiterating the essence of his lifelong work:

In many colleges, courses in the communications arts have been established in the past ten years, and in some of these the habit of observing popular entertainment critically is instilled. The new effort is to give students an intelligent outlook on the mass media, not to make them experts in either the aesthetic or the sociological aspects, but to inform their judgment, to make them more selective in their own choices. Such courses may ultimately increase manyfold the number of people who will not apathetically accept whatever is offered. . . . Our schools and colleges would [thus] "create an audience" of thoughtful people so large that they would become a factor in the plans of the entertainment media.[22]

Seldes' idealistic commitment to the basic didactic function of the critical vocation in a democratic culture had survived since his days at *The Dial*. It was not, however, until after his death in 1970 that evidence began to arise that his faith was neither misplaced nor was it merely the quaint residue of another age.

The publication of Horace Newcomb's *TV: The Most Popular Art* in 1974 was a watershed for television criticism of the type that Seldes had suggested and advocated. A professor of American Studies holding a doctorate in literature, Newcomb had also worked as a daily television reviewer for *The Baltimore Sun*. He had written a book of criticism on popular commercial TV programs organized as a series of genre studies: the domestic sitcom, the afternoon soap opera, the action/adventure show, etc.[23] Dependent upon neither statistics nor stimulus-response theories for any gratuitous cloak of legitimacy, Newcomb did with television what literature critics had been doing with books for thousands of years: he considered text and context; he responded with heart and head.

A year later, Newcomb, as editor, brought out the first edition of an anthology that marked a kind of first flowering of American television criticism. *Television: The Critical View* contained essays by humanities scholars, social scientists, and nonacademic freelancers. The book was a tremendous success in the academic market, finding and filling a real need among a generation of students *and* teachers who were intimately familiar with television language, mythology, drama and manners, but who, for lack of just such a book, could not "officially" consider this common culture in the print oriented world of the classroom. The introduction of the VCR into the consumer appliance market at about this time did much to further promote the rise of academic television studies. Over the next ten years, increasing numbers of professors and students would have these machines at their personal disposal. During this same period, the "video reserve room" gradually became a common component of American college libraries. The videotape was at least gaining the accessibility, if not the respect, of the book.

Though the appearance of the Newcomb volumes seems almost by itself to have initiated a sudden and unexpected beginning for television criticism, it would be a mistake to think that such a wave of critical interest could have developed without regard to television content. There is a picture of Archie Bunker on the cover of *TV: The Most Popular Art* and there is good reason to believe that this character was not arbitrarily chosen over Lucy Ricardo, Sergeant Joe Friday, or Samantha the Witch. As Newcomb observed, the sitcom, after a long incubation as a static, banal genre, had only recently been "changed into a vehicle for biting social commentary" by shows such as *All in the Family*, *M*A*S*H*, *Maude*, and *The Mary Tyler Moore Show*.[24] The genre's expansion into "hot" topics was probably the greatest magnet for the sudden critical attention. An interest in the dramatic concerns of situation comedies led to an interest in the people who were highlighting those concerns and who were thus expressing opinions about them. Identifiable television auteurs began to emerge from the indecipherable shadows of the final credits crawl. Norman Lear was the first nonperforming TV personality to be granted the celebrity status of a *Playboy* interview.[25] The expansion of the sitcom's mimetic agenda accomplished by Lear, Larry Gelbart, and the MTM production team of James Brooks, Allan Burns, Ed Weinberger, and Stan Daniels had fertilized a critical field. As forgotten birthdays, fibs told by children, and reminders of dad's earthy wisdom gave way in the sitcom to abortions, racial epithets, and ironic commentary on the style of modern life, the national drama of prime time television began to "create an audience" in much the sense that Seldes had hoped it would.

Indeed, after a quarter of a century of network television, *All in the Family* was the first weekly series to provoke a sustained critical dialogue. Every racist, ethnocentric, sexist, and sexual preferentialist remark uttered by Archie Bunker seemed to provoke another newspaper column or magazine article during the early seventies. Academic monographs soon followed. Political activists, clergy, and industry operatives joined reviewers, social scientists, and humanistic critics in a debate on the merits of the program. Some thought it a welcome airing of the nation's dirty laundry; others deplored the regrettable opening of a Pandora's box. The paradigm of "The Mass Culture Debate" had decisively shifted from "television vs. culture" to "good television vs. bad television." Moreover, by taking part in this dialogue, intellectuals were freely admitting in public that they were actually watching TV. A penchant for abstract theory was no longer a sufficient credential for a would-be critic of television; the grounding of theory in textual evidence was now required. It was not enough to summarily dismiss *All in the Family* as "dangerous" or as a "sublimation"; you had to know who Meathead was.

Lear spun off a string of sitcom hits from *All in the Family*, including *Maude*, *Good Times*, and *The Jeffersons*, each of which further intensified the suddenly volatile discourse of what had been thought to be among the most arid genres of an intellectually parched medium. In 1979, Richard Adler edited an anthology titled *All in the Family: A Critical Appraisal*, which was perhaps the first attempt at a comprehensive critical assessment of a weekly half-hour situation comedy. In 1984, the British Film Institute book series released *MTM: 'Quality Television'*, a comprehensive anthological treatment of the aesthetic cosmology of an entire commerical production studio.

In *The Producer's Medium: Conversations with Creators of American TV* (1983), Newcomb and Robert S. Alley offer ample evidence that this bursting forth of new energy in the post-sixties sitcom was anything but unselfconscious on the part of the artists who accomplished it. For example, Allan Burns, one of the co-creators of *The Mary Tyler Moore Show*, told Newcomb and Alley:

... [W]e were feeling pretty good about it [*The Mary Tyler Moore Show*], cocky about it. We felt it was going to be *the* show. Then we sat down and watched [the pilot episode of] *All in the Family* and we came out with very mixed feelings. We were very impressed that something was going to be that competitive with us. To be honest we thought it was going to steal a lot of wind from our sails.[26]

While Burns' apprehension was correct and *All in the Family*, with its unprecedented five years in the Neilsen Number One spot, stole most of the headlines, *Mary Tyler Moore* and its spinoffs, *Rhoda* and *Phyllis*, managed to create a critical dialogue of their own, focusing on the changing image of the single working woman in American culture during a period when increasing numbers of women were seeking employment outside the home. Critical comment on *The Mary Tyler Moore Show* became de rigueur for women's magazines ranging from *Family Circle* to *Ms*. The 1979 edition of the Newcomb anthology contained articles on the series by Carolyn Traynor Williams and Dorothy Rabinowitz. Similarly, Gelbart's *M*A*S*H*, with its pungent discourses on war and peace, individuality and bureaucracy, and relations between the sexes, provoked popular and academic comment during (and since) its decade-long production run.

Seldes' argument that any popular TV show deserved serious critical attention just because it was popular had never really won partisans. But the new sitcoms of the early seventies did win attention by directly addressing their content to political and social issues that were already on the minds of many writers and scholars. Television shows became reference points for public rhetoric, thus taking on to some degree the ideal progressive function of a national drama. By the end of the decade, the sitcom renaissance had spent itself. But diverse commentators had at last recognized television criticism as a powerful didactic tool: the practice outlived its initial catalyzing agent.[27]

A thorough understanding of the sudden proliferation of television criticism during the seventies and eighties also requires a look at certain technological and marketing stimuli that abetted the phenomenon. Beginning in the late sixties, with corporate plans for satellite cable already off the drawing board, a conventional belief developed that cable TV would be the force that might finally break the oligarchic stranglehold of the networks on television programming. Dwight Macdonald and many fifties' commentators had argued that the very massness of network television's "infinite" audience precluded quality. But cable seemed to address itself directly to this structural problem. Might not a multiplicity of channels, all aimed at groups smaller and more well-defined than the "mass," result in greater variety? Might not that greater variety, in turn, allow for the emergence of works of quality? Perhaps such works of quality would even provide standards for the entire medium. These so-called "blue skies" predictions for cable television imagined secure places on the enlarged spectrum for both classic and avant-garde art, as well as for suppressed political points of view. The networks would surely continue their cop shows and sitcoms, but all those new empty channels would just as surely allow room for the emergence of a video "high culture" that would be rooted in the historically "legitimate" paradigms that had been handed down through the literary arts.

This is not, however, what happened. Cable TV did improve television drama, but in a way that was not generally anticipated. Instead of taking the high road, the vast majority of cable services proved to be even less concerned with "quality" than the networks had been during their uncontested oligarchy. Exhibition "sports" such as professional wrestling and roller derby, long ago abandoned by ABC, CBS, and NBC, returned to American television—even to prime time television—via cable. Theatrically released soft-core porno and gross-out films became staples of cable fare, even as the Big Three were making concerted efforts to produce their own "issue-oriented" made-for-TV movies. New series, with such poor production values and such weak writing that they were easily recognizable as "subnetwork" appeared, including revivals of long-dead series such as *What's Happening Now?* and *The New Munsters.* The prime time schedules of cable services such as USA or TBS can make ABC look like the BBC. Nick-at-Night and the Christian Broadcasting Network have presented entire prime time lineups consisting almost exclusively of reruns of precisely those fifties sitcoms that had caused FCC Commissioner Nicholas Johnson to coin the term "vast wasteland" in 1961 (ironically, these "schlock" revivals have been a great aid to the proliferation of television studies).

At the same time, as their share of the total national audience diminished, the major networks began to concentrate on attracting richer (and this generally means more highly educated) viewers as the "audience of choice" in the "post-mass" age of video targeting. *Saturday Night Live* was perhaps a stalking horse in the search for this audience. Even those who disliked it could not dislike it for the same reasons that they disliked *I Dream of Jeannie* or *The Brady Bunch*. The allusion-laden, politically-loaded, risqué sketches presented on *Saturday Night Live* by producer Lorne Michaels during the late seventies violated every rule of "least objectionability" that had dominated network TV since its McCarthy Era inception.

Perhaps the biggest breakthrough in prime time "quality" came with the peculiar success of Steven Bochco's *Hill Street Blues*. While *Hill Street's* initial 1981 ratings were fatally low by traditional "mass" standards (only around 9 million people tuned in each week), NBC researchers discovered that among this meager group could be found an astounding number of high-income viewers who had been to college and who, more importantly for network purposes, just might require the convenience of microwave ovens and autobahn cruisers for their painfully fast-paced lifestyles. Even better, the *Hill Street* viewer profile looked curiously like that of the typical pay-cable subscriber. MTM Enterprises, which had done so much to revitalize the sitcom for upscale audiences, had now spawned a cop show capable of similar appeal.

Most critics loved *Hill Street Blues*; a few did not. But virtually no one could ignore this complex, well-crafted drama in a genre better known for its violent pyrotechnics and twisted metal. The spectacle of such high critical praise for a police series had been previously unthinkable. The fact that much of the adoration was based on formal innovations that were derived from afternoon soap operas made *Hill Street*'s critical reception all the more remarkable. The eventual commercial success of the show paved the way for such series as *St. Elsewhere*, *L.A. Law*, *thirtysomething*, and *Wiseguy*. These shows, whose merits have been much debated individually, collectively broke the once immutable mold of traditional, symmetrical, good guy/bad guy comic book TV drama. All written from a point of view that helped to put the work "yuppie" into the language, these series are as much the revenge of articulate TV babies against *Starsky and Hutch*, *Marcus Welby*, *Perry Mason*, *Family*, and *The Untouchables* as they are the substance of what must be considered a middle class public culture in America.

Television programs that are less patently "mass" and more identifiably "class" in orientation clearly get the lion's share of critical attention. The growing importance of authorship in critical studies of TV drama affirms the artistic gentrification of the medium by critics. While archival critical work on "mass era" auteurs and studios such as Paul Henning (*The Beverly Hillbillies*, *Green Acres* et al.) or Mark VII Productions (*Dragnet, Adam–12*, et al.) remains relatively rare, there has been a steady stream of work on "class era" auteurs and studios such as Steven Bochco (*L.A. Law, Hooperman*) and MTM Enterprises (*Lou Grant, St. Elsewhere*). Work focusing on entire cable services, such as MTV, Black Entertainment Television, and the various religious channels has proliferated as well.

To be sure, "The Mass Culture Debate" rattles on in the work of writers

4. See Daniel J. Czitrom, *Media and the American Mind* (Chapel Hill: University of North Carolina Press, 1983). Czitrom describes an almost ritual pattern of response by American intellectuals to the introduction of new mass communications media.

5. Herbert Marcuse, *One-Dimensional Man* (Boston: Beacon Press, 1964), 101.

6. Gunther Anders, "The Phantom World of TV," trans. Norbert Guterman. *Dissent* 3 (1956): 14.

7. T. S. Eliot, "Notes Toward the Definition of Culture" (1949) rpt. in *Christianity and Culture* (New York: Harvest/Harcourt, Brace & World, 1968), see especially "Sect and Cult," 141–57.

8. Walt Whitman, Preface, *Leaves of Grass* (1855).

9. Dwight Macdonald, "A Theory of Mass Culture," *Dissent* 3, rpt. in Bernard Rosenberg and David M. White (ed.), *Mass Culture: The Popular Arts in America* (New York: Free Press, 1957), 62.

10. Michael Ross and Ernest van den Haag, *The Fabric of Society* (New York: Harcourt, Brace and Company, 1957), 101.

11. In Rosenberg and White: David Manning White, "Mass Culture in America: Another Point of View," 13–21; and Melvin Tumin, "Popular Culture and the Open Society," 548–56.

12. Robert Sklar, *Movie-Made America: A Cultural History of American Movies* (New York: Vintage/Random House, 1975), see especially Part I, "The Rise of Movie Culture."

13. J. Fred MacDonald's prolific work includes titles on racial representation, the political character of television drama, and a genre study of the Western.

14. George Lipsitz, "The Meaning of Memory: Family, Class and Ethnicity in Early Network Television Programs," *Cultural Anthropology* 1:4 (November 1986): 355–87.

15. Thomas Cripps, "*Amos 'n' Andy* and the Struggle for Racial Integration," in O'Conner, 33–54.

16. See Walt Whitman, *Democratic Vistas* (1871).

17. For a powerful treatment of this paradigm, see Sherman Paul, *Repossessing and Renewing: The Green Tradition in American Culture* (Baton Rouge: Louisiana State University Press, 1978).

18. Seldes, *The Seven Lively Arts*, 303.

19. Seldes, *The Public Arts* (New York: Simon and Schuster, 1956), 161.

20. *The Jimmy Durante Show* (NBC, 1954–56; CBS, 1957) was part of *The Texaco Star Theatre* series. *The Donald O'Connor Show* aired on alternate weeks.

21. Rev. of *The Beverly Hillbillies*, TV Guide, 15 December 1962, 4.

22. Seldes, *The New Mass Media: Challenge to a Free Society* (Washington, D.C.: Public Affairs Press, 1968), 98.

23. Horace Newcomb, *TV: The Popular Art* (New York: Anchor Press/Doubleday, 1974).

24. *TV: The Most Popular Art*, 57.

25. Barbara Cady and Norman Lear, "Playboy Interview: Norman Lear," *Playboy* 23 (March 1976), 53–69.

26. Newcomb and Robert S. Alley, *The Producer's Medium: Conversations with Creators of American TV*, 174.

27. Another important aid in the facilitation of TV criticism, which I cannot treat adequately here, has been the increasing availability of reference texts. In the last ten years, dozens of books have been published that offer critics the bibliographic grunt work necessary for the easy practice of their art. Two of the most useful of these are Tim

such as Neil Postman, Joshua Meyerowitz and Gerry Mander. But the cri
dialogue on American television that began with the Newcomb books has
erally eschewed the old assumption that television is structurally doome
aesthetic inferiority in comparison to "real" forms of art. The most impo:
change brought about by the rise of television criticism is that blanket conc
nations of the medium that make no distinction between works, auteur:
genres, reveal themselves as bumptious. Any commentator making such a
tions must admit that he or she is incapable of distinguishing between *M*A**
and *Private Benjamin*, between *Crime Story* and *Vega$*, between *Saturday N
Live* and *The Glen Campbell Goodtime Hour*, between *L.A. Law* and *C
Marshall, Attorney-at-Law*. In each case, the "superior" program is not
essarily "objectively" obvious. That is a matter to be settled in the critical
But a critic who cannot or will not make distinctions between works of the :
genre or the same medium loses his or her credibility when issuing mess
warnings about the overall effects of that genre or medium. Such warnings
become tedious echoes of the condemnations of the cinema that were is
from turn of the century pulpits.

Has television drama matured to the point that we may now spea
"highcult," "midcult" and "masscult" programs? If so, what are the s:
features that define these aesthetics? Issues such as self-reflexivity, moral
biguity, and formal innovation are worth considering in this context. Wh:
the implications of the "mass-to-class" evolution of television drama fo
American social class structure? Are new media likely to follow a similar p:
of development? Will historians one day recall (with perhaps a twinge of
ocratic nostalgia) the period of "three-network television" when America
virtually all classes were watching much the same shows? Will demographi
targeted television services such as MTV (youth), Lifetime (18–55 yea
women), and ESPN (men) produce programs in the familiar grammars c
historical network genres? Or will the mythic structures of the sitcom, the g
show, and the talkshow be exploded by audience specificity? And of cours
critic still does well to consider the question that Gilbert Seldes always
himself responsible for: Is there anything good on?

NOTES

1. Waldo David Frank, "Seriousness and Dada" (an exchange of letters betwe
author and Malcolm Cowley during 1924), *In the American Jungle* (New York: I
and Rinehart, 1937), 129.

2. Gilbert Seldes, "Preface to the 1957 Edition," *The Seven Lively Arts* (New
Sagamore Press, 1924), 10–11.

3. The period known as "the golden age of television drama" is perhaps more
known as "the McCarthy era," a coincidence not discussed nearly often enough. F
illuminating study of the ideological conventions forced upon TV dramatists during
golden age," see Kenneth Hey, "Aesthetics vs. Medium in Early Television Dra
in *American History/American Television* (New York: Ungar, 1983), 95–133.

Brooks and Earle Marsh, *The Complete Directory to Prime-Time Network Television Programs* and Alex McNeil, *Total Television*, both of which are massive compendiums of all types of program and industry data. Other reference works focus on more specific types of information, such as episode plot summaries for entire series, network scheduling histories, and biographical information on performers, production operatives, and industry executives.

10

From Mass Man to Postmodernism: Critical Analyses of Television for the Past Half-Century

James M. O'Brien

In the seven years between 1948 and 1955, television became the dominant mass medium in American culture. In 1948, less than one percent of American homes had a television receiver; by 1955, television's penetration was nearly 50 percent and increasing rapidly. In these few years, television became what it remains today: the major consumer of leisure time for all segments of American life; the dominant medium for both news and entertainment, and the bestower of celebrity and notoriety with an unmatched swiftness and intimacy.

The rapid accession of television to the center of American culture was preceded by twenty-five years of electronic development and experimentation. Introduced commercially at the World's Fair in 1939, the medium would probably have followed a more gradual pattern of growth without the hiatus of World War II. Of greatest significance in the growth of television, the radio industry, especially the powerful radio networks, provided economic support, a marketing structure, and a way for the mass audience to relate to the broadcasting experience. The swift ascendancy of television impacted negatively on other mass media: movies, mass circulation magazines, evening newspapers and, most particularly and ironically, network radio.

Radio (understood as a mass medium) also provided the dominant scholarly perspective from which television was to be examined during its early history. With few exceptions, critical analyses of television from a humanistic perspective were absent or negative. Not till the sixties did the writings of Marshall McLuhan and the rise of the popular culture movement justify serious scholarly attention to the medium. By the seventies, this approach began to bifurcate into traditional criticism (in which television is analyzed as an aesthetic object) and contemporary criticism (in which television is regarded as an apparatus or a text, to be deconstructed, "read," metaphored, and otherwise analyzed.) In the social sciences, a similar bifurcation has occurred between the traditional (objective or "value-free") scientists, and those who regard a critical evaluation of ideology and social structure as essential to meaningful media analysis.

By the mid–1980s, approaches to television criticism and analysis had proliferated somewhat chaotically. As Anthony Smith, the director of the British Film Institute, notes:

Television research has grown in a very ramshackle way. During the 1960s and 70s a whole series of academic disciplines, from political science to neurology, began to develop pockets of researchers who attempted to link their particular intellectual habits and attitudes to the massive fact of the presence of television. TV research in the 80s reveals its heterodox historical origins.[1]

"Ramshackle" may be a bit too strong. There are discernible patterns in TV criticism broadly construed, and, while clearly unable to do more than allude to important works, I hope to demonstrate that many current concerns of television criticism may be illuminated by a brief consideration of those same "heterodox historical origins."

THE 1930S AND 1940S: A NEW MEDIUM AND THE MASS MAN

The notion of the "mass man" as a product of modern technology and modern culture gripped the imaginations of both social science researchers and humanist commentators from the thirties well into the sixties. In *The Revolt of the Masses* (1932) Jose Ortega y Gassett, observing the political ferment in post-World War I Europe, complained that the multitude, that is, the average man, had possession of the places and the instruments, particularly the mass media, created by civilization. He saw the rise of contemporary political forms, fascism in particular, as representing the political domination of the masses. Whereas previous forms of government had found room for divergent minorities, "everybody" now represented the masses alone.[2]

Political scientists and sociologists in the United States, transfixed by the rapid accession to power of Mussolini, Hitler, and Franco, noted that, in every case, the dictators dominated and controlled the mass media. They began to turn their attentions to the role of media in the formation of public opinion, and studies of propaganda and voter decision-making proliferated in the thirties. Observers of the U.S. political scene could not fail to notice the effective use of radio by F. D. Roosevelt in rallying the people behind his policies.

Between the late 1920s and the early 1940s the "four pioneers" of communications research (as Bernard Berelson called them in a notable essay), Lasswell, Lazarsfeld, Lewin and Hovland, began a series of studies from the perspectives of their various disciplines, which would lay the groundwork for communications research for a generation to come. The dominant model of communication (elaborated by Lasswell)—source-message-medium-audience-effect—was both linear and medium-powerful by implication.[3] Another influential early work was Hadley Cantril's *The Invasion from Mars* (1940), which summarized the field research done following the most famous and influential radio broadcast of all time: Orson Welles' Mercury Theatre version of *War of the Worlds*.[4]

In the 1940s, beginning with Hovland's studies conducted for the U.S. Army, experimental psychologists designed lab studies in communication, testing hypotheses regarding communication processes and exploring intervening variables in group influence and individual perceptions. Lazarsfeld and Stanton conducted an extensive series of field studies of the radio audience. Engineering studies by Shannon and Weaver (*The Mathematical Theory of Communication*, 1949) emphasized the component of feedback in the heretofore linear model of communication. These works provided a view of the communications process with a powerful scientific ethos and were influential in the developing field. Also in 1949, Norbert Weiner's *The Human Use of Human Beings* elaborated the use of feedback for cybernetics, the scientific analysis of control systems. A major component was added to the communications model, reducing both its linearity and its implied potency. A veritable Pandora's Box of further complications awaited.

This early emphasis on scientific method and "hard" scientific theory undergirding communication research is worth noting. The highly valued ethos of science was seen as necessary to "justify" the attention paid to an otherwise ephemeral and culturally insignificant medium. This scientific emphasis established a tradition of quantitative analysis of mass media which remains vital today in such studies as the Gerbner Violence profile and the annual Roper study of media use and preference.

THE 1950S: ORIGINS OF NEW APPROACHES

Between 1951 and 1953 a series of studies of the content of television programing was made under the aegis of the National Association of Education Broadcasters. Dallas Smythe and various associates conducted content analyses of all television stations in specific markets over the period of a week. The studies were modeled on the famous Payne studies of Hollywood films done in the early 1930s, and came up with familiar findings, that television's dramas represented a simplified and idealized portrait of American society.

After an early burst of optimism at the potential of the new medium based on studies showing that students learn as well from television as from classroom instruction, educators began to lose faith in the power of television to transform the educational process and began instead to rehearse familiar proprint biases. A collection of essays called (rather too broadly) *Television's Impact on American Culture* (1956), edited by William Eliot, focussed on the educational impact and potential of the new medium, but began with the assumption that what television might contribute to culture necessarily came through educational television. Eliot articulates the fears of many educators in the mid-fifties in his forward: "A nation that has ceased to read or that has become merely passive in its absorption of entertainment and education by way of a medium like that of television will have lost the true range of possibilities."[5] Eugene David Glynn, a psychiatrist writing in the same volume, authoritatively articulates another theme of popular psychology in the 1950s—the passive, dependent, oral fixation of the viewer for television which makes him a helpless conformist.[6] This persistent notion is echoed in later writings such as Harlan Ellison's *The Glass Teat* (1970) and Marie Winn's *Television: the Plug-in Drug* (1977).

The 1950s might be called the great decade of popular sociology, stretching from David Riesman's *The Lonely Crowd* to C. Wright Mills' *The Power Elite* (1956). These works were marked by accessibility and connection to the immediate experience of many literate Americans. Typical of such works was Paul Bogard's *The Age of Television* (1956). Bogard posed key questions which continue to shape media inquiry from a social science perspective: How is the medium unique? What is the relationship between leisure and the use of television? What are the criteria for examining the products of popular culture? What is the nature of television's appeal to its audience? And how do people watch television? Finally, and forever, what are the effects of television on youth, politics, sports, other media, and so on?

Mass Culture: The Popular Arts in America (1957) formed a bridge between social science writing on the media and the considerations of various humanists from many perspectives. Stuart Rosenberg and David M. White, respectively a conservative sociologist and a liberal journalist, offered a smorgasbord of some fifty essays which recapitulated previous approaches and pointed the direction for media analysis in the decades to come. The title reveals both emphases: mass culture is a sociological term with a powerful negative bias; popular arts suggests both an aesthetic approach and a positive attitude.

By no means were all humanist writers approving of the popular arts. Dwight MacDonald, the influential curmudgeon of the Left, generated a perversely conservative, antipopulist, antibourgeois attack on popular culture, arguing that the inevitable consequence of mass media was the control of production by a few media barons, with the result that the content of high culture was homogenized into a superficial pap that he labeled "mass culture." MacDonald articulated "Gresham's law of culture" by which a large quantity of cheap inferior products drives out the few works of quality.

Notable on the other hand was Gilbert Seldes, an articulate critic and defender of the popular arts since the 1920s. Seldes argued that the best works of popular culture—operetta and musical comedy, films, and ultimately (and reluctantly) television, could be compared aesthetically to the works of high culture. This point of view would grow into the popular culture movement of the 1960s and is evidenced currently in the work of David Marc and others.

In 1959, when *Public Opinion Quarterly* invited senior communications researcher Bernard Berelson to comment on the state of communications research, he suggested that the approach was "withering away," with the great pioneers in the field, Lasswell, Lazarsfeld, Lewin, and Hovland returned to their own areas of expertise. Wilber Schramm, David Riesman, and Raymond Bauer responded in the same issue with vigorous dissents, citing dozens of studies and lines of research in full flower. In Schramm's words, the field was in ferment. The widely read and anthologized article and the discussion which followed it led to a decade of attempts to define communications and determine the parameters of the "discipline" of communication studies. As it turned out, communication could be satisfactorily defined from a number of perspectives. Since the perspective tended to shape the definition, no commonly accepted definition emerged.

Another profoundly influential work, Joseph Klapper's comprehensive survey, *The Effects of Mass Communication* (1960), funded by CBS, summarized the existing research data on mass media to that date. Klapper concluded that the mass media are rarely the direct and immediate cause of effects in their audiences, but work together with a number of influences, societal and personal, normally in reinforbing the status quo. Klapper's conclusions were good news for television networks and producers, under heavy fire for the increasing and graphic violence evident on the small screen. However, CBS's sponsorship tended to reduce the credibility of Klapper's findings for those media critics who were committed to a negative view of television's impact.

People have always tended to blame the dominant popular medium for the evils of society, and television has absorbed an abundance of scapegoating, as did radio and movies in the 1930s and 1940s. Of the three perennial issues (sex, violence, and negative influence on children), excessive violence leading to antisocial behavior in society has been the most continuous preoccupation. This concern has led to hundreds of lab and field studies exploring violent media diets as a cause of antisocial behavior, most notably Albert Bandura's simplistic but dramatic and influential demonstrations of media behavior modeling in the early 1950s, Leonard Eron's ten-year longitudinal studies linking preference for violent TV fare with antisocial behavior in later life, and George Gerbner's ongoing if mechanistic content analysis counting violent acts on prime time. From the 1950s through the early 1970s, numerous congressional and presidential committees held hearings, compiled data, and issued hotly debated findings.[7]

A number of social scientists were becoming dissatisfied with the rather dehumanized model implied in these studies. Laboratory and field studies in the 1950s supported the concept of audience selectivity in experiencing media products. That is, the audience selectively exposed themselves to congenial media messages, selectively perceived the messages contained therein, and selectively retained them in accordance with their own previously constructed cognitive structure. These lines of study (and many others) began to replace the old "medium-powerful" model of communications with an "audience-powerful" model in the thinking of many researchers. Research beginning with these assumptions, which came to be known as the "uses and gratifications perspective," was grounded in the idea that the media's audience used its messages according to their own needs and for their own various gratifications. In 1974, the publication of Blumler and Katz, *The Uses of Mass Communication: Current Perspectives on Gratification Research*, marked the ascendance of this approach in the communications research community.

THE 1960S: MCLUHAN AND THE POPULAR CULTURE MOVEMENT

Fresh from its success in commissioning Klapper's monumental work, CBS strove to institutionalize its commitment to support critical analysis of the medium by funding a quarterly magazine devoted to television. Though the project was subsequently abandoned, twenty-three essays commissioned for the quarterly were published in *The Eighth Art* (1962). Among various contributors, Charles Siepmann, a television pioneer in both Britain and the U.S., commented trenchantly:

We badly need, as counterweight to such "objective" studies (as those of the social scientists), the stimulus and light of imaginative writings that sets television and its various facets in a broader context than that of a private enterprise and relates it to the times we live in and our true requirements of it.[8]

Siepmann seeks comments on television from multiple perspectives, but finds the record to date limited. He notes E. J. Carwell's early *Television: Servant or Master* (1951), but regards it as flawed by "excessive Christian apologetics." He notes also the work of Reuel Denney (*The Astonished Muse*, 1953), William Lynch, S.J. (*The Image Industries*, 1959), and Gilbert Seldes (*The Great Audience*, 1951), but sees them as atypical and insufficient.

As if in answer to Siepmann, humanistic approaches to various media began to be developed in the 1960s, emerging out of speech, film study, folklore study, American studies, and Popular Culture studies. The application of more rigorous methodologies such as semiotics to film studies, particularly by European scholars, laid the groundwork for a torrent of film and later television analyses from these specialised perspectives. In the mid–1960s, the Popular Culture Association was formed (nominally as a subgroup of the Modern Language Association) and had the effect of institutionalizing the movement. Headquartered at Bowling Green University, the PCA publishes the *Journal of Popular Culture* and the *Journal of Popular Film and Television* among a number of other journals and monographs.

Also during the 1960s, the impact of the ideas of Canadian scholars Harold Innes and Marshall McLuhan, and the wide circulation of McLuhan's *Understanding Media* (1964) spurred multivalenced approaches to the mass media and a boom in graduate studies in communications. Perhaps no other single individual has had more impact on the study of television and other mass media than the Canadian professor of literature at the University of Toronto. Although his writings in the 1950s show a gradually growing preoccupation with popular culture, the publication of *The Gutenberg Galaxy: The Making of Typographic Man* in 1962 first brought McLuhan to international attention. This attention was intensified by the publication of *Understanding Media*, which became a kind of handbook of media jargon for the next decade.

Not surprisingly, academic respectability and approbation were requisite to the proliferation of humanist criticism of popular media, television in particular. This respectability developed (gradually and relatively) with the growth of the Popular Culture movement, a movement that had its roots in American Studies and began developing as an academic discipline in the 1930s. (Yale offered a Ph.D. in American Studies in the mid–1930s.) These programs attempted to draw together the viewpoints of history, literature, sociology, and anthropology into a more unified picture of American culture. The former two disciplines dominated the studies, however, and the emphasis was placed on an analysis of the past rather than the present.

As American Studies programs proliferated, periodicals multiplied, faculties became entrenched, and younger students and teachers in the field grew frustrated with the past-oriented and traditional approach of the American Studies programs. Folklorists, media students, and academic rabblerousers in general began to try to define an area for themselves. After two Purdue University conferences on Folklore and American Culture in the early 1960s, the Popular Culture Association was formed and began publishing texts, collections, and analyses of popular culture artifacts. Literature and historical studies continued to represent the chosen modes of analysis.[9] The Popular Culture movement thus opened the door for academicians, trained in the traditional disciplines of the humanities, to bring their perspectives and methodologies to bear on the material of the media once reserved for social scientists.

John Cawelti, whose writings are seminal to what are now known as genre studies, observed that the new popular culture approach derived in part from dissatisfaction with the mass culture model of communication:

recent mass communication research has shown beyond question that the mass culture model of communication positing a power relationship between an irresistible elite and a helplessly incoherent mass audience is totally inadequate as a description of the real social complexity of relationships between media and their various publics. Recent research stresses the influence of the network of social reference groups which intervene between the media and the audience, shaping the public's perception and reaction to communication in many ways.[10]

Cawelti goes on to note that for the younger generation, popular culture does not seem like a rising tide of garbage, but rather a substantial part of their experience, to which they respond in rich and subtle ways. He suggests that

McLuhan's writings point to this new kind of depth experience created by the electronic media. The insight which Cawelti so well articulates marked a new openness to and freedom for humanistic analyses of the media, particularly television, which would characterize the years to come.

THE 1970S AND 1980S: A PROLIFERATION OF PERSPECTIVES

The graduate students of the seventies were the first generation to have grown up with television as an established fact of American life rather than a sensational new and wondrous technology of information and entertainment access. As McLuhan would have said, the medium had become invisible to them, and media studies permitted them to reenvision familiar experience. As film studies programs which had burgeoned in the 1960s reached a saturation point, many students pursuing graduate programs in cinema studies turned their attentions to television. Scholarly approaches to the medium from a humanist slant, once largely restricted to the popular culture perspective, began to proliferate, with a methodological emphasis on cultural linguistics, especially semiotics, the newly popular critical tool of the decade. Of particular note is Peter Woollen's *Sign and Meaning in the Cinema* (1971), a pioneering work in the application of the tools of semiology to visual images.

These new approaches treat the content of television as a particular kind of literature. Once television "texts" are regarded as a kind of "reading," then the influence of theoretical writers from various linguistic viewpoints can provide substructures for new critical analyses, focussed on the suddenly reenvisioned medium of television. These writers include (but are not limited to) Claude Levi-Strauss (structural linguistics), Vladimer Propp (narrative theory), Umberto Eco, Roland Barthes, and Christian Metz (semiotics, especially Metz' *Film Language: A Semiotics of the Cinema*, 1974), Northrup Frye (genre study), and Antonio Gramsci and Louis Althusser (Marxist analysis). Of particular influence is the work of German sociologist Jurgen Habermas, a Marxist sociologist influenced by the Frankfurt school, especially Max Horkheimer and Theodor Adorno. His shift toward language theory began in a 1968 essay, "Technology and Science in Ideology." Another important work in this tradition, Hartley and Fiske's *Reading Television* (1978) was the precursor of a veritable torrent of linguistically oriented criticism which marked scholarly writing in the 1980s.

In 1984, the British Film Institute held an international Television Studies Conference in London, bringing together over 400 media scholars from across the world. The conference attempted to find patterns in research being conducted. The editors of the conference *Proceedings* noted the characteristic "diversity and openness" of the conference while considering essays about a series of TV related phenomena defined in terms of the paradigms of sociology, politics, economics, literary criticism and semiotics. They distinguished two main currents in the works: political economy (emphasizing that political, economic, and technological conditions create a world communication order profoundly unequal in available technology, capital, expertise, programming support, and influence) and textual analysis (an attempt to unravel the values systems and formal characteristics that mark a particular text or cluster of cultural artifacts).[11]

Papers and discussions at the April 1988 conference of the Center for Twentieth Century Studies at the University of Wisconsin revealed young contemporary television critics' preoccupation with analysis of television as an aspect of postmodernism. This aesthetic category, first elaborated by architect Robert Venturi in the 1960s, was developed in relation to media particularly in the work of Fredrick Jameson and Jean Baudrillard and, according to E. Ann Kaplan, "involves the blurring of hitherto sacrosanct boundaries and polarities, the elimination of any position from which to speak or judge . . . the obliteration of any distinction between an 'inside' and an 'outside' . . . the reduction of all to one level, often seen as that of the similacra."[12] Baudrillard, a semiologically oriented sociologist, whose work is influenced by Habermas and Barthes, posits language as an objective phenomenon, analyzable socially and historically. He focuses on consumption and argues that the true production in postmodern capitalism is the production and manipulation of social signifiers. Television is, of course, the prime instrument of such production.[13]

Presenters at the conference also frequently referred to the work of Raymond Williams, whose *Television, Technology and Cultural Form* (London, Fontana, 1974) argues that television must be understood as a cultural form issuing from culturally mandated technological development. However, the theorist most mentioned was Baudrillard, who may be categorized with Jameson as a neo-Marxist, poststructuralist, postmodernist literary theorist interested in social phenomena. A number of the listeners, among them James Collins and John Fiske, noted in some critics of the postmodernist semiotics orientation a tendency to pursue the meanings of television through the realms of abstract theories and elaborate metaphors, getting farther and farther from the actual experience of watching television.

There are, however, contemporary scholars who analyze specific television programs and genres. Three recent anthologies reveal the lively and diverse state of contemporary television criticism. *Television: The Critical View*, fourth edition (1987), Horace Newcomb's highly successful collection of writing about the medium, is eclectic (by design) tHough somewhat weighted toward genre criticism. The widely used text examines specific shows, genres, and includes general essays about television from both sociological and humanistic perspectives. Twenty-three of the thirty-three essays are new to this edition.

In contrast to Newcomb, *Channels of Discourse* (1987) edited by Robert Allen, surveys the major techniques of contemporary literary, cultural, and cinematic criticism as influenced by the insights into language and culture provided by structural linguistics and its offspring, semiotics. The various "critical languages'' include semiotics, narrative theory, genre theory, reader-response criticism, ideological analysis, psychoanalytic criticism, and feminist criticism. The writers presuppose some prior acquaintance with their perspectives.

E. Ann Kaplan's *Regarding Television* (1983), covers the ground from a literary and feminist perspective. As she writes elsewhere, feminist television (and film) analysis "tries to combine analysis of female images in individual texts with attention to their context of production/exhibition and to the television apparatus," that is, the television industry. Acknowledging the previous domination of scholarly writing by the social scientists, Kaplan explicitly invites focus on television aesthetic—how meaning is produced—or on television as an ideological institution functioning within "a complex consumer circuit that allows only for the production of carefully constricted meanings." The twelve essays are concerned with various TV genres, while occasionally casting a wider theoretical or historical net.

One recent individual work illustrates the critical potential of a (somewhat) traditional approach to televison criticism. David Marc's *Demographic Vistas: Television in American Culture* (1984) vigorously advocates the consideration of television as an aesthetic artifact. He argues that any overarching theory of communication proceeds fundamentally (if unacknowledged) from the aesthetic vision of its creator and attempts to understand the aesthetic vision of the artifact's creator. He concludes with a persuasive look at contemporary television trends, acknowledging (presciently at times) that television "has become aware of itself" as the audience is aware of itself as television-conditioned.

CONCLUSIONS

Despite the multiplicity of perspectives and the continuing controversies within perspectives, some observers detect a certain coming together of concerns on the part of humanist and social scientist. Attention to long-term effects, genre studies, and the infusion of semiotics by humanist media scholars have inspired, in the words of Elihu Katz, "methodological, conceptual and theoretical advances which examine the ways in which television shapes our images of reality."[14] Katz, one of the major founders and researchers in the area of uses and gratifications, notes that the implied "contract" between producers, artists, and audiences explored in humanistic genre studies has returned media researchers to exploring long-term effects such as the media's role in shaping our visions of reality, and to studying the influence of agents of control of other media, an early but neglected area of media studies.

Despite Katz's optimism, a double issue of *Journal of Communication* entitled "Ferment in the Field," published in the summer of 1983 (the very same issue in which he publishes these opinions), reveals that communications scholars from the social sciences rarely or never cite humanist scholars, nor do humanists cite the works of the social scientists. They may be talking about the same subject in much the same ways, but they are not talking to each other.

In a prescient essay in Blumler and Katz's *The Uses of Mass Communications*, James Carey and Albert Kreiling argue that gratifications researchers "fail to link the functions of mass media consumption with the symbolic content of the mass-communicated materials or with the actual experience of consuming them."[15] Thus they are, in effect, forced to ignore the "immediately pleasurable quality" characteristic of aesthetic experience. Carey and Kreiling note the important but generally dismissed work of William Stephenson, whose *The Play Theory of Mass Communication* (1967) develops an approach to the media experience based on the kind of intense aesthetic satisfaction which generates total absorption. They acknowledge in the work of Gouldner (1970) that the tendency to reduce aesthetic or cultural dimensions of experience is typical of "a general disposition among persons in a utilitarian culture to dismiss the reality of things in themselves and to treat them instead in terms of their consequences."[16]

Carey and Kreiling propose three assumptions which will permit gratifications research to treat successfully popular culture:

First, an effective theory of popular culture will require a conception of man, not as psychological man or sociological man, but as cultural man.

Second, that the nature of man, culture, and their interactions leads persons to live in qualitatively distinct zones of experience—religious, aesthetic, scientific—which cultural forms organize in different ways.

Third, that a means-ends model of motivation is insufficient, and that some actions are not purposive, but are engaged in for their own sake.[17]

The Carey and Kreiling essay points to the concerns which continue to preoccupy critics of television, both humanist and social scientist, during the 1980s.

The division between the humanists and the social scientists—possibly unbridgeable—may be understood from the different way leisure is viewed by humanists and social scientists. For the latter, leisure is merely the time left over from work and sleep (or bodily maintenance, in a slightly more inclusive term) and by extension, the activities filling that time. Various functions are assigned to leisure activities, including passing free time, learning, and recovery from work. The concept of play, playing, playfulness, indeed, of any activity undertaken "for its own sake" is extremely difficult to grasp from this perspective.

For the humanist, on the other hand, leisure represents the highest state of civilization, the realization of the larger purposes of work and societies, the "basis of culture" in Josef Pieper's lapidary phrase. While free time activities, recreation, and pastime doubtless have practical functions, they ultimately reduce to two rather bleak alternatives: restorative for work or killing time (i.e., staving off boredom). Leisure, however, neither active and creative, or passive and receptive, represents activity which needs no other purpose than itself to justify or explain it. Either we live to work, and thus all activity must be judged in relation to work, or we work to live, and are confronted with the fact and challenge of leisure. (For an expanded treatment of this concept, the reader is referred to Pieper, *Leisure, the Basis of Culture* (1948); Johan Huizinga's magisterial *Homo Ludens* (1938), or Orrin Klapp's recent and well-received *Overload and Boredom: Essays on the Quality of Life in the Information Age*.)

It seems obvious that television watching can have many functions—informational, social, psychic, sociological—and as such, is a perfectly accessible activity for study by the social scientist. But when television watching transcends these functional activities and becomes pleasurable, fun, involving, even moving and thought provoking; in a word, when television watching becomes aesthetic, the experience is then accessible and comprehensible only from a humanist perspective.

Doubtless, it is frustrating to the social scientist, who is, after all, a multiperspectived human being, to find areas of daily activity effectively excluded from the probing of his/her own analytical tools. It is equally frustrating to the dedicated consumer of soap opera to hear this valued activity described as "escapist" or "vicarious satisfaction" or "substitute gratification." It is only the humanist critic who can access television adequately on an aesthetic or cultural plane.

The division, in turn, between traditional humanist critics and what Robert Allen calls "contemporary critics" with their orientation toward semiotics and literary theory may be rooted in different assumptions about aesthetics and different views of the relevance of aesthetics. Some of the contemporary analyses, while purportedly "about" television, seem so abstract and philosophical-epistemological that, as John Fiske observed at a recent conference, they seem to have lost the sense of the human experience of television. A parallel might be drawn between the elaboration of powerful abstract critical approaches and the development of contemporary statistics, in that significance may be found in almost any data, but the significance may not be very meaningful. Nevertheless, time and the changing winds of intellectual fashion will winnow the substantive from the merely clever.

In the meantime, those who wish to ponder seriously this medium among us have an abundance of riches to consider. If it may truly be said that television is the central artifact of American culture, then the amount and intensity of critical attention paid it is both overdue and appropriate. Television, for better or worse, affects or influences almost every aspect of American life. This suggests the necessity for the examination of television from a multiplicity of perspectives, as seems to be occurring. Given the diversity of perspectives and methodologies, it seems unlikely that any one particular perspective will come to dominate television studies in the near future.

NOTES

1. Anthony Smith, "Foreword," in *Television in Transition*, ed. Philip Drummond and Richard Patterson (London: British Film Institute, 1984), v.

2. Jose Ortega y Gassett, *The Revolt of the Masses* (New York: W. W. Norton & Co.), 11–19.

3. Harold Lasswell, a political scientist, wrote his doctoral dissertation on *Propaganda Techniques in the World War*, published in 1927, and is generally regarded as the "father" of contemporary communications research. Paul Lazarsfeld, a mathematician turned sociologist, is best known for a series of field studies of influences on voter behavior conducted during the early 1940s. The work, conducted by the Columbia Bureau of Applied Social Science Research which he founded, culminated in the classic: *The People's Choice* (with Bernard Berelson and H. Gaudet, 1948) published by Columbia University Press. Kurt Lewin, a social psychologist interested in group process, initiated group dynamics studies, gatekeeper theory, and conducted persuasion studies during World War II. See "Group Decision and Social Change" in E. Maccoby et al., *Readings in Social Psychology* (New York: Holt, Rinehart, Winston, 1958). Carl Hovland, an experimental psychologist moving in the direction of social psychology, also conducted research for the Army during World War II, focusing on attitude change, credibility, and one-sided vs. two-sided messages. His pioneering work was published in *Experiments in Mass Communication*, with colleagues Lunsdaine and Sheffield (Princeton, N.J.: Princeton University Press, 1949). There were, of course, many other pioneers, but these four were "canonized" by Berelson's controversial essay.

4. Hadley Cantril, *The Invasion from Mars* (Princeton, N.J.: Princeton University Press, 1940).

5. William Eliot, *Television's Impact on American Culture* (East Lansing, Mich.: Michigan State University Press, 1956), xvi.

6. Ibid., 182.

7. Leonard D. Eron, Leopold D. Walder, and Monroe M. Lefkowitz, *Learning of Aggression in Children* (Boston: Little, Brown & Co., 1971).

8. Siepmann, "The need for vision," in *The Eighth Art*, ed. Robert Lewis Shayon (New York: Holt Rinehart Winston, 1962), 186.

9. Bruce Lohar, "PC: the journal and the state of the study" in *Journal of Popular Culture* 6(1) (Spring 1972): 6–7.

10. John Cawelti (untitled book review), in *American Quarterly*, 20(2) (Summer 1968): 142.

11. Philip Drummond and Richard Patterson, "Editor's Preface" to *Television in Transition* (London: British Film Institute, 1984), vii–viii.

12. E. Ann Kaplan, "Feminist Criticism—notes" in *Channels of Discourse*, ed. Robert Allen (Chapel Hill: University of North Carolina Press, 1987), 249.

13. Mark Poster, "Technology and Culture in Habermas and Baudrillard," *Contemporary Literature*, 22 (4) (Fall 1981): 462–63.

14. Elihu Katz, "The return of the humanities and sociology," *Journal of Communication*, 33(3) (Summer 1983): 51.

15. James Carey and Albert Kreiling, "Popular culture and uses and gratifications: notes toward an accommodation," in Blumler and Katz, *The Uses of Mass Communication* (Beverly Hills, Calif.: Sage, 1974), 232.

16. Ibid.

17. Ibid.

Bibliography

This bibliography includes only those works cited whose principal subject is television. For bibliographic information about special topics treated by individual contributors, see notes after each chapter.

Allen, Robert C., ed. *Channels of Discourse*. Chapel Hill: University of North Carolina Press, 1987.

Baehr, Helen, and Dyer, Gillian, eds. *Boxed In: Women and Television*. New York: Pandora Press, 1987.

Batra, N. D. *The Hour of Television: Critical Approaches*. Metuchen, New Jersey: Scarecrow Press, 1987.

Blumler, Jay G., and Katz, Elihu. *The Uses of Mass Communication: Perspectives on Gratifications Reseach*. Beverly Hills, California: Sage, 1974.

Bogard, Paul. *The Age of Television*. New York: Ungar, 1956.

Brooks, Tim, and Marsh, Earle. *The Complete Directory to Prime Time Network TV Shows, 1946–present*. 3d. ed. New York: Ballantine Books, 1985.

Czitrom, Daniel J. *Media and the American Mind*. Chapel H of the Evening: Women Characters of Prime-Time Television. Metuchen, New Jersey: Scarecrow Press, 1983.

Davis, Robert E. *Response to Innovation: A Study of Popular Argument about New Mass Media*. New Hampshire: Ayer Co., 1976.

Drummond, Philip, and Patterson, Richard, eds. *Television in Transition*. London: British Film Institute, 1984.

Eliot, William. *Television's Impact on American Culture*. East Lansing: Michigan State University Press, 1956.

Ellis, John. *Visible Fictions: Cinema, Television, Video*. London: Routledge and Kegan Paul, 1985.

Ellison, Harlan. *The Glass Teat: Essays of Opinion on the Subject of Television*. New York: Ace, 1970.

Eron, Leonard D., Walder, Leopold, and Lefkowitz, Monroe. *Learning of Aggression in Children*. Boston: Little, Brown & Co., 1971.

Fiske, John, and Hartley, John. *Reading Television*. London: Methuen, 1978.

Gitlin, Todd. *Inside Prime Time*. New York: Pantheon Books, 1983.

———, ed. *Watching Television*. New York: Pantheon Books, 1986.

Kaplan, E. Ann, ed. *Regarding Television: Critical Approaches: An Anthology*. Los Angeles: American Film Institute, 1983.

Klapper, Joseph. *The Effects of Mass Communication*. Glencoe, Illinois: Free Press, 1960.

Levinson, Richard, and Link, William. *Off-Camera: Conversations with the Makers of Prime-Time Television*. New York: New American Library, 1986.

MacCabe, Colin. *High Theory, Low Culture*. Manchester: Manchester University Press, 1986.

MacDonald, Dwight. *Against the American Grain*. New York: Random House, 1962.

Marc, David. *Demographic Vistas: Television in American Culture*. Philadelphia: University of Pennsylvania Press, 1984.

McLuhan, Marshall. *The Gutenberg Galaxy: The Making of Typographic Man*. Toronto: University of Toronto Press, 1962.

———. *Understanding Media: The Extensions of Man*. New York: McGraw-Hill, 1964.

Meehan, Diana M. *Ladies of the Evening: Women Characters of Prime-Time Television*. Metuchen, New Jersey: Scarecrow Press, 1983.

Modleski, Tania. *Loving with a Vengeance: Mass-Produced Fantasies for Women*. Hamden, Connecticut: Archon, 1982.

Newcomb, Horace. *Television: The Critical View*. 3d ed. New York: Oxford University Press, 1982.

———, ed. *Television: The Critical View*. 4th ed. New York: Oxford University Press, 1987.

Oskamp, S., ed. *Television As A Social Issue*. Newbury Park, California: Sage Publications, 1988.

Postman, Neil. *Amusing Ourselves to Death: Public Discourse in the Age of Show Business*. New York: Penguin Books, 1986.

Rosenberg, Bernard, and White, David M., eds. *Mass Culture: The Popular Arts in America*. New York: Free Press, 1957.

Seldes, Gilbert. *The Seven Lively Arts*. New York: Sagamore Press, 1924.

———. *The Great Audience*. New York: Viking Press, 1951.

———. *The Public Arts*. New York: Simon and Schuster, 1956.

———. *The New Mass Media: Challenge to a Free Society*. Washington, D.C.: Public Affairs Press, 1986.

Shayon, Robert Lewis, ed. *The Eighth Art*. New York: Holt, Rinehart Winston, 1962.

Signorielli, Nancy, ed. *Role Portrayal and Stereotyping on Television: An Annotated Bibliography of Studies*. Westport, Connecticut: Greenwood Press, 1985.

Silverstone, Roger. *The Message of Television: Myth and Narrative in Contemporary Culture*. London: Heinemann, 1981.

Weibel, Kathryn. *Mirror Mirror: Images of Women Reflected in Popular Culture*. New York: Anchor Books, 1977.

Williams, Raymond. *Television Technology and Cultural Form*. New York: Schocken Books, 1975.

Winn, Marie. *The Plug-In Drug*. New York: Viking, 1977.

Index

About the Contributors

KATHERINE USHER HENDERSON is Professor of English and Vice President for Academic Affairs at Dominican College of San Rafael. She is the author of *Joan Didion* and coauthor with Barbara McManus of *Half Humankind: Contexts and Texts of the Controversy about Women in England, 1540–1640*. She has also published articles on women's studies and on contemporary American writers and has served as Director of Women's Studies and as Dean of the School of Arts and Sciences of the College of New Rochelle.

JOSEPH ANTHONY MAZZEO is Avalon Foundation Professor Emeritus in the Humanities and Senior Scholar in the Humanities, both at Columbia University. He is the author of numerous articles and eight books, including *Renaissance and Revolution: The Remaking of European Thought*, *The Design of Life: Major Themes in Biological Thought* and *Varieties of Interpretation*. He has also edited a multivolume anthology of seventeenth century English literature and a series of books on major figures in the history of science and has served on the editorial boards of *Religion and Literature* and *Comparative Literature*.

HARRIET BLODGETT is an Affiliated Scholar at the Institute for Research on Women and Gender at Stanford University. She is the author of *Patterns of Reality: Elizabeth Bowen's Novels* and of *Centuries of Female Days: English-women's Private Diaries*. She has taught at the University of California, Davis, and the University of California, Santa Cruz.

ROBERT CLUETT is Professor of English and former Director of Graduate English at York University in Toronto, Canada. He is the author of *Prose Style and Critical Reading, Effective English Prose*, and, most recently, *Canadian Literary Prose: A Stylistic Atlas*. He has also published articles on subjects ranging from linguistics to arctic travel to winemaking.

JUDITH KEGAN GARDINER is Professor of English and Women's Studies at the University of Illinois at Chicago. Her publications include *Craftsmanship in Context: The Development of Ben Jonson's Poetry, The Politics of Empathy: Jean Rhys, Christina Stead, Doris Lessing*, and articles on Renaissance English writers, twentieth century women authors, and feminist and psychoanalytic theory. Her current research interests include seventeenth century English women writers, self-psychological approaches to literature, and feminist analyses of popular culture.

BARBARA LEE is currently a consultant to major television networks and other organizations. Until recently she was a Director of Social Research in the CBS Broadcast Group. In this position she generated research on television use and effects and reviewed academic work in this area. She is coauthor of *Leading to Reading*, a book on ways parents can use the media to help their children learn, and has an article on the prosocial content of television in *Television As A Social Issue*.

DAVID MARC is Visiting Professor at the Annenberg School of Communications at the University of Southern California. His publications include *Demographic Vistas: Television in American Culture, Comic Visions: Television Comedy and American Culture*, and numerous articles in anthologies, scholarly journals, and the *Village Voice*. He has taught at Brown University and Brandeis University and has appeared on several television programs, including *60 Minutes* and the series *All About Television*.

JAMES V. MIROLLO is Professor of English and Comparative Literature at Columbia University. His publications include *The Poet of the Marvelous: Giambattista Marino, Mannerism and Renaissance Poetry: Concept, Mode, Inner Design*, and numerous articles on Renaissance and Baroque literature and art. He is a member of the Editorial Board of *Literature and the Visual Arts: New Foundations*, an associate editor of *Renaissance Quarterly*, and a member of the executive board of the Renaissance Society of America.

JAMES M. O'BRIEN is Associate Professor of Communication Arts at the College of New Rochelle. He has also taught at Iona College, the State University of New York at Purchase, and the University of Miami. He has extensive experience in broadcast media, including WREX-TV, Rockford, WTNH-TV, New Haven, and the Broadcast Mission Radio Chain in Texas.

MICHAEL SEIDEL is Professor of English and Comparative Literature at Columbia University. He is the author of *Streak: Joe DiMaggio and the Summer of 41*, *Exile and the Narrative Imagination*, and *The Satiric Inheritance: Rabelais to Sterne*. He is currently writing a book on Ted Williams.

MARY SIRRIDGE is Professor of Philosophy at Louisiana State University in Baton Rouge. She has published numerous articles on aesthetics, the philosophy of literature, and expression in the arts in the *British Journal of Aesthetics* and the *Journal of Aesthetics and Art Criticism*. She is also the editor of the Latin edition of Jordan of Saxony's *Commentary on Priscian Minor*. Her research fields are aesthetics and ancient and medieval philosophy.

THEOHARIS C. THEOHARIS is Associate Professor of Literature at the Massachusetts Institute of Technology. He is the author of *Joyce's Ulysses: An Anatomy of the Soul* and numerous publications on drama and fiction in scholarly journals. He is currently writing a book on modern drama.